TRUTH, RELIGIOUS DIALOGUE AND DYNAMIC ORTHODOXY

Reflections on the works of Brian Hebblethwaite

EDITED BY JULIUS J LIPNER

Truth, Religious Dialogue, and Dynamic Orthodoxy

Truth, Religious Dialogue, and Dynamic Orthodoxy

Essays in honour of Brian Hebblethwaite

Edited by
Julius J. Lipner

scm press

All rights reserved. No part of this publication may be reproduced,
stored in a retrieval system, or transmitted,
in any form or by any means, electronic, mechanical,
photocopying or otherwise, without the prior permission of
the publisher, SCM Press.

© Julius J. Lipner 2005

British Library Cataloguing in Publication data

A catalogue record for this book is available
from the British Library

0 334 04009 4

First published in 2005 by SCM Press
9-17 St Albans Place, London N1 0NX

www.scm-canterburypress.co.uk

SCM Press is a division of
SCM-Canterbury Press Ltd

Printed and bound in Great Britain by
Biddles Ltd, Kings Lynn, Norfolk

Contents

Acknowledgements	vii
Notes on Contributors	ix
Introduction	xiii
1 The Truth(s) of Translation *Julius Lipner*	1
2 On Music's Grace: Trying to Think Theologically about Music *Ann Loades*	25
3 Truth and Religious Dialogue *Anders Jeffner*	39
4 Truth and Toleration: Hebblethwaite, Hick, and Bediuzzaman Said Nursi *Ian Markham*	54
5 Philosophical Presuppositions and Biblical Exegesis *Stephen T. Davis*	71
6 A Non-Realist View of God *Don Cupitt*	85
7 The 'Future' of Religion *Douglas Hedley*	96
8 Can Christian Ethics be Universal? A Focus on War *Joseph Runzo*	112
9 Intercultural Christology and Human Values *George Newlands*	136

10 Incarnation and Double Agency *Edward H. Henderson*	154
11 Incarnation, the Trinity, and Fellowship with God *Vincent Brümmer*	165
12 Incarnation, Rationality, and Transformative Practices *David F. Ford*	187
Publications of B. L. Hebblethwaite	203
Bibliography	214
Index	222

Acknowledgements

I am very grateful to all the contributors of this volume: their regard for Brian Hebblethwaite emerges from the time and trouble they took to contribute, and the great patience they have shown while awaiting publication. Many thanks too, to Dr Brian Callingham, Life Fellow (like Brian Hebblethwaite himself) of Queens' College, Cambridge, for generously supplying the excellent photograph that adorns the cover. There is an aura about it that captures well the questing nature of the thinker we are celebrating.

Finally, I am very grateful to Barbara Laing and her production team at SCM for the consistent courtesy, efficiency and professionalism of their work. The book came out in record time.

Julius Lipner
Cambridge, 2005

Notes on Contributors

Vincent Brümmer is Professor Emeritus of the Philosophy of Religion at Utrecht University and past President of the British Society for the Study of Theology and the European Society for Philosophy of Religion. His writings include *Theology and Philosophical Inquiry* (1981), *The Model of Love* (1993), and *Atonement, Christology and the Trinity: Making Sense of Christian Doctrine* (2005).

Don Cupitt is now a Life Fellow of Emmanuel College, Cambridge, the College to which he was first elected in 1965. In recent years his main activity has been overseas, lecturing for the Sea of Faith Networks and various Institutes and Universities. His books, of which there have been 36 in all to date (including *Taking Leave of God*, 1980, *The Sea of Faith*, 1984, *Only Human*, 1985, and *The Way to Happiness*, 2005) are now published in California.

Stephen T. Davis is Russell K. Pitzer Professor of Philosophy at Claremont McKenna College in California. He writes primarily in the philosophy of religion and Christian thought. He is the author of some seventy articles in academic journals and author or editor of 13 books (including *Risen Indeed: Making Sense of the Resurrection*, 1993, *Encountering Evil*, 2nd edn 2001, and *God, Reason, and Theistic Proofs*, 1997).

David F. Ford is Regius Professor of Divinity and Fellow of Selwyn College in the University of Cambridge. He is also Director of the Cambridge Interfaith Programme, and Chair of the Management Committee of the Centre for Advanced Religious and Theological Studies in the Faculty of Divinity. His teaching and research are in systematic theology, hermeneutics, modern theology, and interfaith theology. Among his publications are *Self and Salvation: Being Transformed* (1999), *Theology: A Very Short Introduction* (2nd edn 2000), and (edited with Rachel Muers) *The Modern Theologians: An Introduction to Christian Theology since 1918* (3rd edn 2005).

Douglas Hedley was educated at Keble College, Oxford, and the Ludwig-Maximilians-Universitaet Munich, Germany. He is University Senior Lecturer in the Philosophy of Religion in the Faculty of Divinity, University of Cambridge, and Fellow and Graduate Tutor at Clare College. His books include *Coleridge, Philosophy and Religion: Aids to Reflection and the Mirror of the Spirit* (2000), and a forthcoming monograph, *The Living Forms of Imagination*.

Edward H. Henderson is Professor of Philosophy at The Louisiana State University, Baton Rouge, USA. His BA is from Rhodes College and his Ph.D. from Tulane University. His research focus has been in philosophical theology, with a special emphasis on Austin Farrer, on whom his work includes *Divine Action: Essays Inspired by the Philosophical Theology of Austin Farrer* (1990), edited with Brian Hebblethwaite, and *Captured by the Crucified: The Practical Theology of Austin Farrer* (2004), edited with David Hein.

Anders Jeffner is Professor Emeritus in Studies in Faiths and Ideologies, in the University of Uppsala, where he studied theology and philosophy and received a doctorate in 1966 for his dissertation on Butler and Hume on religion. He is now President of the Royal Swedish Academy of Letters, History and Antiquities. Among his publications in English are *The Study of Religious Language* (1972), *Theology and Integration* (1987), and *Six Cartesian Meditations* (1993).

Julius Lipner is Professor of Hinduism and the Comparative Study of Religion in the University of Cambridge, and Chair of the Faculty of Divinity. He is also a Fellow of Clare Hall. He has published and lectured widely in Hinduism, the relationship between Christianity and other faiths, and the religio-cultural interface between Hinduism and the West in nineteenth-century Bengal. His books include *The Face of Truth: A Study of Meaning and Metaphysics in the Vedantic Theology of Ramanuja* (1986), *Hindus: Their Religious Beliefs and Practices* (1994, 1998), and (Bankimcandra Chatterji's) *Anandamath, or The Sacred Brotherhood: Translated with an Introduction and Critical Apparatus* (2005).

Notes on Contributors

Ann Loades, CBE, is Emerita Professor of Divinity in the University of Durham, UK, where she was the first woman to receive a personal chair. She is President of the Society for the Study of Theology for two years (2005–6). Her most recent monograph (on Mary Wollstonecraft, Josephine Butler, and Dorothy L. Sayers) is *Feminist Theology: Voices from the Past* (2001).

Ian Markham is Dean and Professor of Theology and Ethics at Hartford Seminary, Connecticut. With degrees from the Universities of London, Cambridge, and Exeter, Dr Markham became the first holder of the Liverpool Chair of Theology and Public Life at Liverpool Hope University College, before moving to the United States. His publications include *Plurality and Christian Ethics* (1994), *Truth and the Reality of God* (1998), and *Theology of Engagement* (2003).

George Newlands is Professor of Divinity in the University of Glasgow, and Principal of Trinity College. He was a colleague of Brian Hebblethwaite in the Faculty of Divinity, and Dean of Trinity Hall, Cambridge, for a number of years. His current research is in the area of Christology and human rights, and his recent publications include *John and Donald Baillie: Transatlantic Theology* (2002), and *The Transformative Imagination: Rethinking Intercultural Theology* (2004).

Joseph Runzo is Professor of Philosophy and Religious Studies at Chapman University, California; he was a Visiting Fellow and is now Life Member at Clare Hall, University of Cambridge. He is also Founding Executive Director of the Global Ethics and Religion Forum, Executive Producer for the Forum's documentary project, *Patterns for Peace*, and co-editor of *The Library of Global Ethics and Religion*. The recipient of six National Endowment for the Humanities awards and fellowships, he has published numerous works, and is now completing two books on comparative religious ethics, *War and the Destruction of the Soul*, and *War and Reconciliation*.

Introduction

For nearly forty years, as his bibliography shows, Brian Hebblethwaite has explored the conceptual domains of inter-religious understanding, the nature and pursuit of truth in religion, and issues in Christology with special reference to the Incarnation. And by common consent, whether one agree with him or not, the light of his clear, powerful insights and the long shadow cast by his influence have blended to make a unique chiaroscuro in the conceptual landscape to which he has contributed. It is not possible in one volume to do justice to the magnitude of this contribution. What we have here is but a limited reflection of the inspiration he has generated and the academic esteem in which he is held.

In the context of Brian Hebblethwaite's philosophical and theological concerns then, it is a remarkable fact – for such volumes do not lend themselves to these things – that a unifying thread runs through this work. In the first essay, a methodological issue central to the field of the comparative study of religion is considered: the nature of translation in the broad sense of this term, and of the kind of truth(s), that is, the contextualized gains, that this layered epistemic transaction might yield. Without the enactment of translation in the senses discussed, we cannot overcome the conceptual boundaries and cultural barriers that the pursuit of intellectual exploration in comparative and other contexts demands.

Ann Loades' essay, which follows, is an expression in another register of this pursuit but from a heuristically Christian point of view. She considers how music translated into the lives of people of faith, far from being a simple embellishment of their experience, actually 'makes worship *possible*', not only the worship of liturgical prayer, but also the worship of directing life's rhythms to their highest end. 'An identifiably "incarnational" understanding of music must needs attend to its sheer physicality through corporeality in time, with a destiny, if Christian faith is true, of being re-clothed in "holy and glorious flesh"...'. This is the 'incarnational' truth of music which she analyses, at times to poignant effect.

Anders Jeffner's discussion of truth and religious dialogue comes next. The question that looms large for Jeffner is a fundamental one – one that has exercised Hebblethwaite himself crucially over the years: 'Do true and false religious doctrines exist, and, if so, how are they distributed between the world religions?' Jeffner makes use of a methodological device he derives from Nathan Söderblom: the idea of 'windows towards reality' which intimates that 'we as humans have the opportunity to get a view of reality that at least partly corresponds to what is the case'. In the context of the 'stream of pessimism in epistemology from ancient sceptics through Kant to postmodernism', this is a refreshingly realistic position to hold, but Jeffner does not deploy it naively. In terms of what he calls an act of *basic faith* which is required at various levels of an epistemological grasp of the world, he considers different forms of experience, including that of religious interpretations of transcendence. Clearly acknowledging his own Christian commitment, Jeffner explores how the claims of other faiths might open up his own. Honest, seemingly insuperable differences notwithstanding, 'we can . . . gain a considerable amount of mutual understanding and learning from each other by comparing experiences of transcendence and different ways to devotional experiences' by seeking to formulate, each of us within the context of specific religious traditions, a *coherent* view of the world – a view in which *all* forms of human knowledge are integrated into the whole: a Hebblethwaitian trait *par excellence*.

Almost on cue, in his contribution Ian Markham takes up the debate between Hebblethwaite and John Hick concerning the adequacy of a pluralist response to religious truth and diversity. As Markham puts it, for Hick, 'all the major religions in the world are equal and valid responses to the "Real"' (or Transcendent), whereas for Hebblethwaite, 'a commitment to the truth of Christianity [is] not incompatible with an equally strong commitment to the need for peaceful relations, dialogue, and mutual understanding with other faith traditions', based on an understanding of the world that makes use of all the epistemic resources at our disposal. Elsewhere, Markham has described this approach as a 'dynamic orthodoxy', a felicitous expression which we have used in the title of this book. In his essay, Markham seeks to demonstrate the appropriateness of Hebblethwaite's approach by analysing the views of the Muslim thinker Bediuzzaman Said Nursi (1873–1960), who argued from a so-called

Introduction

inclusivist point of view against the use of violence by Muslims towards non-believers (violence in this regard being a sign of lack of confidence in the beauty and truth of Islam), and for peaceful coexistence with non-Muslims (in particular, Christians and Jews). The thrust of Markham's thesis is that the kind of approach Hebblethwaite adopts represents a far more adequate and *realistic* starting point for interreligious dialogue than that of Hick: Nursi's own thinking on this subject is a case in point.

We already have an emergent picture of the *kind* of approach – philosophically, theologically, and comparatively – that Brian Hebblethwaite himself adopts. And Stephen Davis in his essay makes this picture clearer. He considers the central issue of the relationship between philosophical presuppositions and biblical exegesis and argues strongly for the view that 'the holding of certain philosophical positions is *essential* to interpreting the Bible, at least in Christian exegesis' for there is no such thing as 'a view from nowhere'. What are these positions, and the presuppositions on which they are predicated? As to the latter, Davis argues for the unity of the Bible – 'more like a thematic or organic unity' – and that it should be open to philosophical enquiry; as to the former, he mentions the following: that metaphysical monism and metaphysical materialism are false, that time is linear and moral values are objective, that human beings are morally responsible for what they do, and that epistemological scepticism is false and linguistic realism is true. On this basis we have the means 'to integrate all that we know, our faith and our learning, the teachings of scripture and the results of our research'.

That '. . . our moral values are objective'. Indeed, the emphasis of the volume so far has been on two pervasive features of Hebblethwaite's approach: the 'incarnational' nature of his thinking – its characteristics of contextualization and integration of knowledge into a coherent whole – and his stress on openness coupled with 'objectivity', that is, on the potential for universal applicability of his system's fundamental insights. We shall return to 'incarnation' in due course, but the next three essays enquire into the scope of the 'objectivity' of such an approach.

Don Cupitt, alone of all the contributors to have once taught Hebblethwaite, first puts forward the case for undermining the very basis of his now errant pupil's philosophical stance. Without mincing words, he advocates 'A Non-Realist View of God', clarifying what he means by his 'non-objectifying theology' and declaring that he was right 'to try to break with the old metaphysical belief in an objective transcendent personal God out there'. Such a theology inculcates a false consciousness: 'If you insist upon theological realism, if for you faith has got to be a way of communing with a great Spirit via a direct hotline inside your head, then for you the religious believer must be a person who lacks a crucial bit of critical self-awareness.' His non-realist view, he continues remorselessly, by implicitly rejecting all traditional ideas of religious authority, affirms the autonomy of religion, of 'religion without prostration – the religion of a free and upright person'. It endorses the formation of a new body of knowledge as 'something entirely created by human beings who engage in systematic enquiry'. This is a body of knowledge that is 'at every point disputable, and subject to change'. The objectivity of sacred revelation and all that it stands for is dispersed by the epistemic winds of the New Reason of scientific method and deconstructive theory: 'We are the only makers of our world . . . The world is built by language: only we have language, and only we, therefore, make the world what it is . . . a world of endlessly conflicting interpretations.'

In 'The "Future" of Religion', Douglas Hedley springs to the aid of the 'objective' view by vigorously contesting the underlying approach of the Masters of Suspicion – Nietzsche, Marx, and Freud – and their successors, Lacan, Derrida, Foucault, etc., and Cupitt himself. 'I wish to question the cosy assumption of the theological avant-garde that their appeals to the Masters of Suspicion evince a superior awareness of the problematic and complex nature of God-talk. Indeed, I wish to propose that the intellectual high ground claimed by those who wish to subvert the philosophy of religion has its foundations in the crude biological obsessions of the nineteenth century, and in particular, the influence of Darwin.' Arguing for the authenticity of 'religion' as a category of academic enquiry, Hedley warms to his theme of debunking in particular Marx, Nietzsche, and Freud in the context of the slavish deference to Darwinism that influenced their times: ' "Darwinism" has sown the seeds of a radical disenchantment theory. Whereas Marx, Freud and Nietzsche are parasitic upon some kind of idea of evolution as a progressive tendency, some residual eschatology, and the "illusion of the future", Darwin grimly reinforced Hume's critique of natural theology . . . Darwin is less of a theory of evolution than Marx, Nietzsche, or Freud.'

Joseph Runzo, 'following the spirit of Hebblethwaite's work', then asks whether Christian ethics can be universal, and focuses on war as a topical case-study. In comparative context, he considers the question of the uniqueness of Christian ethics, and then reviews how Christians

Introduction

xvii

in the past have viewed the prospect of war: 'Historically, the Christian ethics of war contains two strands: pacifism and just war theory. If Christian ethics is to be universal [in senses discussed earlier] there must be a shared aspect of these pacifist and just war views within Christianity which can be universalized.' Then, skilfully weaving narrative accounts which depict the hellishness of war into his argument, he concludes that just war theory falters before ethical scrutiny, and that the world religions combined with a moral appeal to the non-religious person 'are potentially powerful allies in the quest to limit the number and intensity of wars, and to condemn the dishonourable soldier's actions'.

The remaining four contributions return to a theme central to Hebblethwaite's project, that is, not only the 'incarnational' emphasis of Christian theology as such – its embodiedness in temporality, context, and integrated knowledge – but the incarnation of Christ itself as the model for our relationship with God and each other, and our approach to the world. In 'Intercultural Christology and Human Values', George Newlands launches us into the deep waters of a non-hegemonic Christology in an increasingly globalized yet fissiparous world in which Christology interacts with culture(s) both as product and prophet. Newlands speaks of the need to move away from Christian triumphalism towards an unsentimental Christology – not least in Europe itself – which retrieves a God for us who in the doctrine of the Incarnation expresses a distinctive solidarity with all humankind through the attributes of vulnerability and generosity, which, Newlands contends, are 'central to the Christian contribution to culture at all levels'. These attributes are highlighted in particular in modern emancipatory theologies. Newlands illustrates his thesis 'with reference to the relevance of some aspects of Black Theology in Britain today', for, he suggests, 'the forms of kenosis which the modern emancipatory theologies mediate to us, the kenosis of the crucified peoples of the earth, may help us to imagine the political, economic, and social implications of the divine kenosis'.

But can 'the high Christology of Christian orthodoxy' – a version of which Hebblethwaite supports – make sense philosophically with special reference to God's action in the world through Jesus? Edward Henderson tackles this question in his contribution, 'Incarnation and Double Agency'. 'If Jesus is the incarnation of the eternal Son of God, then Jesus cannot rationally be thought to be truly human. But, continue most critics, it is the humanity we can most reasonably believe; therefore, we must deny the divinity. I want to join Brian

Hebblethwaite in arguing against this line, and I shall do so by bringing Austin Farrer's ideas about double agency to bear . . . for I believe the idea of double agency enables us to think a non-docetic incarnation in which both humanity and divinity are maintained.' Henderson mounts a detailed argument with a view to showing how this might be the case, exploring the ideas of 'the non-coercive *persuasion* of one creature by another' as an analogue for non-coercive divine agency, of the scale of double agency with reference to God's action in the world and in Jesus, and the manner in which we can say that though God acts in Jesus differently from the way God acts in us, this does not entail that Jesus' humanity is a sham.

Vincent Brümmer continues reflection on this theme of God's action in Jesus, but extends it to Hebblethwaite's contention that through the Incarnation 'Christianity claims to meet the problem of evil' in the world. He outlines objections to the way Hebblethwaite deals with this claim, arguing that 'What is needed . . . is that we *first* examine the doctrine of atonement or divine reconciliation and show why and in what sense it functionally requires the doctrine of the Incarnation.' So after providing an incisive analysis of the notion of forgiveness and its christological implications, Brümmer arrives at the last part of his essay: how divine reconciliation works through the two natures of Christ in relation to our world, and how 'God's action in reconciling the world to himself involves all three persons of the Trinity and not only the incarnate Son'.

Finally we come to David Ford's essay, 'Incarnation, Rationality, and Transformative Practices', in which the author comments on Hebblethwaite's Henley Henson Lectures given at Oxford in 2002, 'the broadest, richest, and most sustained exposition so far of his Incarnation-centred account of reality'. Ford, in his own distinctive way, reviews the role of rationality, history, the relationship between faiths, the integration of knowledge, social context, and the creative tensions between these poles, in Hebblethwaite's incarnational position, offering numerous suggestions as he goes along. He concludes by considering two large connected issues: the role of the Universities with respect to interfaith relations, and the Resurrection of Jesus 'where questions of God, incarnation, history, rationality, empirical fact and religious experience come together' since 'Hebblethwaite's cumulative apologetic gives considerable weight to this'. This essay is a fitting conclusion to the book as a whole in that it seeks to carry forward Hebblethwaite's 'fundamental concern for a wisdom that unites the theoretical and the practical in arriving at a quality of comprehensive judgement fed by feeling, imagination, and intuition as well as critical reflection'.

The twelve contributions in this book by well-known philosophers of religion and philosophical theologians are not an exegesis of Hebblethwaite's work. Informed and inspired variously by this work though they may be, they seek at times to criticize it constructively, or to justify, extend, or deepen its presuppositions and implications in a number of salient ways, combining to produce a unique contribution to scholarship in the context of a distinctive approach to our human reality. As a result, we are minded not only to return again and again to Hebblethwaite's considerable body of writings in their own right, but also to reflect and build on these ideas for ourselves. Can there be a more fitting tribute to the person honoured in this volume than this?

1. The Truth(s) of Translation

JULIUS LIPNER

One of Brian Hebblethwaite's major concerns over the years has been the conceptual interaction between cultures, the careful attention to the discernment and possible exchange of truth between religious faiths. As a philosopher of religion, Hebblethwaite has pursued this goal in the personal conviction that it is better to be a servant of truth than a master of often pointless, discursive speculation. But as Brian Hebblethwaite knows perfectly well, the pursuit of truth across cultures involves a philosophy of translation, a grasp of the truth(s) that translation might yield.

The Architecture of Translation

By 'translation' I do not mean in the first instance what we may call the narrower meaning of the term, the conveying of semantic content from one written or spoken tongue to another. To be sure, this is the most obvious sense of 'translation', and I do not exclude it; it will occupy much of our attention in this essay. We are exposed to the ubiquity of translation in this sense all the time, in circumstances that range from the mundane to the more sublime, from the array of languages on a packet of detergent all purporting to give the same 'Directions for Use', or the subtitles in a Bollywood movie, to the conversion from one language to another of a literary work. The sheer momentum of living in an increasingly interactive global environment marked by a bewildering diversity of linguistic backgrounds seems to produce this growing demand for the 'translation' of different genres of text.

But this is a token, the surface display, of a deeper meaning of the term, namely the passage of a set of developing and defining cultural traits and themes via the undercurrents of more or less distant stretches of space and time. It is thus that we can say, however elusively, that a particular mind-set is currently 'Western' rather than 'Islamic', 'traditionally English' rather than 'Bengali'. Such affirmations of identity, the end-result of a chain of historical transactions, conceptual shapings, and linguistic determinations between peoples, are the product of translation too, the translation or 'carrying across'[1] of a set of enduring cultural specifics from past times through to the present.

In his monumental work, *After Babel: Aspects of Language and Translation* (1975), George Steiner puts it thus:

> We are so much the product of set feeling-patterns, Western culture has so thoroughly stylized our perceptions, that we experience our 'traditionality' as natural ... The themes of which so much of our philosophy, art, literature are a sequence of variations, the gestures through which we articulate fundamental meanings and values are, if we consider them closely, quite restricted. The initial 'set' has generated an incommensurable series of local variants and figures (our 'topologies'), but in itself it seems to have contained only a limited number of units ... Our Western feeling-patterns, as they have come down to us through thematic development, are 'ours', taking this possessive to delimit the Graeco-Latin and Hebraic circumference. (p. 462)

It is important to note, given the vagaries of the geographical and linguistic transactions between peoples through time even within a particular cultural circumference, that the fixing of a mind-set by means of the 'carrying over' of certain specifics relies inevitably on the translation, in the first sense, of foundational texts. Steiner indicates how *Weltanschauungen,* philosophical preoccupations down the ages, the very 'shape' of cultural assumptions, notwithstanding their thematic and other variations amid a diversity of linguistic and ethnic identities, derive from the translation – the carrying over – of the formulated experience of *Ur*-texts across internal and external linguistic boundaries. This involves the sometimes not inconsiderable changes over time of word and meaning within a particular tongue, as well as the divisions that characterize historically closely related languages. The two forms of translation seem to be inextricably linked. More particularly, by analysing some of the foundational texts

---

[1] From the Latin verb *transferre*; past participle: *translatum* ('content conveyed').

of the Graeco-Latin and Hebraic heritage, Steiner endeavours to give us a glimpse of this process, i.e. not only of the literary architecture of Western, Judaeo-Christian civilization, but also of the architecture of translation as such.

But there is an even more grounded sense of the word 'translation' for our purposes. This pertains to the way the brain acquires, collates, and processes its sensory and other input (that 'translation' that bridges the gap between the transmission of external data and their internal reception), and to the way the mind then experiences and seeks to communicate semantic content. This calls for a mode of translation as well. The communication of individual meaning in a particular instance – in conversation, through a gesture, in written form – is enabled by the shaping of meaningful content selected from a vast matrix of 'banked' material in which the mind's various capacities – memory, imagination, intelligence, education, etc. – all have their integral roles to play.

This arises by means of a dual conditioning: the one generic, the other individual. The first derives from the cultural circumference out of which one speaks (adverted to by Steiner above), the specific mind-set determined by a particular culture or subculture: 'Spoken like a true Englishman/New Yorker!' or whatever. The second arises from within this circumscription, the individuated expression of a particular life-history: 'Ah! It is *Hebblethwaite* who speaks!' Our utterances are complexioned by this twofold determination. We do not, cannot jump out of our cognitive skins in the conveying of meaning.

There is a double hiatus here as well: first, the hiatus between experiencing, feeling, *knowing* what it is we wish to communicate and the actual expression of this content. How often we experience frustration at being unable to 'translate', to actualize the felt or mental content of personal, formulated experience, in being 'at a loss for words', not because we have nothing to say, but because we do not have the words at hand to say it. We are unable to translate what we feel, think, know into the adequacy of semantic content. But beyond this, there remains the added problem of transferring individuated meaning across personal boundaries, from self to self. Have we been effective in getting ourselves understood, we may ask, in translating meaning from one personal nexus to another?

At this point perhaps it is worth clarifying that, for our purposes, the semantic unit of translation in its most obvious sense is the 'sentence' rather than the phoneme, or verbal root, etymon, term, etc. In other words, by 'sentence' in this discussion I understand the minimal quantum of meaning in any context purporting to make *coherent* sense. This quantum of meaning need not be conveyed by a plurality of words. It may be expressed by a single word, namely 'Yes' (i.e. 'Yes, it is raining'), or 'Magenta' (i.e. 'I prefer the magenta one'), or by a single meaningful gesture.

It is not difficult to grasp that all three strata of translation are structurally of a piece. We cannot satisfactorily translate the Greek of Plato into English or the Sanskrit of Kālidāsa into German unless we have first contextualized Plato or Kālidāsa in terms of received cultural idioms with respect to ancient Greek and modern English, or classical Sanskrit and contemporary German, and we could not do this without allowing for the limitations and possibilities in conveying meaning of what we might call the idiolects of individual translators. Over a century ago a Jowett would translate the same extract of Plato into English rather differently from a Cornford of a later generation, though each attempt might be considered a satisfactory translation in its way. We shall return to this point in due course.

Thus far we might say that our discussion points to a (tripartite) truth of translation, irrespective of the stratum being considered: (1) its *inherent possibility*. Translation is possible from thought to speech, from one human tongue to another; indeed, this must be the case; (2) nevertheless, translation carries a stamp of *incommensurability*. This is because of its hiatal nature; ontically, translation resists closure. This raises the question as to what adequate translation might be; and (3) notwithstanding its intrinsic possibility and incommensurability, or rather in the attempt to reconcile these two extremes, translation becomes inherently creative; it engenders a new self, a reflected other. But this is too opaque a conclusion as it stands, and we must seek to explain it further.

1 Translation as Epistemic Act

In an early lecture, when discussing Descartes' and Foucault's understanding of madness vis-à-vis the role of rational discourse (or the play of *logos*), Jacques Derrida observes that 'if discourse and philosophical communication (that is, language itself) are to have an intelligible meaning, that is to say, if they are to conform to their essence and vocation as discourse, they must simultaneously in fact and in principle escape madness. They must carry normality within themselves . . . for [this] belongs to the meaning of meaning . . . By its

The Truth(s) of Translation

essence, the sentence is normal. It carries normality within it, that is *sense*, in every sense of the word – Descartes's in particular.'[2]

In a community of human beings, however primitive, who express forms of solidarity among themselves by formulating rites of passage, acquiring and storing food and information, devising means of shared entertainment, and reproducing and otherwise perpetuating their identity as a community, there can be no such thing as a 'monadic' language, a language so private that it remains essentially incommunicable beyond the group. As human beings the group are subject to the same natural laws that govern other human groups elsewhere in the world, in terms of which body and mind need to develop and reach out as human. To use Derrida's famous concept, the *différance* between this group and others cannot be impervious *per se* in so far as the groups are characterized as human. It is in this sense that the language of our group is inherently 'normal': normal not only for carrying out the transactions of everyday life within the group, but normal also in so far as it is the inalienable vehicle for conducting transactions that are *human*. Such a system of transactions can only be carried out in terms of a stable logic that is recognizable as such – that is, in terms of a 'rationality'. In this context, madness – the realm of the irrational – becomes the limiting symbol of quotidian normality.

This does not mean that other groups, perhaps distanced culturally through space and time, cannot find the customs or language of such a community strange or even impenetrable – ('strangeness' is a very culture-bound notion indeed!) – but this could be so only contingently, not necessarily. The semantic expression of such a culture, even though it could not be replicated in certain respects (perhaps because the group has been isolated environmentally for such a long time that it has developed vocalizations that other humans cannot easily reproduce), would still be inherently communicable beyond the group, once the conditions for this translation were right (e.g. a written language, or mechanical means of reproducing the vocalizations with the appropriate technology). In so far as the group is human, and perpetuates itself in the form of a *community,* with all the ongoing solidarities that this implies (even though the whole group could be regarded as 'mad' or bad in certain respects by other

---

2 From 'Cogito and the history of madness', in *Writing and Difference* by Jacques Derrida, translated with an Introduction and Additional Notes by Alan Bass, 1978:53–4.

groups[3]), it carries within it, through the agency of a purposeful language, the very basis of 'normality'.[4]

A universal point is being made here about the nature of formulated human experience and the communication of semantic content. It is the foundational point implicit in the *raison d'être* of anthropology and ethnology as social scientific disciplines (not to mention cognitive and other forms of psychology). More romantically, it underlies the unquenchable thirst of human beings down the ages to penetrate other cultures, and even to dominate them, not only or primarily by force of arms, but by the manipulation of meaning. As to the last, this is exactly what the colonial project was essentially about.[5] Theoretically, there are no no-go areas, no hermetic boundaries, in the transmission and comprehension of human meaning.[6] And so it is that the resourceful continue in search of Rosetta Stones of one sort or another, either between different tongues or between fields of learning, and comparative philologists still strive to decipher the Indus Valley script of the second millennium BCE, one of the last barriers to a fuller understanding of a great and ancient civilization.

This understanding of human speech is predicated on the ineluctable assumption that language is the expression of a collective self in the first instance, in and through which the individual self is shaped, that, in other words, human beings are intrinsically relational beings. Today, this intuitive truth derives support not only from the accumulated wisdom of the comparative study of various civilizations, but also from ongoing scientific research. Further, it extends to the awareness that it is language in its various agencies that constructs both the collective and the individual self in their societal context. But where there is construction of meaning, there is the contingency of contextuality, and the temporality of interpretation.

---

3 There is a polysemy to the term 'madness' which can be disconcerting, from a sense of impenetrable or dangerous irrationality, or unconventional behaviour (which may prompt one to observe that 'there's a method in his/her madness'), through to expressions of anger ('Are you mad with me?').

4 'It is through this relationship to the other as an other self that meaning reassures itself against madness and nonmeaning' (Derrida, 1978:59).

5 See, e.g., Inden's account of Britain's attempt to exercise intellectual hegemony over colonial India: R. B. Inden, *Imagining India*, (1990) 2000.

6 The translation of meaning across the species-barrier, namely between humans and non-humans, is a related but separate issue.

2 The Incommensurability of Translation

The articulation of self to own-self and to self as other, both collective and individual, in their historical unfolding, necessitates the deployment of a hermeneutic of meaning. The life-growth of the individual as self-aware, the development of the collective (whether this be the nation or some smaller group) – these translations of the embodiments of meaning and purpose through time – cannot be achieved without a complex dialectic of interpretation which becomes possible only through a corresponding development of complexity in the formation and use of language. The very multi-layeredness of language (and here I include gestures and wordless signs) gives ample scope to the ambiguities of intentionality (which are being explored so well through modern literary and critical theory). But to speak of the inevitability of interpretation in the transmission of meaning, of the inherent multi-layeredness and intentional ambiguity of language, is to speak of translation as an exercise in incommensurability. In other words, though the translation of meaning across internal and external barriers of articulation may be inherently possible wherever there is human speech, it cannot be achieved perfectly, namely in terms of some exact match of synonymity. This requires further elucidation.

Hear Steiner again:

> A 'perfect' act of translation would be one of total synonymity. It would presume an interpretation so precisely exhaustive as to leave no single unit in the source-text – phonetic, grammatical, semantic, contextual – out of complete account, and yet so calibrated as to have added nothing in the way of paraphrase, explication or variant. But we know that in practice this perfect fit is possible neither at the stage of interpretation nor at that of linguistic transfer and restatement. (1975:407)

Not only 'in practice', but also in principle. Not only for contingent reasons (e.g. linguistic deficiencies of the translator, confusions or obscurities in the source-text), but because of the nature of translation as such. We *could not* achieve a perfect fit even under optimal conditions. This is my point.

The reason for this resides in the ontic uniqueness of each individual's formulation of experience. This uniqueness extends to each stratum of translation distinguished above. The assimilation and storing of information is conditioned by the individuality of one's experiential faculties. There is only one perspective on the world in the name of our Brian Hebblethwaite: a singular composite of shaped and initiating consciousness, of a particular history of psycho-physical conditioning. Consequently, his attempted translations (and their idiosyncratic limitations) of formulated experience into word/gesture will also be unique. This applies both to the conversion of experience from mind/brain to intentional sign, whether this be by word or gesture (here personal internal physical and psychical hiatuses need to be bridged), and to the translation of meaning across personal hiatuses that are external, namely from own-self to self as other. Because Brian Hebblethwaite is Brian Hebblethwaite and no other, because of his numerical identity (a wonderful fact of our world!), his articulation of meaning in any capacity must necessarily bear the stamp of Hebblethwaitian uniqueness, of his singular perspective on the world.

But, we may ask, is not this originality ironed out in the daily interchanges of a shared language, in the common currency of words and ideas by which we relate to one another? If uniqueness held sway, and acted as a barrier to successful communication, how could we effect the fruitful cognitive interchanges of an increasingly globalized world?

Doubtless the transmission of meaning could take place only on the basis of shared semantic content. In this sense cognitive 'universals' are a requisite for verbal self-expression and communication.[7] But such universals are only the raw material, so to speak, of meaningful interaction. For it is individuals who transmit meaning, who act in terms of their own particularity of context and experience on the semantic template handed on to them and then passed on. Just as the various items of the coinage of a land remain inert, *in potentia* as it were, until they are subsumed as the active ingredients of endless unique interchanges of greater or lesser worth between persons ('unique' because no two interactions can be exactly the same), so the cognitive universals of which we speak enter into the common currency of unique transactions of meaningful expression between individuals. But whereas in fact coinage is subject to only insubstantial physical change through everyday wear and tear, ideas (if not always their phonetic embodiments) can undergo radical transformations of

---

7 Whatever we may make of the conclusions reached about the nature of 'universal ideas' in various debates of the past. I have in mind especially the medieval Scholastic controversies about the 'universal' in the West and the classical Sanskritic debates about *sāmānya* in the Indian subcontinent.

The Truth(s) of Translation

content with the passage of time, though important traces of semantic continuity may remain. The idea of *religio* used in a Ciceronian peroration was quite different from what it had become in the treatises of early Scholasticism, and this in turn metamorphosed appreciably as the modern meaning of 'religion' began to develop in the West from about the sixteenth century onwards. This is why no two concatenations of meaning that represent the translation of the same passage from one language to another in different hands can ever be the same: each sums up a unique resolution of meaning across internal and external hiatuses of space and time in different individuals.[8] From the point of view of the philosophy of translation, it is not a trivial matter that there is only ever one of each of us. Cumulatively, the consequence of this is that the shared repository of idioms and themes handed down in a particular culture or subculture is configured anew by each generation, so that their semantic continuities and discontinuities give rise continuously to subtle, sometimes eventually radical, shifts of emphasis and meaning.

Thus translation as a linguistic form resists semantic closure. Its hiatal nature urges continually towards the breakthrough, straining to the limits of meaning, encouraging the stretching and play of words. Curiously, or perhaps not, it is in the attempt to translate certain forms of scripture that one encounters a recognition of translation's ontic resistance to closure.[9] This can occur in a number of ways. Consider the case of the Qur'ān. Translation of the Qur'ān

> has often been hampered . . . by theological hesitations about the translatability of God's word.
>
> Three such hesitations may be identified. Firstly, for the theologians, the Qur'ān is . . . inimitable . . . Since this quality pertains to its Arabic diction as well as to its meaning, no translation can be said adequately to represent the original. Secondly, the Muslim belief that earlier scriptures had been compromised by interpolation and distortion (*taḥrīf*) led many to defend God's Book from the *traduttore* [translator] who might turn *traditore* [traitor]. Thirdly,

---

8 This does not preclude the possibility that two translators will come up with exactly the same set of words when translating the same passage (the shorter the passage, the greater the chance this could happen). But this outcome is exactly that: a chance occurrence of the physical manifestation in words of two quite distinct, individually conditioned fields of subjective experience.

9 Also, of course, in the translation of poetry, certain kinds of humour, idioms, etc., and indeed, musical scores. On the last, see Ann Loades' essay in this book.

twentieth-century Arab theologians sometimes feared that translation into European languages would entail a diminution of the religion's perceived Arab particularity, leading to its symbolic conquest by the colonialist Other.[10]

These are different kinds of theological hesitation, no doubt, yet in each case the theologians need not have striven so anxiously to protect either the deity's unique revelation or the inalienable status of the Qur'ān as inimitable text. For even in the case of an endless number of other literary texts, similar hesitations about their translatability might be expressed as I have indicated, even though they may not be regarded as having proceeded directly from the deity. As the word of God, the Qur'ān may be a unique text in a special way, but it is not the case that it cannot be perfectly or even adequately translated, without semantic loss, *because* it is the Qur'ān. So long as God's word is expressed in a human tongue, it remains inevitably subject to the inherent limitations of translation as such.

Let us consider another, interestingly different, instance of incommensurability in the translation of scripture. This pertains to the Vedas, canonical Sanskrit scriptures of the Hindus. Scholars date the ongoing redaction of the four Vedas from c.1200 BCE to about the beginning of the Common Era, but traditional Hindu theologians believe(d) that the Vedas are timeless. This timelessness does not necessarily refer to the reception of the Vedic text among humans, but to the composition of the Vedas and to their Sanskritic literary form. As such the Vedas are supposed to be *a-pauruṣeya*, i.e. *not* composed by any personal agent (this includes a/the deity); this means that the sequence of Sanskrit words that makes up the Vedas as a whole is autonomous: timeless and unchanging. Their *Sanskritic* utterance in certain circumstances[11] has the power to produce and change the reality, or aspects thereof, of our world.[12] Traditional Hindu theologians were not particularly perturbed by attempts to translate the *meaning* of Vedic passages. Here they continually resorted to paraphrase, restatement, commentary. It was just that (Vedic) Sanskrit was

---

10 T. J. Winter, 'Qur'ān: Translations', in the *Concise Encyclopedia of Language and Religion*, ed. John F. A. Sawyer and J. M. Y. Simpson, 2001.

11 Especially in the sacrificial ritual or *yajña*; this includes prescribed gestures (*mudrā*) by the officiating priests as well as other features of priestly role-playing.

12 For one classical Hindu theologian's view of this process, see the author's *The Face of Truth: A Study of Meaning and Metaphysics in the Vedāntic Theology of Rāmānuja*, 1986, ch. 1.

The Truth(s) of Translation

a privileged scriptural language because it was its *utterance* in certain circumstances that had effective power with respect to the production and change of being. In this sense the Vedas were unique and untranslatable into other verbal expressions (including the Sanskritic). Though the Vedas represent a form of intelligible discourse (and have been subjected, either in whole or in part, to numerous translations into various languages), it was primarily their utterance in their correct context and sequence that was sacrosanct and effective, not the meanings. In this sense, it is not clear if we are dealing with an instance of (un)translatability proper. But in so far as their meanings were sought to be transferred across the linguistic boundaries we have been considering, they too fall under the inherent limitations of translation *per se*.

Finally, consider the Bible, or more precisely the New Testament, in the hands of Christian missionaries. Whatever literary judgements may have been made over the centuries about the inimitable beauty and power of God's word in the form of the Bible, there have been no major theological objections to translating it. On the contrary. One of the first things missionaries contemplate when encountering a new language or unevangelized people is the translation of biblical text into this new context. The narrative of Christian expansion is replete with this endeavour. Indeed, important advances in the history of printing and the formation of various scripts and their grammar can be attributed to this programme. So, the 'truth' of the Qur'ān and the Vedas for the eyes of faith apart, is it not the case that the 'truth' of the New Testament is constituted only in and through its very translatability?[13] And yet it is through this compelling feature, in the ceaseless striving for adequate reformulation and restatement, that the Bible's truth must remain, humanly speaking, ever unfulfilled and elusive.

Thus the translator deals in approximations; and from one point of view (we shall consider the other side of this truth presently) the task is to narrow the gaps to the best of one's ability, to be ever sensitive to context and valence, to what might be lost in the cognitive silences between words.

---

13 Surely this has to do in Christian theology with the translation of the Word of God into human form in the person of Jesus Christ, a translation explained in terms of emptying on the one hand ('he emptied himself . . . becoming as human beings are'; Phil. 2.7) and filling on the other (e.g. Col. 1.19: 'because God wanted all fullness to be found in him', and 2.9: 'In him, in bodily form, lives divinity in all its fullness').

3 The Translation Self as 'Other'

So much for the incommensurability of the translational act. But it is this hiatal characteristic that gives another dimension to translation, enabling it to exploit these very silences in creative ways, and rendering the good translator one of the most valuable assets in the enriching of human speech and experience. It is to this demiurgic property of translation that we now turn in the third and final part of our discussion.

Dryden's observation in the Preface to his translation of the *Aeneid* is well known: 'I have endeavoured to make Virgil speak such English as he himself would have spoken, if he had been born in England, and in this present age.' Of course, if Virgil had been born in England in Dryden's age, not only would there have been no *Aeneid*, but there is a good chance that the very course of the history of Western literature and, perhaps more significantly, of certain deep-set features of Western culture would have taken a different turn. For may not the *Aeneid* be regarded as one of those foundational texts whose verbal and conceptual translations down the ages have played an important part in giving shape to Western perceptions of the world? Perhaps Dryden's point could have been expressed more pithily in the words of Ronald Knox: 'A good translation should have the freshness of an original product.'[14]

We speak of a 'good' translation here. In the same essay, Knox distinguishes between the 'artisans' and the 'craftsmen' of translation, that is, between the 'jobbing carpenters' of the art, those producers of subtitles and 'Directions for Use', the pure functionalists, and the Chippendales of translation, those who are 'concerned to produce something useful but not merely functional ... the rendering, like the original, is to be a literary production'.

His focus is on the craftsman, and so is ours. In a lecture entitled 'Reflections of a Translator',[15] Professor Nicholas de Lange, a colleague at Cambridge, speaks of three models of a translator: the first is the translator as mere 'copyist'. Here the translator seeks to imitate the original as faithfully as possible, the result intended being 'like the reproductions of paintings and artifacts that you can buy in

---

14 In ch. 3, 'On English translation', in his *Literary Distractions*, 1958:50.
15 Published as The Sixteenth Annual Rabbi Louis Feinberg Memorial Lecture in Judaic Studies, Judaic Studies Program, University of Cincinnati, 1993.

The Truth(s) of Translation

museum shops'. Clearly there can be no freshness of product here, and if this is all that the translator sets out to accomplish, it is arguable that the vitality, the distinguishing feature of the original, must be lost. In seeking to duplicate, the translator comes up with a crib, with all the dismembering of the original that this term entails. Where translation is concerned, the attempt to duplicate can only result, ironically, in translation as glaring approximation between original and copy. This is not what good translation is about.

Secondly, there is the model of the translator as 'servant'. Here, the job of the translator is to work 'completely unnoticed, like the perfect butler'. According to de Lange the weakness of this approach is 'that the successful translator is the one who has eradicated from his text every arresting feature, every sign of originality. Is that really what we want from our translators? Do we want Dante or Kafka to read like the latest pulp novel?' For my part, I see the point of the distinction between these two models as that between soulless externalizer and internalizer. The copyist has not entered into the heart of the original, so that there is no dialogue between subject and object. Consequently, there is only objectification of the original, and the translation dies the death of inanity. In the case of the perfect servant, however, the translator internalizes the original to such an extent as to be completely immersed in it, surrendering every vestige of subjectivity. The objectification here is of the translator, with equally ineffectual results for the translation. In neither case is there that meeting of hearts and minds in the interaction between original and product that is the prerequisite of a good translation.

Finally, there is the model of the translator as 'creative artist' whose role is rather that of 'a poet or novelist [who] takes an incident or an idea and works it into an original and exciting piece of writing'. According to de Lange this is unsatisfactory too, if it is held up as the sole ideal of what translation must be. For what is invariably lacking here is that mark of fidelity to the original so essential for a good translation. We are not unfamiliar with 'translations' in this mould, where the translator has taken such liberties with the text as to have produced not a 'fresh' piece of work (in every sense of this word), but virtually a new creation. This too is to fail in the act of translation. In terms of our earlier analysis, it is to submerge the objectivity of the original, its inalienable givenness, in the voracious subjectivity of the renderer (who becomes one who 'rends', namely, disembowels and tears up), so as to make of the original an ingested non-entity in the translational act. As a separate work of creativity it may be highly commendable, but as a work of translation it is an act of perfidy: *traduttore* here has turned *traditore*.

The ideal for Professor de Lange is to blend all three models of translation. 'The good translator must be copyist, servant, and creative writer. The trick is a balancing trick: to succeed in all three at once . . . I would liken the translator to a performing musician.' The translator must be attuned to the original so as to enter into 'a double relationship and a double responsibility, to the composer on the one hand and to his listeners on the other'.

From what has been said so far, we may conclude that there are three salient characteristics of the good translation, the good translator: *fidelity* to and *respect* for the original, and *integrity* between original and product.[16] All the marks of good translation analysed hitherto are summed up in these three qualities, and the supervening model here, in my view, is that of the translator as '*suhṛd*' (pronounced, more or less, '*su-hrid*'). *Suhṛd* is a Sanskrit term that is itself hard to translate. The *suhṛd* is a friend, a confidante, a well-wisher, something of a soul-mate.

'Suhridic' Translation

In a way, suhridic translation is an act of midwifery, displaying through the passage of restatement what was (sometimes only germinally) present in the original. It is an act of enablement which gives new life – 'freshness' – to what was already there. In this way semantic content is not transgressed, but re-born, renewed.

This process seems to be twofold. First, a striving to enter into the heart of the source-text. One can do this only by submerging the ego-self, by bringing all one's skills into play – linguistic, psychological, noetic – in exploring context and intention. It is important to note that authorial intention does not exhaust the intentionality of the source-text. Authorial intention can be unclear (both to author and to reader), stratified, explicit and implicit, at odds with itself. In his stimulating work, *Translation and Understanding*, Sukanta Chaudhuri points out that:

> Translation can release an alternative, subversive potential of the

---

[16] These properties apply no less to translations in the realm of music. Though I shall not focus on the analogy of translator as performing musician, in what follows my argument will apply, *mutatis mutandis*, to musical renderings too.

text, turn it inside-out to bring its deconstructive factor to the fore. The new language draws out possibilities beyond the original writer's intention or awareness, possibilities he might have consciously rejected. Going beyond authorial intention, they might be possibilities that his own language could not admit but that are instilled in the new text by the structures of the target (or, as I would prefer to call it, 'host') language. (1999:2)

This respectful, explorative journey into the source-text, attentive to its intentionalities, context, resonances, achieved both by the subjection of the ego and by giving it rein to enact the modalities of the text, I shall call the phase of *kenotic interrogation*. It requires an emptying, a pouring out of the translator's self, the assumption of an actor's role. The translator 'must, in fact, get inside somebody else's skin before he undertakes the rendering of a single sentence . . . All translation is a kind of impersonation; make a success of that, and style and idiom will follow' (R. Knox, 1958:54–5). Here, the translator has taken on the identity of the text.

But this is one limb of the dialectic, and faithful restatement is necessary. If the translator remains in kenotic mode, the amity of the relationship between translator and text will be impaired, for friendship requires a dialogue between individuals. Good translation is not a crib; as Chaudhuri's statement indicates it 'releases' the original without distorting it. In the second limb of the dialectic, the subjectivity of the translator is engaged, and the material absorbed in the first phase by immersion, is released through the personality, the idiolect, of the translator. Good translation entails a dynamic equilibrium between kenosis and plenitude, between emptying-out and re-issuing, through the fullness of the translator's skill and individuality. 'His style must be his own, his rhetoric and his emphasis must be that of his original. And, always, at the back of his mind, he must imagine that he is the original' (R. Knox, 1958:57) – but the original restated and renewed. He is not to be the original purely by way of an identity of insinuation where he has lost his individuality (or his 'identity' according to a certain way of speaking), he is to be the original in his own right. Or if you wish to frame it musically, in the hands of a Toscanini or a Simon Rattle, Beethoven's Seventh will sound recognizably the same, down to the last note if they work to the same score, yet each rendering will take on a life of its own, and neither would be what Beethoven himself could hear in his mind's ear.

I am reminded here of a Buddhist analogy. As is well known,

Buddhists do not believe in a substantival self (an *ātmā*), yet they believe in the rebirth of an individual, or rather, in the serial transfer of an individual's karma from birth to birth, till enlightenment is attained. But if there is no enduring self, who continues to be reborn, and how is the transfer of karma effected? A striking analogy is often given in reply. Just as a burning oil-lamp transfers its flame to an unlit lamp, so the individual and their karma pass from one birth to another.[17] Is it the same flame or another on both sides of the divide? The Buddhists answer: 'It is neither the same nor another.' In other words, there is an integrity – a real continuity of history and nature – between the two flames, but not a simple numerical identity. This is the ideal of suhridic translation: there is a historic identity, an integrity, between original and translation, but each remains an individual in its own right.

We may get a sense of this integrity, I hope, by reference to the following instance of a translation from Sanskrit into English. The original is a verse from the *Kumārasambhava* ('The birth of Kumāra'), a heroic poem by the great classical poet, Kālidāsa (*c.* fifth century CE). Rati is mourning the unexpected loss of her husband Kāma, the god of love, who has suddenly been reduced to ashes by Lord Śiva for daring to disturb his meditation. This verse is part of Rati's lament to Kāma. It is necessary to start with the Sanskrit:

*kva nu māṃ tvadadhīnajīvitāṃ
vinikīrya kṣaṇabhinnasauhṛdaḥ/
nalinīṃ kṣatasetubandhano
jalasaṃghāta ivāsi vidrutaḥ//* (Canto 4, v. 6)

First a (truncated) crib:

kva: where; *nu*: (strengthening particle) Oh; *māṃ*: me; *tvad-adhīna-jīvitāṃ*: you-dependent on-living for; *vinikīrya*: having abandoned/cast off; *kṣaṇa-bhinna-sauhṛdaḥ*: (in) an instant/short time-cut off-friend/companion(ship); *nalinīṃ*: a lotus, a cluster of lotuses, a lotus-pond; *kṣata-setubandhanaḥ*: broken-dike/dam; *jala-saṃghāta(ḥ)*: water-mass; *iva*: like; *asi*: you are; *vidrutaḥ*: flowing quickly, dispersed.

Construal: Oh, where (are you), friend(ship) cut off in an instant,

---

17 Cf. St Augustine, *Epistola* 190, where he considers the possibility that souls are transmitted from parents to offspring 'like [a flame that is passed from] oil-lamp to oil-lamp (*tamquam lucerna de lucerna:*)'.

who has abandoned me who has been living for/dependent on you? You have gone away like a mass of water flowing quickly through a broken dam leaves a lotus flower /cluster of lotuses.

The crib is hardly a translation; it is unfinished business. Note the shredding of text, the awkward piecing together, the lack of nuance – and the consequent inanimation of meaning. Like the unfortunate Humpty Dumpty, the text is in some disarray.

But this, I trust, is a translation:

> Oh, where are you – our love lost in a moment –
> Who's abandoned me even as I lived for you?
> You've left me like a torrent of water
> Rushing through a broken dam leaves
> A cluster of lotuses.

The untoward absence of Kāma ('love lost in a moment'), the sudden, almost physical hurt his apparent abandonment gives to the blameless yet bereft Rati (who is lotus-like), the ephemerality of their relationship, these latent nuances of meaning which devolve in large measure on the sense of dispersal, rapid movement-away, connoted by *vidruta*, now come through, and the integrity of the original has, to some extent at least, been restored in the translation. (One can see that it is translation of verse in particular, with its attention to the measure and flow of words, that is akin to the playing of a musical score.)

The ideal, we have argued, can be approximated only more or less perfectly. And it is in the cognitive silence(s) between the equilibriating poles of this integrity that the creative resonances of translation reside, where the tension between fidelity and respect releases the multivalent potential of the source-text, of the semantic content in new form, of the play and stretching of words. Chaudhuri mentions some of these possible acquisitions:

> In translation, the verbal transference carries its own disjunctive function, makes the translation something other than the original, reveals in the original the potential to be something other than itself ... Each translation from a marginal or subaltern language into a dominant one can counter the imbalance [between the dominant language and its subaltern counterpart] – often subtly, sometimes dramatically. It validates the subaltern culture quite literally in terms of the dominant one; but thereby draws out the dominant language beyond its entrenched confines. (1999:10, 16)

The Historicity of Translation

In good translation the source-text acquires a new identity, becomes another, and yet, as we have intimated above, remains the same; this is better put negatively: 'neither the same nor another'. One facet of this transformation is that translation is embedded in historicity. It is a salient marker of historical transience, for every translation, by virtue of its contingency as *this* translation, *this* concatenation of words rather than some other, demonstrates its contingency. By its vulnerability to time and change, translation, like history – to extend an idea of Sudipta Kaviraj – shows not only how the world came to be what it is, *but also how close at times it was to being quite different*.[18] Translations, however good they might be, cannot mark time; they are harbingers of change, of a continuous process of re-translation, of the re-birth of texts and ideas.

This has repercussions for languages and cultures that may have a history of subalternity. Through translation, the subaltern of today can become, if not the hegemon, then the resistant interlocutor, of tomorrow. I am not sure if we can call Bengali a subaltern language. It has a colonial history, yet it is spoken today, in its various forms, by many millions of people; it has produced a Bankim Chandra Chatterji, the first to develop the novel-form in an Indian language, and a nobel laureate (albeit in translation!) in Rabindranath Tagore. Nevertheless, it would be fair to say, I think, that to a Eurocentric West, or an Anglophile world, it remains a closed, somewhat marginal, language. Translations, good translations, of literary works from Bengali into English, therefore, will perform a dual function: on the one hand, they will valorize Bengali language and culture as the vehicle of a refined humanity which has many fresh things to say about the enrichment of human relationships, about how to assume fruitful new perspectives on the world. They also help us reveal those cultural differences that define and at the same time celebrate the particularities of certain kinds of identity. All this will encourage some to learn Bengali (not least in the Universities) with serious intent, and many to hold on to their linguistic heritage in the face of an omnivorous challenge from English. But, on the other hand, these translations will also bring about a change for the good in English. They will insinuate new thought and life into English-based perceptions, new loan-words, new

---

18 *The Unhappy Consciousness: Bankimchandra Chattopadhyay and the Formation of Nationalist Discourse in India*, 1995, see p. 109.

cultural idioms. Through this exchange, in time English will be changed for ever as part of the broadening global interactions between peoples. One must not underestimate the constructive value of good translation.

However, it is not always easy to ascertain what a good translation is, whether translational fidelity has been transgressed in the interests of educing the whole meaning of the original, and integrity impaired. Let us consider what might appear to be a simple example.

On that fateful morning in the Praetorium, when, according to John's Gospel, Jesus stood before Pilate and they spoke of truth, what exactly did Pilate's last remark mean before he went out again to the waiting Jews? We cannot even be certain in what language he spoke. We have a New Testament version of his words in Greek: *ti estin aletheia?* (John 18.38). The New Jerusalem Bible translates: ' "Truth?" said Pilate, "What is that?" ' Have we departed here from the seeming blandness of the Greek? Is there not a touch of sarcasm in Pilate's English words? One can almost see the half-sneer on his lips. Yet if Pilate spoke thus, the Greek seems devoid of his intonation. Were these words uttered with a gesture? A world-weary shrug perhaps? Or were they said in jest, or with a spark of serious intent, or indeed in irony or sarcasm? The Greek seems to be silent on this. Yet it is out of the depth of this silence that we have the English translation, and many others, of course.

Consider the Sanskrit of The Bible Society of India and Ceylon (1962): *pilātas tam āha, satyaṃ kim?* 'Pilate-said-to-him-what-is-truth?' Like the Greek, the Sanskrit too seems a 'stuffed-owl' (Knox's expression) rendering, devoid of expression, more silent than telling. But the Bengali of the acclaimed S. Bandyopadhyay and C. Mignon edition published not so long ago,[19] is different: *pilāt tāke ballen: satya! satya ābār ki?* ('Pilate said to him: "Truth! Now/Well, what is truth?" '). Note the exclamation mark after the first 'truth' (*satya*), and the intrusive (?) use of *ābār* ('Now/Well'). There is a mocking irony here, a raising of the eyebrows perhaps, or that faint arrogance of a superior who knows that he comes from a civilization whose philosophies have searched deep into such matters and still await an answer.

Now which is the good translation, and how can we tell? The stuffed-owl rendering, or the other with interpretative content? And do these interpretations succeed in bringing out what was present

---

19 *Maṅgalbārtā*, Calcutta, 1st edn 1984.

germinally in the original? The answer lies not in some whim or fancy of the translator ('I'll make it interesting!', or 'Pilate must have meant that'), but in faithful attention to context and detail. Fidelity, respect, integrity. These terms have moral connotations too, and their qualities are pursued by dint of that dialectic between kenosis and subjectivity in the translator that results in an *accountable, informed* response. What can we know of Pilate both inside and outside the text, of the intention(s) of John's Gospel as a whole, of the role of truth in it? Only after these questions have been properly addressed, can a responsible translation be attempted. And it may well be that wisdom lies in preserving what could be the reticence of the original, in offering a dead-pan rendering, so that the imagination of the reader (hearer too?) may set to work and engender a personal engagement with the text.

We are nearing the end of our discussion. Let us draw some of its strands together by considering a final, more substantial example.

The *Bhagavadgītā* ('The Lord's Poem', *c.*100 BCE–300 CE) has come down to us as one of the foundational texts of devotional Hinduism. Composed in metrical Sanskrit, and consisting traditionally of 18 chapters and 700 verses, it represents a discourse between Krishna, the supreme deity in human form, and his friend and disciple, the warrior Arjuna. In the *Gītā*, Krishna reveals his true form and the nature of *dharma* or righteous living as the performance of selfless action, in accordance with one's vocation in life, out of unswerving devotion to the Lord. Other teachings of the *Gītā* – the nature of the human person and of the world in their bearing on the deity, the motives of the wicked, the forms of spiritual discipline, etc. – hinge on this central doctrine. The *Gītā* has been translated, commented upon, and paraphrased again and again in its long history down to the present day, continually being adapted to circumstance, and configuring and re-configuring the spiritual ideals of Hindus and the perceptions of non-Hindus about Hindus. It has been repeatedly translated, of course, into English.

Let us consider some examples of the translation into English of two verses taken from ch. 4 (vv. 7–8).[20] These verses have reverberated through history, for here for the first time in the words of Krishna to

---

20 *yadā yadā hi dharmasya glānir bhavati Bhārata/ abhyutthānam adharmasya tadātmānaṃ sṛjāmy aham//*

paritrāṇāya sādhūnāṃ vināśāya duṣkṛtām/ dharmasaṃsthāpanārthāya sambhavāmi yuge yuge//

The Truth(s) of Translation

his disciple Arjuna (= Bhārata, viz. descended from the lineage of king Bharata), the teaching of divine descent (*avatāra*) into human affairs is announced. This is a teaching which for generations of Hindus has revealed the deity's active and continuing concern for the welfare of the world, and which has acted as the basis for the development of key aspects of Hindu devotionalism (and, in the nineteenth century, of Hindu nationalistic consciousness). Further, it is with this teaching in mind that in recent times important comparisons and contrasts have been drawn between Hindu and other faiths.

We can begin with a verbal analysis by Winthrop Sargeant:

v. 7: *yadā yadā*: whenever; *hi*: indeed, truly; *dharmasya*: of righteousness, of duty, of law; *glānis*: exhaustion, decrease; *bhavati*: it is, it exists, it comes to be; *bhārata*: Descendant of Bharata, epithet of Arjuna; *abhyutthānam*: rising up, emerging, standing up; *adharmasya*: of unrighteousness, of undutifulness, of unlawfulness; *tadā*: then; *ātmānam*: self, myself; *sṛjāmi*: I give forth, I let go, I create; *aham*: I.

v. 8: *paritrāṇāya*: to refuge, to protecting, to preservation, to deliverance [*sic*]; *sādhūnām*: of the righteous, of the good, of the virtuous ones; *vināśāya*: to the destruction, to the loss, to the perishing (sic); *ca*: and; *duṣkṛtām*: of evil doers, of doers of wicked deeds; *dharma*: righteousness, duty, law; *saṃsthāpana*: the establishing; *arthāya*: for the purpose of, with the aim of, for the sake of; *sambhavāmi*: I come into being, I originate myself; *yuge yuge*: from age to age, in age after age.

Sargeant's translation:

v. 7: Whenever a decrease of righteousness
Exists, Descendant of Bharata,
And there is a rising up of unrighteousness,
Then I give forth myself

v. 8: For the protection of the good,
And the destruction of evil doers;
For the sake of establishing righteousness,
I come into being from age to age. (1984 edn)[21]

---

21 *The Bhagavad Gītā*, 1984:207–8.

Here are some other renderings:

> For whensoever right declines, O Bhārata, and wrong uprises, then I create myself.
> To guard the good and to destroy the wicked and to confirm the right, I come into being in this age and in that. (W. D. P. Hill, 1928)[22]

> When righteousness is weak and faints and unrighteousness exults in pride, then my Spirit arises on earth.
> For the salvation of those who are good, for the destruction of evil in men, for the fulfilment of the kingdom of righteousness, I come to this world in the ages that pass. (Juan Mascaro, 1962)[23]

> Whenever and wherever there is a decline in religious practice, O descendant of Bharata, and a predominant rise of irreligion – at that time I descend My Self.
> In order to deliver the pious and to annihilate the miscreants, as well as to re-establish the principles of religion, I advent My Self millennium after millennium. (Swami A. C. Bhaktivedanta, 1968)[24]

> Whenever there is a falling away from the true law and an upsurge of unlawfulness, then, Bharata, I emit myself.
> I come into being age after age, to protect the virtuous and to destroy evil-doers, to establish a firm basis for the true law. (W. J. Johnson, 1994)[25]

Since space is limited, we cannot give a detailed comparative analysis, or argue which of the above translations is most closely tethered to the original. Each claims to be a serious attempt to divine the purport of the text; none has been without influence in the history of *Gītā* translation. There is little doubt as to what the general sense of the passage is: it is about the repeated descent of the deity into our world to restore *dharma,* and to overthrow *adharma.* But when we seek clarity as to what *dharma* and *adharma* might mean, complications arise. 'Right' and 'wrong' do not have the same connotations as 'righteousness' and 'unrighteousness', or 'the true law' and 'unlawful-

---

22 *The Bhagavadgītā: Translated from the Sanskrit with an Introduction, an Argument and a Commentary,* 1928:138.
23 *The Bhagavad Gita,* 1962:62–3.
24 *The Bhagavad Gita as it is,* 1968:113–15.
25 *The Bhagavad Gita,* 1994:19.

ness', or indeed 'religious practice' and 'irreligion', respectively. Further, who are the targets of Krishna's intervention? 'The good', 'the pious', 'the virtuous', on the one hand, and 'evil doers', 'the wicked' and 'miscreants' on the other. From these comparisons, nevertheless, we do get a sense of the rich semantic texture of the term *dharma* (and by implication of *adharma*), and the (correct) impression that they carry what would be social, moral and religious connotations in current English discourse. The polyvalency of the terms brings to mind a wise piece of advice I received from my doctoral supervisor many years ago: when dealing with translations consult more than one serious translation of the same text, for it is in the disparities that interesting questions arise.

We may question further: do the translations give us a clear sense of how the *avatāra* comes about? 'I give forth myself (v. 7) . . . [and] I come into being (v. 8)', says one rendering of Krishna's words, 'I create myself . . . [and] I come into being' says another; or is it: 'My Spirit arises on earth . . . [and] I come to this world', or (more curiously), 'I descend My Self . . . [and] I advent My Self', or indeed, 'I emit myself . . . [and] I come into being'? It seems clear that Krishna initiates the action, but it is not clear what the nature of this action is. As to the frequency of the descent, with the exception of the somewhat idiosyncratic Swami Bhaktivedanta (there is hardly justification here for a 'millennial' count), the word 'age' is most often resorted to. This word and the repeated expression 'I come into being' indicate that translators tend to keep track of each other's work, at times forming a line of succession in the rendering of certain expressions. It is not uncommon for a false move to be inherited in translation and then to be passed on (though not necessarily in this case).

Where form is concerned, most do not attempt to reflect the metrical style of the original. Mascaro's well-known translation (the third above) most obviously takes recourse to poetic licence, but it is precisely for this reason that he has been severely criticized by other scholars. One could hardly fail to notice the biblical resonances of his 'For the salvation of . . .' and 'for the fulfilment of the kingdom of righteousness'. Indeed, we could ask whether the tenor of his translation has not Christianized the *Gītā* in some sense. And if it has, could we say that this theologically negotiated translation reveals the latent truth of the *Gītā*? These questions take us too far afield, and we cannot deal with them here. But in the final analysis, the three qualities identified earlier – fidelity, respect, integrity – must remain the acid test of a good translation. There is no room for sentiment here.

Throughout his career, not least in his comparative analyses of religious thought,[26] Brian Hebblethwaite has shown unfailing fidelity, respect and integrity wherever they have been required, eschewing sentiment with an unassuming rigour. In this sense, he has been a translator of ideas, of a message he holds dear, *par excellence*. Through his numerous writings, he has had many illumining things to say, and over the years I have learned a great deal from him as a person and as a thinker. This essay is a small token of the warm esteem in which I shall always hold him.

---

26 See, e.g., *Evil, Suffering and Religion*, 2000.

2. On Music's Grace
Trying to Think Theologically about Music

ANN LOADES

Making Worship Possible

In writing this essay I have no pretensions to being a professional musician, and cannot talk about music as though I were one. Like Brian Hebblethwaite, however, I find that the experience of listening to music, participating as a member of an audience at musical performances, including those in the professional theatre, and participating in music in the context of worship is integral to my life. With respect to the latter, it needs to be said at the outset that I do not think that music-making is simply a matter of enriching worship, though indeed it may do that. Rather, it is about making worship *possible*, as members of congregations well know, even if their ministers and professional theologians do not (with some notable exceptions). I assume, of course, that worship is the root of theology. If music does indeed make worship possible, it is crucially important that musicians do not lose their nerve, and be over-intimidated by ministers and theologians, since with one or two honourable exceptions, not only have the latter not been thinking hard about music, they have not done much thinking about worship as adoration either, and the theological work which might have encouraged them to do so has been pushed to the margins of study.

The development of 'liturgical theology' in the USA especially may in time help to remedy this state of affairs, as it may rejuvenate academic theology as a whole.[1]

---

[1] See, for example, Don E. Saliers, 'The integrity of sung prayer', *Worship* 55(4), 1981:290–303, and 'Singing our lives', in Dorothy C. Bass *et al.* (eds), *Practicing Our Faith*, 1998: 179–215, and essays in E. Byron Anderson and Bruce T. Morrill SJ (eds), *Liturgy and the Moral Self: Humanity at Full Stretch Before God*, 1998.

It seems sometimes too easily thought that congregations are absent from services at which there is normally music, and especially those at which the musical fare may normally be of high quality, because they only come 'to worship the music'. The point may well be that to attempt to worship God without music of any kind is artificial and distinctly odd – hence the importance of the gift of poetry and song to the Northumbrian Caedmon, as recounted by Bede, and Denise Levertov's poem about Caedmon, which concludes, '. . . and nothing was burning,

> nothing but I, as that hand of fire
> touched my lips and scorched my tongue
> and pulled my voice
>   into the ring of the dance'.[2]

There seems to be little good reason for attempting to worship God without music, except if and when worship has turned into theatre or concert, as may sometimes be so, in which case some corrective but temporary steps need to be taken. The same might equally be true when a preacher or celebrant has been allowed to become a sort of liturgical soloist, in which case music without words might be a particularly helpful option to explore for a time. The norm, however, one supposes, is to make music in order to worship. Would Jews, for instance, welcome and delight in the Sabbath without some version of *Lekhah dodi*?[3] For the devout, it seems that music is a 'means of grace' which helps us to be opened up to a richly personal divine presence, and to be graced by that presence, perhaps unexpectedly. For instance, those who attend to the Qawwali ('utterance') of Ustad Nusrat Fateh Ali Khan (even in a 'concert' setting, if this is the nearest approximation to worship that can be achieved) discover that the complexities of chant, bodily movement and rhythmic clapping, without knowledge even of the words, may grace both performer and listener with closeness to God.[4]

---

2 In David Impastato (ed.), *Upholding Mystery*, 1997:128–9.

3 See 'The meaning of a tune', in Jeffrey A. Summit, *The Lord's Song in a Strange Land: Music and Identity in Contemporary Jewish Worship*, 2000:33–104, and Michael Fishbane's 'Joy and Jewish spirituality', in his book, *The Exegetical Imagination: On Jewish Thought and Theology*, 1998:151–72.

4 See also the essays by Seyyed Hossein Nassr, 'Islam and music', and Regula Burckhardt Qureshi, 'Sounding the Word', in Lawrence E. Sullivan (ed.), *Enchanting Power: Music in the World's Religions*, 1997:219–35, 263–97.

From the conviction of that possibility absolutely nothing follows as to what kind of music may be a 'means of grace', or in what context that grace may be mediated, or by what means precisely. In a world graced by God, it may not be music which is identifiably from a 'sacred' tradition or in a 'sacred space' or in the context of worship which will say 'God' to someone. So far as the evidence goes, it seems that there is in fact a whole range of music which can help people on their pilgrimage through life. As Thomas Day wrote a quarter of a century ago:

> One simple yet profound piece of wisdom finds its way into the decrees of the Council of Trent, the *Constitution on the Sacred Liturgy*, and the twentieth-century papal encyclicals on music: Worship involves the efforts of human beings who possess that curious imperfection known as human nature. The authors of these statements never once entertain the idea of forbidding musical innovation or freezing liturgical music in some archaic style; they realized that human beings were hopelessly changeable when it came to matters of taste and the kind of music that would inspire them.[5]

In the context of worship, music clearly does not have to be complex, or performed by highly trained musicians, as the music associated with Taizé or the Iona Community or St Gregory's Episcopal Church in San Francisco or collections of 'World Praise' exemplify.[6] What is central is the care taken in its preparation, and the conviction that everyone present is involved, that is, those who listen are as important as those who perform, that listening is itself a skill, and that each of these is as important as those who celebrate, preach, and lead prayers, which may, of course, be part of the problem: does someone feel 'upstaged'? That said as a preliminary statement of my convictions, let me elaborate a little, so as to mark out some more theological parameters as it were.

---

5 Thomas Day, 'Twentieth-century church music: an elusive modernity', *Communio* 6(3), 1979:236–56.
6 See, e.g., Brother Jean-Marie, 'Prayer and song in Taizé: opening the doors to an inner life', *Ecumenism* 124, 1996:16–18.

The Saying of Music

No doubt it is 'orthodox' enough to recall the divine 'otherness', that is to say, that God is unnameable, unsafe, beyond our idolatries, including what we take to be 'real' even of God in godself – beyond our self-intoxication, self-preoccupations, delusions, needs and harms, both necessary and unsayable. On the other hand, Christian believers seek to engage with God because they believe that God seeks them (Gen. 3.9, and God's hunt for and call to God's earth-creatures in the garden, and Christ's conversation with the Samaritan woman in John 4). And this God not only flesh-makes but flesh-takes, and on one view of the matter even puts godself on our tongues to taste. That is, the unsayable God becomes Word-made-flesh, to some degree 'sayable' in the seeking. We catch the echoes of Christ's own struggle to say and sing 'God' in the Gospels and arguably in other, non-canonical texts too.[7] 'Grace danceth. I would pipe; dance ye all' is a line from the apocryphal 'Acts of John', part of which was set to music by Gustav Holst as his Opus 37, *The Hymn of Jesus*. The whole text may well capture the echo of Christ's words (Matt. 11.16–17/Luke 7.31–2) as it were, given the intricate relationship between word, proclamation and chant in Jewish liturgy, with many forms of which Christ must have been familiar. The 'Hymn' itself, of course, comes from a context somewhat removed from that of the 'historical' Jesus.[8]

The point here is that problems to do with saying or singing 'God' are neither novel nor finally resolvable, but that appeal to revelation via a text does not necessitate word-without-music any more than it necessitates wordlessness in human response to God's seeking, since Christ himself arguably indicates both the difficulties and the search for ways to negotiate them within his milieu. In ours, in turn, we learn to stammer and sing 'Trinity' one way or another,[9] and listening to the The Sixteen singing a piece of sixteenth-century polyphony by John Sheppard may be more profoundly illuminating than a textbook on doctrine, polyphony using a deceptively simple text: *Libera nos, salva nos, justifica nos, O beata Trinitas*.

Music, with or without words, is one means, and a central one, of

---

7 See the editors' essay, 'The divine poet', in David Brown and Ann Loades (eds), *Christ: The Sacramental Word*, 1996:1–25.

8 See James Miller, *Measures of Wisdom: The Cosmic Dance in Classical and Christian Antiquity*, 1986:81–7, 98–110.

9 Fergus Kerr, 'The Trinity and Christian life', *Priests and People* 7(6), 1993:233–37.

saying 'God', and a means by which God may grace human creatures. In addition, we may add that there is a long and ancient tradition in Christianity of thinking of a whole range of activities, particularly but not exclusively in connection with music, as 'sacramental' in the sense of a 'means of grace' (as above). The list of such activities could and did include saying or singing the Lord's prayer, chanting or saying the liturgy, especially the creeds, singing and reciting hymns and psalms and other texts, making the sign of the cross, sounding bells, standing, kneeling or prostrating oneself in prayer, placing and using the hands in certain ways, genuflecting, lighting candles and burning incense, using water, ashes and oil as well as bread and wine, preaching, reading, carrying the scriptures from one part of a church to another, processing and dancing, feetwashing, collecting and distributing cash, embracing, shaking hands, dressing up in certain ways.

A key phrase here is *koinonia hagion*, understood as making the common holy and making the holy common, or with Karl Rahner, discovering or rediscovering the divine depth of ordinary life, explicitly celebrated in worship, but not restricted to worship.[10] And liturgy, public work and service no less, in any case is undertaken by the Church for the sake of the world, as the ancient *Ite, missa est* reminds us to this day, even in its vernacular and sometimes banal paraphrases. The boundaries of poetry and music-for-worship and not-for-worship here are fluid, fragile and permeable, and there is much to be learned from the supposedly 'secular' world. Tim Rice's song for Mary Magdalene, 'I don't know how to love him' from Andrew Lloyd Webber's *Jesus Christ Superstar* is a case in point, contributing to one of the richest seams of Christian tradition which is especially associated with this saint.

Much existing writing on the relationship between music and worship rehearses disquiet in the biblical text or in non-biblical theologians about the 'place' of music in worship and someone's discomfort with it. Certainly, where worship is concerned, human beings may well be at their silliest, most superstitious and idolatrous, and from time to time much has to be sent into an iconoclastic disposal-bin, as it were, music and musicians as well. Critics often have their usefulness, and what needs articulating in a situation of iconoclasm is what can be learned from it, for such periods always provide us with a priceless opportunity. In the case of the absence of music we can

---

10 See Rahner's essay, 'On the theology of worship', in *Theological Investigations*, vol. 10, 1984:141-9.

relearn habits of total silence and physical stillness. We can relearn the capacity to be patient, to be attentive with concentration within silence. Psalm 40.6 is accurately translated as 'ears thou hast dug for me' (transmuted via the LXX in Hebrews 10.5 into 'a body hast thou prepared for me' which has its relevance to music, as I shall suggest later on).

Elijah at Horeb heard a silence beaten fine – like a very highly pitched note, perhaps, only just within the capacity of a human being to hear. It is at least arguable we are at last emerging from a period of theological iconoclasm about music and risking 'catholicity' again, in the sense of becoming attentive to a whole realm of possibilities, but with no guarantees that whatever we attempt will not end up pompous, banal, shoddy and shabby, chaotic, incoherent, intrusive or sentimental (problems also familiar with the preached word and with forms of liturgy). For instance, some Christmas carols need serious reviewing for the nonsense they perpetrate about one particular Child and about children more generally, whereas Timothy Dudley-Smith's 'Child of the stable's secret birth' is a doctrinally rich hymn about the Incarnation and its significance which should be true of all carols sung in connection with Christ's Nativity. The response to what may, can and does go wrong is not to do nothing, or to relapse always into a wordless silence, or into words-without-music, as if words do not furnish our most cherished inanities, but to pray to worship God better: 'Cleanse the thoughts of our hearts by the inspiration of thy Holy Spirit, that we may perfectly love thee, and worthily magnify thy holy name . . .', and hope that we can laugh at ourselves and our best efforts sometimes.

The Wonder of Music

If by this time non-theologians are uncomfortable with the above theological claims, let me endeavour to suggest where we might find common cause: in the closing paragraphs of Mary Midgley's *Beast and Man* (1979: 361–2). Human beings, she writes, are a vulnerable species, but with a place on this particular planet, and nowhere else. Much less often mentioned than the vulnerability is that 'we are receptive, imaginative beings, adapted to celebrate and rejoice in the existence, quite independent of ourselves, of the other beings on this planet'. Our natural sympathy reaches easily beyond the barrier of our own species, and we also rejoice in the existence of plants and lifeless bodies '*not* regarding them just as furniture provided to stimulate our pampered imagination'. The world does not need us, and it is constantly capable of surprising us, and is as such the proper object of wonder. Hugh MacDiarmid takes us one stage further:

> Come, follow me into the realm of music.
> Here is the gate
> Which separates the earthly from the eternal.
> It is not like stepping into a strange country
> As once we did. We soon learn to know everything there
> And nothing surprises us any more. Here
> Our wonderment will have no end, and yet
> From the beginning we feel at home.
>   At first you hear nothing, because everything sounds.
> But now you begin to distinguish between them. Listen.
> Each star has its rhythm and each world its beat.
> The heart of each separate living thing
> Beats differently, according to its needs,
> And all beats are in harmony.
> – Your inner ear grows sharper. Do you hear
> the deep notes and the high notes?
> They are immeasurable in space and infinite as to number.
> Like ribbons, undreamt-of scales lead from one world to another,
> steadfastly and eternally moved.[11]

Other relevant expressions of comparable wonder could include Kathleen Raine's 'Word made flesh' in *The Pythoness*, and Elizabeth Jennings' 'Thunder and a boy' from *Growing-Points*, on God's 'timpani'. Mary Midgley cites parts of God's reply to Job out of the whirlwind (Job 38 and 41), and suggests that the Lord 'only said what any true naturalist may say to himself, whether he believes in any god or not'. That said, a believer may well add Psalm 104,[12] or the so-called 'Hymn of Creation' from the LXX version of Daniel, once familiar in Christian liturgy as the *Benedicite* or blessing of God from out the burning fiery furnace, settings of the *Te Deum*, Francis of Assissi's 'Canticle of the creatures', William Draper's 'All creatures of

---

[11] Hugh MacDiarmid, *Complete Poems 1920–1976*, vol. 2, ed. Michael Grieve and W. R. Aitken, 1978:87.

[12] Perhaps Robert Jackson's transformative reading of it in *The Lincoln Psalter*, 1997:116–18.

our God and King', or Britten's setting of Christopher Smart's texts in *Rejoice in the Lamb*.[13]

These examples do not simply express wonder at the world, but specifically enable believers to adore God in doing so. The virtual loss of the *Te Deum* or the *Benedicite* from revised liturgies may signify a real spiritual impoverishment for adults. For a time at least children may find their own resources, so long as spontaneity and curiosity, the ability to enjoy the world, and an apparently limitless capacity to receive its graces have not been stifled out of them – 'singing a rainbow' in response to the shower of colour from a stained-glass window, for instance.[14] Singing colours is like using metaphor in speech and meshing it with music, and the children's response is one of insight and recognition. They will remember how it felt, seeing the light streaming colour through to them. If deprived of ways of responding in wonder and delight to the world specifically as God's world, ways provided by religious tradition, adults too will find alternative foci for their attention, these not necessarily as benign as coloured glass, nor their response to it as immediate and refreshing as that of children.

Precisely because 'singing' the world and music-making are so central to our response to God, there will almost inevitably be difficulties made about it, not least in cultures where the advent of print meant, in the course of time, not simply that 'religious texts' went into home or academy for study, but that it was easily forgotten where they came from and why they existed in the first place. Where ways of studying narrowed down to only one way of studying them (historical-critical method, for example), detachment from worship might seem almost inevitable. There are, however, clues in Reformation tradition which remind us that music and theology might both be regarded as divine gifts, as in the words of Martin Luther's musician-colleague, Johann Walter:

For music and theology
Were given by God concurrently.
The former with its lovely sound
Was in the latter hidden found.

---

13 See the essay by William Kumbier, 'Benjamin Britten's *Rejoice in the Lamb*: figural invention, "impression" and the open text', in Clement Hawes (ed.), *Christopher Smart and the Enlightenment*, 2000:215–31.

14 See Coral Davies, 'Music in general education', in J. Astley, T. Hone and M. Savage (eds), *Creative Chords: Studies in Music, Theology and Christian Formation*, 2000:210–18.

God let his peace on both arise
So that each might the other prize.
To closest friendship they have grown;
They are as loving sisters known.
Where God's Word lives in human heart,
One finds there harmony's sweet art
In which there is the Spirit's love,
The proof it came from God above.
No other arts with it compare,
For it breathes purest Gospel air,
Exalting Holy Writ on high,
And earning highest praise thereby.[15]

Music and Temporality

From the days of Walter and Praetorius onwards, exploration of the relationship between thinking, saying, singing and playing was undertaken theologically in Lutheranism in a way perhaps unparalleled in other branches of the Christian tradition, though this would need to be researched in much detail. It is certainly the case that in twentieth-century English-speaking theology, brief essays apart, the one person who has made a really significant shift in thinking theologically about music is Jeremy Begbie in a series of essays and books (most notably *Theology, Music and Time*, 2000). He argues that music's engagement with and amidst time helps us to understand the dynamism of temporality as our proper condition and context, thus by accident making common cause with Mary Midgley, one might say. It is in this context that God engages with us, as indeed Christ's incarnation should have enabled us to insist. God's engagement with the world does not require us to evade time or defeat it or attempt the folly of trying to escape from it, but also to engage with it. Rich harmony, non-identical repetition that both closes an event and yet provokes desire for a further 'repetition', multiple layering and connection and the apparent inexhaustibility of musical creativity make us attend to the sheer complexity of our world and divine engagement with it. Or as Annie Dillard puts it,

---

15 Johann Walter, 'Lob und Preis der loblichen Kunst Musica' (1538), trans. Samuel Jantztow, in Carl Schalk, *Music in Early Lutheranism*, 2001:189. Vigorous defence of music in worship is also to be found in the work of Michael Praetorius, such as his 1619 *Syntagma Musicum*, references I owe to the Revd M. Hendrickson.

> material complexity is the truth of the world, even the workable world of idea, and must be the truth of the art object which would imitate, order and penetrate that world: complexity, and contradiction, and repetition, diversity, energy and largesse. I am as attracted to purity as the next guy. But it must not happen here.[16]

Complexity for Jeremy Begbie is superbly represented by the significance of musical improvisation, and not only in jazz – the sheer alertness of the players, enabled by their skill and discipline and their limitless attentiveness to one another makes it possible for them to take risks, change roles, and to experience freedom within their experience of their skills deployed in temporal sequences, however complex these are. There may well be much not only for theologians but for liturgists and musicians concerned with the 'sacred' to draw on here, since such richly textured freedom is as much witness to the mystery of God in kataphatic mode as the utter simplicity of negation in apophatic mode.

Jeremy Begbie's critics have wanted him to explore many different kinds of composers and forms of music other than the ones he mentions, but I would want to pursue his discussion in a rather different direction, following up a clue that he himself provides when referring to the work of David Sudnow.[17]

If theologizing about music may become over-intellectualized, Sudnow reminds us that music is the creation of human bodies, and that temporality needs attention to intensely physical experience. If God engages with us in temporality, he engages with us in our 'corporality'. Sudnow, writing of 'hands' at the piano, finds that he has to write about the involvement of the whole human body.

> I sing with my fingers, so to speak, and only so to speak, for there is a new 'I' that the speaking I gestures toward with a pointing at the music that says: It is a singing body and this I (here, too, so to speak) sings. (Sudnow, 1978:152)

To say the obvious, it may be not only fingers specifically, but tongue, lips and teeth which constitute the new 'I' of the singing body, the experience of temporality and spatiality which are both internal and

---

16 *Living by Fiction*, 1982:172.

17 David Sudnow, *Ways of the Hand: The Organization of Improvised Conduct*, 1978; and *Talk's Body: A Meditation between Two Keyboards*, 1979.

external, whatever instrument being used dissolving 'into an inner acquisition of spaces to speak with' (Sudnow, 1979:7). It will be rarely that the performer's 'I' is not a 'corporate body', or, we might say, a 'Pauline' body. For musicians depend crucially on the way music is written on their respective faces, in eyes, mouths and brows, heads rising and falling with hands. 'The looks cannot be differentiated from the sounds. They are both displays of movements that run everywhere through the participating bodies. The musicians look at the music as they look at each other' (Sudnow, 1979: 91). What is true of the quartet is true also of the 'concerted sociability' (ibid.:104) of the orchestra, a 'Pauline' body we might say, in which the conductor's single 'orchestral' body both mirrors the 'sounding movements' of all the instrumental 'voices' as together they give substance to the music which as experienced cannot be differentiated from any one of their particular contributions to its being played.

An identifiably 'incarnational' understanding of music must needs attend to its sheer physicality through corporeality in time, with a destiny, if Christian faith is true, of being reclothed in 'holy and glorious flesh' as Dante put it on the lips of Solomon in Canto XIV of 'Paradise' in *The Divine Comedy*. One cannot pray the 'Jesus Prayer' without learning to breathe in a certain way (breathing in to say 'Lord Jesus Christ' and out to say 'Have mercy on me, a sinner') which also calms one's body by natural rhythm.[18] One cannot perhaps even begin to lay hold on what the transformation of that body might be like without the aid of music. Once upon a time at Easter the Chapter at Chartres Cathedral would have danced the labyrinth within the cathedral, taking themselves on 'pilgrimage' through the twists and turns of life, as it were, singing '*Victimae paschali laudes*' as they tossed a ball to and fro between themselves and their Dean, standing at the centre of the labyrinth, dancing their conviction that Christ has indeed risen from the dead.

Luther's 'Christus lag in Todesbanden' based upon the Latin text was transformed into an organ chorale by Bach, which provides a thread of continuity back to such a literally moving appropriation of resurrection. Without the actual treading and singing orientated as at Chartres towards a great window of Christ and the saints in glory, the sung text or the hearing of the chorale may not take us in our own times far enough beyond merely 'hearing' resurrection, whereas what

---

18 John Michael Talbot, *The Music of Creation: Foundations of a Christian Life*, 1999:63–6, provides a brief discussion.

we need is to experience it in a more visceral way. Here perhaps the most significant writing among all those available is the 'Dance Chorale' and 'Coda' from James Macmillan's *Veni, Veni Emmanuel* first performed in 1992 which has a pulsing heartbeat which identifies Christ risen, beyond betrayal by those he loved the most, and embracing not only the victims of horror and those who mourn them, but the humanity of those who harm and destroy. For the 'company of heaven' includes those who delight in a re-possessed paradise, graced into a life beyond our present imagining, but of which the resources of composer and performers may, as it were, catch an echo. For all the alleged secularism of Western societies, the combination of his musicianship with Macmillan's own publicly and passionately held Christian conviction about the Resurrection as a Roman Catholic, and its musical expression in *Veni, Veni Emmanuel*, has clearly been recognized by those who listen to it, receiving five hundred performances within its first five years in concert halls alone.[19]

The Praise of Music

Music in relation to theology has another importance, however, at which I hinted in my earlier reference to the 'Hymn of Creation' sung in the 'burning fiery furnace'. Central to worship is learning to adore God in order to be able to go on doing so no matter what, continuing to praise God in extremity. Music may cut through the forms of piety which deny the tragedies and horrors of the world, as for instance in Shostakovich's Piano Trio No. 2 in E minor, Opus 67. This explores in its final movement with its Jewish melodies and folk tunes the horrors of the dances near-skeletons were forced to perform on the edges of their own graves in extermination camps. We can juxtapose this with an all-too-vivid image from Yaffa Eliah's account of 'the first Hannukah Light in Bergen-Belsen'.[20] The prisoners constructed a makeshift *hannukiah* from a wooden clog, strings and shoe-polish to serve as oil. Living skeletons surrounded by the bodies of the dead, including those of their own families and loved ones, they nonetheless assembled to kindle the lights. The Rabbi might well hesitate, but he

---

19 Some other examples are briefly discussed in John Bowden, 'Resurrection in music', in Stephen Barton and Graham Stanton (eds), *Resurrection*, 1994:188–97.

20 Michael Downey, 'Worship between the Holocausts', *Theology Today* 43, 1986:75–87.

proceeded with the third blessing, in which God, addressed as Lord and King of the universe, is blessed for keeping, preserving, and enabling the covenant people to reach this season. If God has a people still living, their faces expressing faith, devotion and concentration, though death stares at them from every corner, then the prayer is justified.

We learn through such music as Shostakovich's just what courage the praise of God requires, as well as through such narratives as that from Bergen-Belsen or the re-hearing of such texts as 1 Chronicles 29.10 ff., or Ecclesiasticus 39.5–8, or the *Te Deum*. Another example is rehearsed by Kathleen Norris, quoting an account of a massacre that occurred in December 1981 in El Salvador, in the hamlet of El Mozote.[21] Most of the peasants killed there were evangelical Christians, and one was a young girl among the women raped before being murdered. Throughout it all 'this girl had sung hymns, strange evangelical songs, and she had kept on singing, even after they had done what had to be done, and shot her in the chest'. With the blood flowing her singing was weaker, and she was shot again, and still sang, until they hacked though her neck, so the singing stopped. In relation to these circumstances, human beings learn that valuable though human justice is, it may never and could never be sufficient, so human beings need the full resources of such texts as the Psalms (unabridged) or if not the Psalms, of something comparable if they are going to be able to rage, weep, grieve and, possibly, leave some things to the God they praise.

Music for rage and grief is also a means of grace, for if God does not descend into human hell, human beings may not of their own resources be able to emerge from it. Human beings need both music without words which will tap into the depth of their affections, and the words and the chant which will enable people to get to the 'guts' of their grief if they are eventually to let go of it. Both the praise and the grief are in their different ways manifestations of the fact that music in worship enables us to be clear that worshippers are involved in the manifestation of divine political authority, of central importance for the future of the human community. The *Kyrie Eleison*, and the *Sanctus* as well as the Creeds, put the 'lords' of the world in their place, however good or bad they may seem to be. It follows that prayer for the 'enemy' is therefore required – intercession for the death-bringers – among whom we ourselves may be found. Without such

---

21 *The Cloister Walk*, 1996:204–5.

intercession human beings may not be able to find the resources of hope to go on making and sharing the best of which they are capable with one another, believing that God offers them a life beyond the worst which any of us may inflict on one another.

This essay, like too many liturgies, is in danger of collapsing into solemnity and stuffiness in all-too-familiar North European mode, so I conclude by referring to one particular means of grace, which is the music composed by Duke Ellington in the last years of his life for three 'sacred concerts', which have been performed from the mid-1960s onwards. These, most emphatically, were not written as jazzed-up-mass, but nonetheless a selection of the music has been incorporated into celebrations of the Eucharist, and most recently, in concert performance, some of it has been heard again (23 November 2001 at the Royal Academy of Music in London). As commentators rightly perceive, words and jazz and religious conviction in the case of Ellington's work combine religion with fun, exuberance, delight, and general *joie de vivre*. Music making worship possible has not only to do with the depths of grief and rage, but with conviviality and companionship, and, one supposes, the life glimpsed in such texts as the second-century book of *Jubilees* and some parts of the book of Revelation. In the case of Ellington, whether or not it takes the place of *Ite, missa est* or is simply the conclusion to a 'sacred concert' performance, 'David danced before the Lord' has been not only played and sung but 'jazz-tapped' by Will Gaines, born in Baltimore in 1928 and still able to 'sound' his body through his feet to the words of this number which include 'Psaltery, cymbals/ harps and cymbals/ played out loud and clear./ Chanting, singing/ trumpets ringing/ joy to every ear/ David upped and danced . . .' in hilarity which is also solemnity.

In this essay I have not been concerned to argue for my convictions, but to assert them, and most of my examples come from the tradition and culture I know best. I hope, however, to have touched the edges of 'grace-in-waiting' by thinking about music and theology, and while Brian Hebblethwaite might not relish all my examples, I hope I share his sympathies in this matter.

3. Truth and Religious Dialogue

ANDERS JEFFNER

The field of inter-religious dialogue has been thoroughly explored during the last decades. Books and articles and journals dealing with or practising dialogue have reached a respectable number. When it comes to its theological or theoretical parts there exists in Christian theological circles a fairly well established typology covering relations between Christianity and other religions. A research student of mine wrote a dissertation in which he described in detail the arguments between an 'exclusivist' view represented by Lesslie Newbigin, a 'pluralistic' view represented by John Hick and an 'inclusivist' view represented by Gavin D'Costa.[1] I think most people interested in the field have met the positions indicated by these descriptions. In this article I will, of course, touch upon some of the arguments brought forward in recent international debates, but my entrance will be from the Swedish tradition and I am not going to analyse the present state of the dialogue. My aim is both more modest and more ambitious. I want to formulate tentatively some reflections that could calm my own worries when I look around in the religious world. In doing this, however, I must risk being pretentious and deal with the fundamental classical problems of philosophy and theology though I often cannot do more than point out a line of thought. What worries me is the very basic question behind all attempts to establish closer relations between religious standpoints: the question of truth. Do true and false religious doctrines exist and, if so, how are they distributed between the world religions? These problems lie hidden behind all friendly dialogues and have been mirrored in book titles like *Truth and Dialogue*.[2] Those who are familiar with the discussion will easily see that I have many arguments in common with John Hick but that I deviate from him in

---

1 Dag Bjarnhall, 'Pa vag mot en kristen religionsteologi', 1999.
2 John Hick (ed.), 1974. This early collection of essays has been important for many later authors, including myself.

a more traditional and less Kantian direction.[3] I do not like to label my basic standpoint 'pluralistic'.

Nathan Söderblom's Heritage

My starting-point is in my own religious tradition, but I hope that my further arguments hold regardless of theological suppositions. The Swedish archbishop Nathan Söderblom (1866–1931) was famous for his pioneering work in the ecumenical movement, but his importance covers a much wider field. Nathan Söderblom started his career as a professor of religious history in Paris and in Uppsala. His doctoral thesis dealt with the Persian religion.[4] He was also a systematic theologian well orientated in contemporary theology, especially the tradition of Schleiermacher, and he had a broad overview of the sciences of his day.[5] Natural science was important to him. It does not give us complete knowledge of reality but it highlights certain important aspects.

In his extensive theological and religious writings, he often tried to combine his Christian faith with his knowledge of and respect for other religions and for scholarly and scientific work. There are in his books clear contours of an early theology of religions, which has many similarities with later views in the field. A key concept in his theology is revelation. The religious view of reality, which follows humankind, was interpreted as a response to God's revelation. In Söderblom's view of the world God is seen as continuously revealing himself to humans and the different religions are interpretations of this revelation. There are certain channels or openings through which revelation reaches humans. Söderblom calls them doors to revelation, the two most important being the sense of the infinite and the human striving towards ideals, i.e. conscience. The first of these led Söderblom to a special study of mysticism in different religions. For the responses to revelation in human societies, the use of reason is of the utmost

---

3 John Hick gives a summary of his view in *The Metaphor of God Incarnate*, 1993: ch. 14: 'Christian truths and other truths'. The controversy between John Hick and Brian Hebblethwaite concerning the doctrine of incarnation will not be dealt with in this essay.

4 'La vie future d'après le Mazdéisme', 1901.

5 What is referred to in what follows is based on his Swedish book, *Uppenbarelsereligion*, 2nd edn 1930. See further his *The Living God* (1979), *The Nature of Revelation* (1933), and E. J. Sharpe, *Nathan Söderblom and the Study of Religion* (1990).

Truth and Religious Dialogue   41

importance and Söderblom ascribes a special role to the genius in the religious world. As one might expect, Söderblom saw a special clear revelation in the Christian tradition, but it is interesting to note that he reckoned with a deepening of Christian religious insights by analysing parallels between the biblical tradition and revelations in other religions. In one of his many religious tracts he says that even the heretical rites that the women conducted before Tammuz according to Ezekiel 8.14, are important for an understanding of the passion of Christ.[6]

Söderblom's theology and his heritage from theologians like Ritschl deserve special study, but here I will just use Söderblom as a help to find a starting-point for my own thoughts, so he cannot be blamed for what follows.[7] Let me first connect to his general picture of the cognitive situation of humans: the real world becomes accessible to us through certain openings. As humans we are open towards reality. Söderblom speaks about doors. In order to make clear that I deviate from Söderblom, I will use another word and talk about 'windows' towards reality. My second loan from Söderblom will be the broad concept of revelation, and further, his positive view of reason and science in the formation of religious faith.

Windows Towards Reality

Let me start with what seems obviously to be a window towards reality – our senses. Not just the sensory organs, but also the whole psychophysical apparatus which makes it possible for us to see, hear, feel, taste. This window is taken for granted in our daily life. The scientist looks closely through the window and with the help of reason describes, explains and makes foresight possible. Our culture is based on empirical science. But a great part of our philosophical tradition consists of doubting this simple picture. What naively can be described as a window becomes often in philosophy a complicated and partly unavoidable filter created by our cultural tradition, psychological constitution or inbuilt cognitive structures. Windows tend to become mirrors. There is a stream of pessimism in epistemology from ancient sceptics through Kant to postmodernism. Truth about reality in the corresponding meaning cannot be reached. The opposite view lies closer to common sense, but it need not involve a naive belief in

---

6 *Kristi pinas historia*, 1928:411 f.
7 For more details, see my *Six Cartesian Meditations*, 1993.

empirical science as the final truth about reality. An optimist believes that we can formulate true propositions about reality that express what is the case, but that the way to scientific truth is long. We have a window towards reality but we are still on the way towards truth in our understanding of what we see.

The choice between pessimism and optimism is, of course, essential for the whole problem of truth. I think that radical scepticism and relativism are self-destructive positions but there are also reasonable pessimistic positions when it comes to our ability to formulate true propositions that correspond to real facts, that of the philosopher Nelson Goodman being an example.[8] The optimistic view can also be reasonable. No conclusive arguments hinder us from accepting that our empirically based beliefs and theories can tell us at least partly something true about the world we live in. I cannot see that the choice between pessimism and optimism in the sense indicated here can finally be made on the basis of clear, reasonable and binding arguments. There is an unavoidable moment of unguarded choice to be made here. If we opt for the optimistic side, I shall say that we have *basic faith*. Basic faith belongs to common sense. Connecting to Wittgenstein in a non-Wittgensteinian way, we can say that it belongs to 'the given'. Religious people generally have basic faith. To think otherwise is to believe that our Creator has locked us in or deceived us, as Descartes says in his *Meditations*. I myself have a bit of basic faith. I believe that we as humans have the opportunity to get a view of reality that at least partly corresponds to what is the case. Our impressions and empirical science open a window. Basic belief makes religious dialogue, involving questions of truth, urgent. It might be tempting in a postmodern cultural climate to say: I have my perspective and my truth, you have your perspective and your truth, let us respect each other. I cannot see this being compatible with either common sense or the truth-claims of living religions. If the postmodernist says that compatibility is a modern and outdated concept, all kinds of meaningful dialogue have come to a dead end.

The next question then must be: Are there more windows? Do we get information about reality in our everyday life via other methods than sense experiences? If we try to answer unaffected by too much philosophy, I think the answer will be affirmative, but to look through other windows may demand another adjustment than sense experiences, namely an attitude of engagement as existentialist

---

8 *Ways of Worldmaking*, 1978.

Truth and Religious Dialogue 43

philosophers have noted. It could be argued that our knowledge of other persons is of a different kind from what we get by ordinary observations but that it is still knowledge. When I look into the eyes of my wife, I have a window into reality closed to physics and physiology. If I see a defenceless child being seriously beaten, another new aspect of reality becomes apparent, an aspect which goes far beyond sense experiences. I know that what is happening is *wrong*. I have unveiled a moral relation in reality. If I were a supporter of philosophy of the empiricist kind, I would say in this case that I had not discerned something real, but that I had a certain kind of emotion towards reality. Here moral reactions are seen as subjective in a way that sense impressions are not. But are there really reasons to become a pessimist in this realm of our experience? Normal people discern the same as I do when they see the action of hurting a child, and we say that it is wrong to torment a child. It seems to be a real structure in the world.

No doubt the moral experience is also a reaction in our mind just as sense-impressions are, but why couldn't we believe that we discern an aspect of reality through our moral reactions as well as through our sense reactions? We can say that moral reactions are more varied and culturally dependent than sense experiences. That is true, but it is difficult to deny that there are common human moral insights. This has been apparent not least in modern inter-religious dialogue. It is also popular nowadays to say that morality has been created by evolution and has become important because it promotes our survival. But the same can be said about science and it is hardly an argument against its connection with reality. If we have basic faith in our senses and in empirical science, we must consider extending it to moral reactions. We can go further and ask if aesthetic reactions also give access to real relations in the objective world. And what shall we say about the enormous amount of human experience of something divine or holy? Let us call it devotional experience and include the experiences of the mystics. My hypothetical answer is that no conclusive arguments speak against believing in true aesthetic propositions and truth about holiness in reality. Mathematical and logical experience can also in a Platonic way be interpreted as windows into reality, but perhaps the complications are greater in these cases and I must leave the whole problem of conceptual realism here.

There are, of course, many difficulties in accepting an extended basic faith that includes I/Thou experiences and experiences of right and wrong, beautiful and ugly, holy and profane. The greatest difficulty as I see it is that it takes out of our hands the effective weapons against superstition which Hume among others introduced. I will return to this but I have no opportunity here to go deep into the enormous field of problems lying behind the simple reflections made above. My intention has been only to sketch a view of our cognitive situation which I think can be defended and which makes it reasonable to talk about truth. It is not more than a cognitive scenario and I have not said that it can be proven or even made theoretically probable, but later on I will hint at some arguments that may strengthen basic faith in our possibility to reach out to a real world of matter, fellow humans, and moral and aesthetical relations as well as holiness.

Experiences of Transcendence

The next step on my way towards religious dialogue will be to argue that we as humans can have and often do have a certain kind of experience that can be called an experience of transcendence when we are looking through a 'window'. The sense experiences of common sense contain an awareness of limitation. When we look and hear and taste, we know that we cannot reach the totality of the real sensuous world. Even if we do not think about it most of us know that there are aspects of reality that we cannot reach in our actual sense experiences. There is a reality before and after our present experiences, and our sense organs and concepts are far from perfect. The sensuous world transcends our sense experiences. Thomas Luckmann, who has fruitfully discussed the role of experiences of transcendence in religion writes: '[W]henever anything transcends that which at the moment is concretely given in actual, direct experience and can itself be experienced in the same manner as that which it now transcends, we may speak of the "little" transcendence of everyday life.'[9] Luckmann also discusses other forms of experiences of transcendence. When something is encountered which cannot be experienced directly and which is not part of ordinary reality, he calls this a 'great' transcendence. I will adopt his terminology, but it must be observed that Luckmann does not make any ontological claims, which I do in using the symbol of a window.

Now the window of our senses can give us also experiences of great transcendence. These come through empirical science. If we add together the fragments of scientific theories that have become more or

---

9 'The new and old religion', in *Social Theory for a Changing Society*, ed. Pierre Bourdieu and James S. Coleman, 1991:173.

Truth and Religious Dialogue 45

less common property we get the following picture of the world.[10] The basic structures of elementary particles building up the atoms have once upon a time been combined into bigger structures – the molecules. One type of molecule has a structure that forces them to copy themselves in an extremely effective way. We are now at the starting-point for life. The further development of RNA and DNA molecules can be explained by evolutionary theory and research into the DNA structures called genes. In due course these genes formed for their future existence very complicated organisms and some of them attained consciousness as a by-product of great importance for their survival. This curious creation of evolution reached its all-time high in human beings, and in humans matter now can understand itself, explain how it has evolved and how in certain structures it has got the power to experience, reason, judge, fear, hope and love. If this picture, or part of it, represents a true theory, we must say that we have come across a mystery – the mystery of matter. That matter can have this wonderful power lies completely outside our understanding. It is a *mysterium tremendum et fascinans*. It can give us a sense of the infinite, which Söderblom speaks about. So by looking the best we can through the window of our senses we can gain an experience of 'great transcendence'.[11]

If we go to the window of our I/Thou relationships, we can find a new form of transcendence-experience. Luckmann calls these the intermediate transcendences of everyday life. The minds and personalities of our fellow humans transcend our sense-experiences but we are familiar with minds and people and these belong to everyday reality.

The window of moral sense confronts us with a kind of transcendence which in a way belongs to everyday reality but which also can tend towards great transcendence. It is well known that experience of the moral law for Kant opened up a depth of reality. Even if we do not see moral experiences in the Kantian categories of law and if we refer them to everyday life we must admit that they widen our picture of reality. Perhaps even an emotivist can agree about this, but the emotivist refuses to acknowledge our picture of windows and the connected view of possible true moral propositions.

---

10 See further my booklet, *Biology and Religion as Interpreting Patterns of Human Life*, 1999.

11 I think that this is the same kind of experience that we can find in a rationalized form in classical teleological thinking, and it is not the new scientific discoveries that have made the old physico-theology out of date.

To discuss in a more qualified manner the sense of beauty and the transcendence in aesthetics, we ought to go into a discussion of Romantic philosophy or analyse a philosopher like Shaftesbury, but this would lead too far afield and I will do no more than point out its similarity to moral transcendence.

The window of devotion is of course the place for experiences of great transcendence. In prayer, rites and meditation people meet privately or in common a reality of a totally different kind, a divine reality. These experiences have followed humans at all times and in all places.

Religious Interpretation of Experiences of Transcendence

A religious view of the world is to a great extent based on experiences of transcendence. This could be argued as a phenomenological theory without claims to a religious reality. But I will go a step further. I will adopt the religious interpretation and argue that experiences of transcendence really give us access to a religious reality. Taking this step is analogous to accepting basic faith. Its correctness can be neither proved nor disproved, but it lies close at hand, which we see when we realize how a religious interpretation of reality has followed humankind. When we have basic faith and then also believe in certain cognitive experiences of transcendence, I shall say that we have *religious faith*. These experiences of transcendence then become together religious experiences, and it should be observed that religious experiences here are not restricted to the window of devotion. Now it is obvious that there are many various interpretations of these experiences of transcendence giving as a result the rich world of religious myths, doctrines and rituals. I will soon return to this fact, but first I would like to point out a phenomenological characteristic of such experiences of transcendence. They come to us. We do not produce them. In a way we produce the interpretations, but not the experiences. We can say that the basis of religious faith is given to us. Here we have the anchorage for the concept of revelation. Revelation is one of the forceful religious concepts that are used in various religions for interpreting religious experiences.

I think Söderblom was right when he saw the belief in revelation as a unifying trait in the religious world. For the Christian it is easy to adopt the language of revelation and I shall accept it as a first step on the way of religious interpretation. To reveal is to do something – to act, and actions are bound to actors. The force that reveals something to us can easily be seen as an actor or as actors of a kind totally different from those we meet in everyday life. Then we have reached an interpretation which can provide a common basis for most great religions of the world: God or the gods reveal themselves to humans, making themselves known. As a result, believers know about a world outside the everyday reality.

The claim to have access to a revelation is a religious truth-claim. Being religious in a Christian, Jewish or Muslim way, among others, involves accepting this truth, though revelation for many is restricted to fewer of the windows than those discussed here. We have now come across a religious truth-claim. But a living religion does not consist of various propositions about the transcendent which are held to be true. Expressing religious faith is a far more complicated process.

Religious Language

God or gods cannot be adequately described in ordinary language. All religious people who are aware of the problems of language tend to agree about this. Statements and narratives about God(s) and divine actions can only point in the direction of divine reality. For the philosophically-minded believers they are sometimes seen as ladders that can be thrown away after an encounter with the divine. There are various well-known theories about the linguistic mechanism that allows narratives and pictures to hint at a non-describable reality, and in religions with a developed theology we come across subtle theories about metaphors and analogies in statements about the divine reality. Separating the real religious content from the surface meaning of a religious narrative or term is an activity that can be found in many religions. Bultmann did it in a very radical form. The many diverse problems of religious language will not be discussed here. Just one aspect that is of utmost importance for the present subject will be taken up. It is the extent to which a religious utterance contains propositions that can be true or false in the 'correspondence' sense.

I think we can roughly reckon with four classes of language units when we focus on this aspect. The first one is narrative that helps the believer towards experiences of transcendence. These can point out a certain trait in reality or provide a new *gestalt* to well-known things, an example being Nathan's story told to David according to 2 Samuel 12 which led David to a striking moral experience. These stories are not true or false but more or less effective. To the same category belong many religious hymns and liturgies. They prepare the singer or listener primarily for a devotional experience. Rituals and the accompanying texts often have the same function. I will call this first category experience-promoting texts.

The next group of language units are narratives, stories and hymns that have as their point a propositional content. They may not be explicit or clear but at least they attempt to say something true of the factual transcendent world. The narratives of a last judgement belong to this group. Normally their point is at least a denial of the proposition: Nothing happens to humans after death. Many liturgical texts have a propositional point together with its experience-promoting function. The second group will be called indirectly propositional. It may be remarked that the frequent performatives in religious language are normally indirectly propositional though the linguistic analysis is different in these cases. It can be difficult to make the propositional content precise, and you can therefore agree about the cognitive importance of narratives like the parables in the Christian Gospels but disagree about their propositional content.

Let us now move on to the third group, which is doctrinal statements. We have already met the statement that there is divine reality and divine revelation. When we describe religions or confessions we often concentrate on the theological or doctrinal part. But as remarked above it can be doubted that these lie in the centre for ordinary believers. Doctrines can be interpreted in a non-cognitive way as is well known in Western theology and philosophy. Doctrines then become similar to the first category above. But in the normal use doctrines are used as religious propositions. They claim to say something true about the divine reality, such as that there is only one God. But in philosophically developed theologies the propositional content is carefully circumscribed by the incomprehensible mystery, St Thomas' theory of metaphors and analogies being the standard example. As a fourth category of this rough division, I will mention the moral precepts which accompany most religions. The books and texts that presume to be sacred or revealed can contain all the four categories of religious language, and the special problems connected to holy books will be dealt with below.

Something important to observe now is the applicability of logic to religious statements. It is obvious that logical criteria cannot be applied to the first group. Two narratives can contradict each other and still both be fruitful and fulfil their religious function. Not all the statements of the other groups may be submitted to logical tests, but the cognitive point made by narratives or pure doctrinal statements must follow the rules of logic after their analogical character has been recognized. If not we could not argue theologically, and different theologies could not contradict each other. I will also suppose without further discussion that there is a logic to moral precepts.

Realms of Theological Dialogue

It is always better that people talk rather than fight. Therefore it is tempting to say that all kinds of inter-religious dialogue are good. But it is not enough that inter-religious dialogue as such may contribute to a more peaceful world. I will not deny the utmost importance of this but I think we must demand more of a fruitful theoretical dialogue between believers of different religions, such as recognizing what is common in their beliefs, helping one another to interpret experiences and holy texts, identifying the propositional content in respective religious texts and practices, helping each other to develop a religious worldview, recognizing real contradictions between religions and respecting contradicting truth-claims by explaining why they seem to be false.

One starting-point for a dialogue which reckons with religious truth is to establish a common front against those who deny basic faith and religious faith in the sense explained above, this being a big task in an age of cultural relativism and philosophical materialism. Thereby the possibility of mutual moral understanding gets religious significance, and adherents of different religions can help each other to form the contours of a religious worldview. I think then that we can also gain a considerable amount of mutual understanding and learning from each other by comparing experiences of transcendence and different ways to devotional experiences. Comparing experiences may strengthen the importance of the concept of revelation and thereby establish a common understanding of the relation between the divine and the human reality. Such discussions lead to understanding without syncretism. I can respect what I at first glance find curious in Indian cults, and Hindu believers can understand why I refuse to throw butter on the crucifix. I can also easily see in an honest dialogue that the same experience of transcendence can be interpreted and expressed by many different linguistic tools. Also, when it comes to discerning the religious and propositional points in the rich flora of religious narratives, there is room for mutual learning. Most religions have stories about the creation, for example, that sometimes need doctrinal interpretation. The same holds true for interpreting the intricate statements about God. Is there a genuine contradiction between the Christian doctrine of Trinity and the monotheism of Judaism and Islam? Are there paradoxes in the various doctrines, and how are they to be interpreted? But, as has been said many times, we reach a point where there are obvious contradictory straight truth-claims in different religions. Is there really a way ahead at this point? I will soon come to a positive answer against the background I have sketched. First, however, I must deal with a big and well-known obstacle on the way, which I have not mentioned so far. This is the idea of a holy text as a final criterion of truth.

If the final test of the adequacy of a religious story or the truth of a religious proposition is its adherence to one of the many holy books, then there is no common ground for theoretically fruitful discussions. This kind of scriptural belief, however, is a very common religious standpoint and even the claim that the holy book is a true revelation can be defended by reference to the book itself. The criteriological view of holy books creates a theoretical reservation for believers and I find it difficult to develop a coherent view of God and the world from this position. I will return to this. However, to deny the scriptural criterion of truth is not to deny the holiness of some religious books. As a Christian I believe in the Bible as Holy Scripture. Through the Bible I get access to a wonderful tradition of human responses to divine revelation and I get help to interpret my own experiences. I find religious truth-claims which I think there are reasons to accept, and I learn about Christ as a person clarifying the windows toward transcendent reality, both little and great.

The Bible gives help in the search after truth, but nothing is true just because it is found in the Bible. After a hundred years of Christian discussion of the authority of the Bible and similar questions, I think that this is a fairly common view among Christian theologians, Barthians included, but I have no overview of the situation in other religions. Certainly there is a great difference between educated and non-educated believers. In the Christian tradition already Origen had problems on this point with 'fides simpliciorum'.[12] However, a fruitful dialogue leading to theological results must involve an attempt to overcome the idea of a simple scriptural criterion of truth. I think it must go so far that believers clearly dissociate themselves from certain parts of their holy texts.

---

12 See Gunnar af Hällström, *Fides Simpliciorum according to Origen of Alexandria*, 1984.

An example for a Christian often referred to in religious dialogues is Acts 4.12: 'for of all the names in the world given to men, this [Jesus Christ] is the only one by which we can be saved'. Without doubt this is a statement of a very exclusivist position in early Christianity. Attempts to disarm it by some form of hermeneutic magic do not seem to me to work. A Christian who thinks that a believer can have good Christian reasons to deviate from St Luke may adopt a way of reasoning like this: When a human being has got a clear and overwhelming revelation, which the disciples had, it seems natural to interpret the revelation as the only way to truth and salvation, but later on the interpretation of the revelation and further religious experiences can lead to an insight that God is greater and has many ways to save humans, ways unknown to us. Pointing out such a psychological structure, common for most believers, may avoid a dead-end to further theological dialogue, and it does not profane the holy texts.

Ways Ahead

Let us now return to the clear fact that people from different religious traditions who are honest, open-minded, educated and reasonable have contradicting truth-claims about God and salvation. I have promised to point out a way of further dialogue in this connection and I will do so briefly in this last section. According to the sketch I have given about human cognition and the real world, we are confronted with various experiences of reality, including experiences of transcendence. If we now have religious faith and take the experiences seriously, we face the challenge to bring them together to form a picture of reality – of human beings in a material universe transcending all familiar experience. This challenge seems to be built into our minds. It is difficult and unsatisfactory for most humans to live with fragments. In trying to combine our pieces of reality we meet a well-known criterion of truth that must be applied to the propositions we think of accepting. It is the criterion of correspondence or coherence, the importance of which is very much underestimated in theology.[13]

Logical reasoning is a common faculty in human reason and we cannot exist in daily life without logic. Openness to the use of reason

---

13 Theologians who put great stress on logic can still avoid the force of the principle by diminishing the cognitive content of religious statements, John Hick being sometimes an example. For a further discussion of theological language and logical criteria, see my *Kriterien christlicher Glaubenslehre*, 1976.

in religion was part of my heritage from Nathan Söderblom. Now I think that in all religions there is a theological problem, namely, combining theological propositions with everyday sense experiences, scientific results, experiences of persons, moral and aesthetic propositions, and so on, in a coherent way. This is an enormous task and here lies the real kernel of a fruitful theological dialogue between religions. Believers can help each other on the way to form a coherent whole. The principle of coherence is also a forceful common guard against superstition, which always threatens those who reckon with many windows into reality. A serious dialogue involving the principle of coherence must involve mutual criticism and a willingness to change the propositional part of one's own religious tradition – not, however, necessarily the stories, rites, and metaphors.

The reason to leave the criteriological view of Holy Scripture on the way to dialogue is just that it leads either to contradictions or to the necessity to shut some of the windows. It must be observed, at the same time, that rejecting the whole idea of holy texts can also involve shutting a window. Real theological dialogue leads necessarily to a change in religious doctrine. Many religious people think that all changes are heresies: there is a common idea that there was an original pure religion. But the truth is that religious doctrines very often change over time. There are also religious strategies for defending such changes – the deepening of truth under the guidance of the Holy Spirit being a Christian example. If we look at the doctrine of creation in Christianity we can easily see how it changes in conjunction with the development of science, and the believers and theologians try to guard the real religious kernel of the doctrine. This question, how to maintain the religious truth of doctrines of creation without contradicting scientific truth, is an elementary example in a field of possible fruitful dialogue involving truth between many religions. The conflict between growing common ethical experiences and the traditional religious ethical rules is another arena for common discussion. Can it lead to a revision of the ethics of the Qur'ān and to a rethinking of the Christian idea of atonement? I do not find it completely unrealistic and it is very important from a general theological point of view. I have taken my examples from exclusivist religions like Christianity and Islam. Dialogues with more inclusivist Indian religions may be very different, but I think that the common key problem to reach coherence in the view of the world remains, and also that there are many lessons to learn from each other.

Does now this view of dialogue and truth lead to a common world religion in the future? I am not so deeply cut off from the real world that I think such a scenario is possible in the foreseeable future. However, it is part of the Christian eschatological hope that all people will one day share the same truths about God and the world and that all will be astonished on this occasion. But for the present, religious people will belong to one of the established, or perhaps 'new', religions. Not least the social side of religious practices makes this necessary. There is also a good argument for belonging to one particular religion even if the believer is aware of the need for revision and thinks that there are some deeper religious insights in other religions. It is the case that one's established religion works in everyday life, which means that it makes it possible to interpret the experiences of transcendence and opens up ways to arrive at a coherent picture that makes it possible to become meaningfully orientated in the world. There is a kind of testing of religions in everyday life – an experimental way of approaching the question of truth. This kind of testing may also be applied to the steps taken towards basic faith. If we accept the idea of experimental testing in everyday life, we can also see that dialogue respecting truth is not an argument against all kinds of mission. The reasonable task for a Christian missionary is to offer an invitation to test, thereby repeating what Philip said to Nathanael, according to John 1.46: 'Come and see.'

4. Truth and Toleration
Hebblethwaite, Hick, and Bediuzzaman Said Nursi

IAN MARKHAM

Introduction

As one looks at the history of twentieth-century British theology, Brian Hebblethwaite figures prominently. He was a key contributor to the *Myth of God* debate.[1] Hebblethwaite made substantial contributions in both *The Truth of God Incarnate*[2] and *Incarnation and Myth*.[3] His defence of the coherence of a kenotic account of incarnation was very attractive to many. Later when his colleague Don Cupitt was causing a controversy with his vision of a non-realist form of Christianity, Brian Hebblethwaite constructed an elegant defence of theism called *The Ocean of Truth* (1988). As we look back on these two controversies, most commentators would agree that Hebblethwaite was on the winning side.

In this chapter, I shall reflect on one other controversy where Hebblethwaite has been at the forefront. His co-edited volume of essays with John Hick on the issue of religious pluralism proved to be remarkably prescient (1980).[4] He anticipated the controversy that was going to grow. Hebblethwaite took the position that a commitment to the truth of Christianity was not incompatible with an equally strong commitment to the need for peaceful relations, dialogue, and mutual

---

[1] This was the debate about Christology triggered by a collection of essays edited by John Hick. See John Hick (ed.), *The Myth of God Incarnate*, 1977.

[2] Edited by Michael Green, 1977. Hebblethwaite's contribution was entitled, 'Jesus, God incarnate'.

[3] In this volume, advocates for and against the Myth position were represented. See Michael Goulder (ed.), *Incarnation and Myth: The Debate Continued*, 1979.

[4] A second edition has been published. See John Hick and Brian Hebblethwaite (eds), *Christianity and Other Religions*, 2nd edn, 2000.

understanding with other faith traditions. I shall now demonstrate that his instincts on these questions and his difficulties with John Hick's pluralist hypothesis are shared by leading thinkers in other faith traditions.

Hebblethwaite, I am sure, would be the first to concede that truth often appears to be incompatible with toleration. The problem is that a commitment to a worldview as 'true' necessarily implies that others are 'wrong'. Historically, the temptation for those who are powerful is to insist that those who disagree with them (and therefore from their perspective are in 'error') must be censored or even killed. So, the argument goes, a commitment to the truth often ends up being intolerant.

In this chapter, we shall start by examining the approach of Hebblethwaite's early conversation partner, the English philosopher John Hick. Hick argues for a 'pluralist hypothesis' according to which all the major religions in the world are equal and valid responses to the 'Real'. I shall show that although one should welcome the underlying charitable disposition, the position itself is very problematic to any orthodox believer of any major religion. Indeed, I shall argue, in a way that I am sure Hebblethwaite would commend, that the logical implication of the pluralist hypothesis is that all the distinctive truth-claims of each tradition are mistaken. There is the danger, I shall show, that only liberals can be tolerant, and that this toleration comes at the price of denying the possibility of truth in religion.

Now it is not just orthodox Christians who have a problem with John Hick's pluralist hypothesis. It is a problem for almost all 'orthodox' adherents in the main religious traditions. To illustrate this, we shall look at the thought of Bediuzzaman Said Nursi. In his *Risale-i Nur*, we find an approach to religious diversity that is firmly committed to the truth and particularities of Islam. We shall look at three features of his response to religious diversity. The point is that the Hebblethwaite-approach to religious diversity is more helpful not only for Christians, but also for Muslims.

The Pluralist Hypothesis

We start then with the approach of John Hick.[5] Hick's solution to the problem of religious diversity arises in the context of the 'Christian

---

5 Hick's views are found in a number of writings. The most systematic presentation occurs in his Gifford Lectures, *An Interpretation of Religion*, first published in 1989 (and republished in 2004 with a new Introduction). Some of this summary is taken from my article, 'Christianity and other religions', in Gareth Jones (ed.), *The Blackwell Companion to Modern Theology*, 2004.

Theology of Other Religions debate'. Building on the taxonomy suggested by his student, Alan Race,[6] Hick argues that 'exclusivist' and 'inclusivist' responses to religious diversity are inappropriate. Instead, we should all become 'pluralist'. This debate is provoked by the problem of soteriology in Christian doctrine, namely, if Jesus is the only way to salvation, then what about those who are not Christian? The exclusivist argues that orthodox Christians are committed to the biblical claim that explicit belief in Christ is the only way to be saved (see John 14.6). This is the reason for the missionary imperative to reach those outside the Church. The inclusivist takes the line that the saving activity of God in Christ does not necessarily need conscious recognition. It is possible for a person to be saved by Christ through obedient observance of a different religious tradition (e.g. Islam). Such Muslims, explains the Roman Catholic theologian Karl Rahner, are really 'anonymous Christians'.

Hick rejects the exclusivist position as incoherent and unjust. It is incoherent because Christians believe that God desires the salvation of all people (1 Tim. 2.4) and that desire is unrealizable if only one (acculturated) religion is legitimate. It is unjust, says Hick, because the majority of people, owing to no fault of their own, are born into non-Christian cultures. A loving God, argues Hick, would not condemn to hell the majority of people just because they were born into the wrong culture. Hick rejects the inclusivist position because it is epistemologically too self-confident and insulting. From the epistemological point of view, Hick argues that no human can be completely sure about the nature of God and God's relations with the world. The inclusivist is confident that the Christian drama is closer to the truth and that all other religions only have (at best) a partial knowledge of that truth; Hick cannot see anything that justifies that self-confidence. It is insulting and patronizing because it does not acknowledge the 'self-definition' of a person (as, say, a Muslim) but instead turns that person into an 'anonymous Christian'.[7]

---

6 Alan Race, *Christians and Religious Pluralism*, 1983.

7 Given that we are considering Islam in this essay, it is worth noting that the Muslim Bilal Sambur has written that the concept of an 'anonymous Christian' 'does not have any contribution to make to interfaith relations, because people have freely chosen religion as their independent religious identity. Furthermore, that concept includes the disrespectful approach to human freedom and humiliates the religion of the other.' It is my view that Said Nursi would not concur with these criticisms of inclusivism. See B. Sambur in 'Is interfaith prayer possible?' *World Faiths Encounter*, July 1990.

Truth and Toleration

So Hick's solution is the so-called 'pluralist hypothesis'. The heart of the pluralist hypothesis is a single reality that is accessed and partially revealed in all the major religions of the world. Now what is that reality like? Hick's initial writings suggested a 'theistic pluralism', that is, a single God, who was loving and good, was underpinning all the major faith traditions. But later, he recognized that 'theistic pluralism' could not accommodate Buddhism. Buddhism takes many different forms, but there are significant strands that hardly talk about 'God' at all. Further, God hardly figures in the four Noble Truths, which are the central teaching of the Buddha. So in his Gifford Lectures, Hick argues for a 'Real', which no tradition can describe or claim to know exactly. In this way, the significance of *nirvana* in Buddhism can be accommodated in the experience of the Real.

Thus we are left with the following picture: the Real is the objective sense of the Transcendent, which is interpreted differently in each culture. For those living in India, they might call the Transcendent 'Krishna', while Muslims in Turkey talk of 'Allah', and Christians in North America call it 'Christ'. Hick acknowledges his debt to the Kantian distinction between the noumenal and the phenomenal. The noumenal is knowledge of the divine as 'it is in itself'. The phenomenal is knowledge of the divine as 'it appears to mind'. The noumenal is inaccessible. All we know is that each culture is interpreting an 'objective' experience of the Real in its own language and concepts. We cannot claim that any particular culture is more or less right, because none of us can transcend our own culture and find out exactly what the Real or Transcendent really is like.

Although one might appreciate Hick's charitable affirmation of religious diversity, the conclusion of his logic might disturb many committed believers in the major world faiths. His conclusion is that all we know about the 'Real' is that it exists; apart from that we have to be agnostic. For Hick, any distinctive doctrine that conflicts with the pluralist hypothesis has to be rejected. So, for Hick, Muslims are mistaken to claim that the Qur'an is the final and definitive revelation from God, as are Christians when they claim that Jesus is the incarnation of God. These doctrines, as traditionally understood, are incompatible with the pluralist hypothesis. For if the Qur'an is true, then the Qur'anic worldview is truer than the alternatives and, in particular, polytheists and Trinitarian Christians are mistaken.

This means that if we accept Hick's solution to the issue of religious truth and toleration, we all must become 'liberal' adherents of our faith traditions. All the distinctive truth-claims within each tradition must be radically reinterpreted. Brian Hebblethwaite puts it well when he explains that 'Hick's characterization of the transcendent object of all religious experience is becoming more and more vague and empty of content as he struggles to accommodate the diverse plurality of the religions of the world within a single global perspective.'[8] For Hebblethwaite, truth must coexist with toleration. Hick's manoeuvres, which deny a traditional incarnation, are deeply problematic. In Hick's theology, Jesus instead of being the incarnation of God is simply one of many different prophets; and the Qur'an, instead of being the final definitive disclosure from God, is simply one of many holy books – all of which witness to the reality of a transcendent entity about which we know virtually nothing.

Said Nursi on Truth and Toleration

It is at this point that we turn to the writings of Bediuzzaman Said Nursi. The world of Bediuzzaman ('Wonder of the Age') Said Nursi (1873–1960) is one that moved from the concluding years of the Caliphate and Ottoman Empire, through the tragedy of the First World War, to the emergence of the Republic of Turkey in 1923 with its initial strong commitment to aggressive secularism. His major conversation-partners were the West (which he saw as both 'secular' and 'Christian') and the many different forms of Islam. Primarily because of Nursi's situation, Judaism only gets passing references. I shall show that the achievement of the *Risale-i Nur* (the Treatise of Light) was to set an approach to Islam which is both committed to the truth of that tradition and yet, simultaneously, committed to toleration of religious diversity. It is to the thought of Said Nursi that we now turn.

There are three features of Nursi's position that I wish to examine. These are as follows: first, Nursi is committed to the truth of Islam and the importance of persuading others of that truth. Second, Nursi finds in his tradition several reasons why it is important to commit to constructive coexistence with other faith traditions, and third, Nursi believes that the resort to violence by Muslims against non-Muslims demonstrates a lack of self-confidence in Islam. Self-confident Muslims who are strong in their faith do not need to resort to violence.

Let us consider the first point. Islam, for Nursi, is not just a cultural religious option. Instead, Islam is the final, definitive, and most elegant

---

8 *The Ocean of Truth*, 1988:122.

description of the nature of God and the expectations that God has for humanity. So, for example, when Nursi describes the significance of Muhammad, he writes:

> Peace and blessings be upon our master Muhammed thousands and thousands of times, to the number of the good deeds of his community, to whom was revealed the All-Wise Criterion of Truth and Falsehood, from One Most Merciful, Most Compassionate, from the Sublime Throne; whose Prophethood was foretold by the Torah and Bible, and told of by wondrous signs, the voices of jinn, saints of man, and soothsayers; at whose indication the moon split; our master Muhammed! Peace and blessings be upon him thousands and thousands of times . . .[9]

It is important to note how embedded in this piety are certain truth-claims about the nature of Muhammad and his relationship with the Torah and Bible. In the 'Fourteenth Droplet', Nursi moves his focus from Muhammad to the Qur'an. Here he writes:

> The All-Wise Qur'an, which makes known to us our Sustainer, is thus: it is the pre-eternal translator of the great Book of the Universe; the discloser of the treasures of the Divine Names concealed in the pages of the earth and heavens; the key to the truths hidden beneath these lines of events; the treasury of the favors of the Most Merciful and pre-eternal addresses, which come forth from the World of the Unseen beyond the veil of this Manifest World; the sun, foundation, and plan of the spiritual world of Islam, and the map of the worlds of the hereafter; the distinct expounder, lucid exposition, articulate proof, and clear translator of the Divine Essence, attributes, and deeds; the instructor, true wisdom, guide and leader of the world of humanity; it is both book of wisdom and law, and a book of prayer and worship, and a book of command and summons, and a book of invocation and Divine knowledge – it is a book for all spiritual needs; and it is a sacred library offering books appropriate to the ways of all the saints and veracious, the purified and the scholars, whose ways and paths are all different.[10]

Said Nursi believes that there are compelling rational arguments for

---

9 Said Nursi, 'Thirteenth Droplet', in *The Words*, 1999:249.
10 'Fourteenth Droplet', in *The Words*, 1999:250.

60   Ian Markham

the truth of Islam. There is a constant sense pervading his writings that anyone reading the Qur'an cannot but acknowledge the divine origin of the text. Indeed, the impact of the Qur'an is so great on the reader, says Nursi, that he uses a *reductio ad absurdum* argument to defend its divine origins. After noting how the 'common people' cannot help but admit that the Qur'an is totally different from any other book, he explains:

> The Qur'an, then, is of a degree either above all of them or below all of them. To be below them is impossible, and no enemy nor the Devil even could accept it. In which case, the Qur'an is above all other books, and is therefore a miracle. Therefore, the Qur'an is the Word of the Creator of the universe. Because there is no point between the two; it is impossible and precluded that there should be.[11]

So, unlike John Hick, Said Nursi starts with a strong commitment to his tradition. He believes that Islam is true. It is not simply true for him, but for the entire world. We do not find anywhere in Nursi's voluminous writings the suggestion that there are many 'truths' about God and that the Qur'an is just one such 'truth'. There is no postmodern cultural relativism in the *Risale-i Nur*. Nursi makes this explicit when he explains how important it is to convert the 'People of the Book'. He writes:

> When urging the People of the Book to believe in Islam, the Qur'an shows them in this verse [Qur'an 2:4] a familiar aspect and a facility. That is, it implies: 'O People of the Book! There is no difficulty for you in accepting Islam; do not let it appear hard to you.' For the Qur'an does not order you to abandon your religion completely, it proposes only that you complete your faith and build it on the fundamentals of religion you already possess. For the Qur'an combines in itself the virtues of all the previous books and the essentials of all the previous religions; it is thus a modifier and a perfector of basic principles.[12]

---

[11] 'The Addendum to the Fifteenth Word', in *The Words*, 1999:204.

[12] Said Nursi, *Isârâtü'l-I'câz*, 1995:50, as quoted in Niyazi Beki, 'The Qur'an and its method of guidance', in *A Contemporary Approach to Understanding the Qur'an: The Example of the 'Risale-i Nur'*, 2000:105. In the *Letters*, 1997: 201, Nursi explains why the Torah and the Bible are not as good as the Qur'an. He writes, 'The words of the Torah, the Bible, and the Psalms do not have the

Truth and Toleration

Because of Said Nursi's commitment that Islam represents the truth about the world, we can see two further commitments in this passage. These are: a conviction that non-Muslims should be invited to convert to Islam, and a sense that the Qur'an 'completes' Christianity and Judaism. This 'fulfilment theology' is also found in Karl Rahner's description of the relationship of Christianity to non-Christian faiths.

This 'tradition-constituted' starting-point (to use an expression taken from the work of Alasdair MacIntyre) has one major advantage over the liberal approach of John Hick. The advantage is this: the vast majority of Muslims in the world start in the same place. The commitment to diversity, conversation, and toleration cannot start from semi-unbelief, but needs to be grounded in the particularities of the faith tradition. We need the 'orthodox' believers in each tradition to commit to toleration. Hick's approach will only appeal to those who are already liberal and semi-detached from their tradition. Said Nursi's approach is much more hopeful.

We turn now to the second feature of Nursi's position on truth and toleration. This is his recognition that there are many positive reasons, explicitly grounded in the tradition, that encourage a positive attitude to coexistence with non-Muslims. Given that consideration of this feature alone could give rise to a substantial paper in its own right, I shall simply confine myself to a small number of illustrations. One major illustration of this feature is Nursi's celebration of the importance of love. This passage from *The Damascus Sermon* sets the tone well:

> What I am certain of from my experience of social life and have learnt from my life-time of study is the following: the thing most worthy of love is love, and that most deserving of enmity is enmity. That is, love and loving, which render man's social life secure and lead to happiness are most worthy of love and being loved. Enmity and hostility are ugly and damaging, have overturned man's social life, and more than anything deserve loathing and enmity and to be shunned. (1996:49)

For Nursi, this very basic commitment to love does entail a commitment to peaceful coexistence with others. A good illustration of this

---

miraculousness of those of the Qur'an. They have been translated again and again, and a great many alien words have become intermingled with them. Also, the words of commentators and their false interpretations have been confused with their verses.'

has been documented by Thomas Michel.[13] When Kurdish tribesmen in Eastern Anatolia are worried about permitting Greeks and Armenians to be free, Nursi is adamant that the 'freedom of non-Muslims is a branch of our own freedom'.[14] Furthermore, the fear about acknowledging the legitimate freedom of the Christian is grounded in ignorance, poverty, and enmity. As Michel puts it: 'The message of Said Nursi is as valid for our own day as it was when he wrote these words almost 80 years ago. At the roots of tensions and conflicts between Muslims and Christians today lie not so much the evil nature of the other as our egoistic desires to dominate, control, and retaliate' (2000: 557). Nursi is clear: there is a Qur'anic obligation on Muslims to respect the freedom of Christians.

Thus we find in Said Nursi's writings, a strong commitment to love, coupled with an equally strong commitment to respect the liberty of the other. These two dispositions should shape our relationships with non-Muslims. Although Nursi believes that it is important to explain to the Christian the truth of Islam, he recognizes that at the end of the age there will be many sincere and good Christians who have not converted to Islam. In the cosmic battle against the Dajjal (the promotion of 'naturalist and materialist philosophy, [which] will lead to the total denial of God'; Michel, 2000:560), there will be a group of sincere Christians who will work with the Muslims to defeat Dajjal. So Nursi writes:

> Moreover, in the world of humanity, the secret society of the Dajjal will overturn civilization and subvert all mankind's sacred matters, with the intention of denying the Godhead. A zealous and self-sacrificing community known as a Christian community but worthy of being called 'Muslim Christians', will work to unite the true religion of Jesus (upon whom be peace) with the reality of Islam, and will kill and rout that society of Dajjal, thus saving humanity from atheism. (*Letters*, 1997:515)

This co-operation, towards the end of the age, is also linked to the return of Jesus. Nursi explains:

> At that point when the current appears to be very strong, the

---

13 Thomas Michel, 'Muslim–Christian dialogue and co-operation in Bediuzzaman's thought', in *A Contemporary Approach to Understanding the Qur'an: The Example of the 'Risale-i Nur'*, 2000.

14 Said Nursi as quoted in ibid.:557.

religion of true Christianity, which comprises the collective personality of Jesus ... will emerge. That is, it will descend from the skies of Divine Mercy. Present Christianity will be purified in the face of that reality; it will cast off superstition and distortion, and unite with the truths of Islam. Christianity will in effect be transformed into a sort of Islam. Following the Qur'an, the collective personality of Christianity will be in the rank of follower, and Islam, in that of leader. True religion will become a mighty force as a result of its joining it. Although defeated before the atheistic current while separate, Christianity and Islam will have the capability to defeat and rout it as a result of their union. Then the person of Jesus ... who is present with his human body in the world of the heavens, will come to lead the current of true religion, as, relying on the promise of One Powerful Over All Things, the Bringer of Sure News has said. Since he has told of it, it is true, and since the One Powerful Over All Things has promised it, He will certainly bring it about. (ibid.:79)

Although there are some sensitive Christian souls who will resent being told that the 'superstition and distortion' of present Christianity needs to be cast off and that then Christianity will 'in effect be transformed into a sort of Islam', the significance of this passage lies in the fact that there are still 'authentic' Christians at the end of the age. In other words, Said Nursi's beliefs about eschatology are a safeguard to a continuing Christian population now. Although he would love to see all Christians convert to Islam, he recognizes both sociologically and, more importantly, theologically that this will not happen. Christians and Jews have roles at the end of the age: for reasons already identified, Muslims have a duty to protect Christian and Jewish communities in the present. Although a Christian and a Jew might not like the theology, the social and political consequences of this theology are good.

Of course, there are more challenging texts in the Qur'an, for example, the verse that seems to prohibit the taking of Jews and Christians as friends (5:51). Said Nursi is interesting here: he concedes the validity of the text, yet insists that it is not a blanket prohibition. Instead, it is confined to moments when Jews and Christians are a threat to a Muslim.[15] Nursi explains thus:

---

15 Or rather, as Nursi writes, when Jews and Christians reflect their 'Jewishness and Christianity'. I interpret this as overt antagonism to Islam. For a slightly different interpretation see Michel, 2000:559.

A mighty religious revolution occurred in the time of the Prophet, and because all the people's minds revolved around religion, love and hatred were concentrated on that point and they loved or hated accordingly. For this reason, love for non-Muslims inferred dissembling. But now . . . what preoccupies people's minds are progress and this world . . . In any event most of them are not so bound to their religions. In which case, our being friendly to them springs from our admiration for their civilization and progress, and our borrowing these. Such friendship is certainly not included in the Qur'anic prohibition.[16]

In other words, friendship is possible when the goals are constructive and appropriate. Said Nursi recognized throughout his life the importance of good relations with the people of the book.

The net result is a set of arguments, firmly grounded in the Qur'an and hadith, which require Muslims to have positive and constructive relations with non-Muslims. These arguments are not intended for the non-Muslims; they assume the truth of the Islamic worldview. But the outcome is that we have a strong Islamic argument for diversity, conversation, and peaceful coexistence with the other.

This leads to the third point. For Said Nursi, the resort to interreligious violence reflects a lack of confidence in the truth of Islam. For Nursi, only the weak resort to violence, for Islam is sufficiently strong that good arguments can bring about victory. Sükran Vahide in her biography of Nursi explains his position thus:

[T]he way of the Risale-i Nur was peaceful *jihad* or '*jihad* of the word' (*mânevî jihad*) in the struggle against aggressive atheism and irreligion. By working solely for the spread and strengthening of belief, it was to work also for the preservation of internal order and peace and stability in society in the face of the moral and spiritual destruction of communism and the forces of irreligion which aimed to destabilize society and create anarchy, and to form 'a barrier' against them.[17]

In other words, Nursi is committed to handling disagreement with

---

16 As quoted in Osman Cilaci, 'Comments on the Holy Bible in the *Risale-i Nur*', in *A Contemporary Approach to Understanding the Qur'an: The Example of the 'Risale-i Nur'*, 2000:585.

17 Sükran Vahide, *The Author of the Risale-i Nur: Bediuzzaman Said Nursi*, 1992, Part 3:352.

peaceful means not because he shares a Western scepticism about the truth of religion, but because of the truth of religion. He wants an Islamic renewal; he wants Muslims to realize the power of their tradition. And in so doing, he believes, the power of argument and reason is sufficient to hold those who already belong and to attract others who are seeking God. He calls this a *mânevî jihad*, which is a 'jihad of the word' or a 'non-physical jihad'. One of the reasons why the *jihad* can be non-physical is because he is confident that God will bring about the necessary victory through such a peaceful witness that uses arguments rather than violence. The God Said Nursi believes in can work wonders with the sincere effort of faithful Muslims.

Thus when it comes to secularists and followers of other traditions, Nursi calls for non-violent witness to the beauty and coherence of Islam. Within Islam, Nursi insists that it is an obligation on all faithful Muslims to stand united. So he writes:

> Practice the brotherhood, love and cooperation insistently enjoined by hundreds of Qur'anic verses and traditions of the Prophet! Establish with all of your powers a union with your fellows and brothers in religion that is stronger than the union of the worldly! ... Do not say to yourself, 'Instead of spending my valuable time on such petty matters, let me spend it on more valuable things such as the invocation of God and meditation'. For precisely what you imagine to be a matter of slight importance in this moral jihad may in fact be very great.[18]

Once again, there is an interesting argument embedded in this text. However tempting it might be to evade disagreements and squabbles in the Islamic community by an act of piety, Nursi insists that it would be wrong to do so. Living in among these arguments is religious duty, for we do not know what the implications of the disagreement signify for the 'moral jihad'.

Nursi accepts the reality of pluralism (i.e. that there are many religious traditions), and the inevitability of disagreement both within and outside the Islamic community. However, his response is not to call for a 'recognition that Islam is just one truth among many' (the strategy of John Hick), but to call for a deeper faith more committed to its distinctive claims and beliefs. For Nursi, part of the renewal he

---

18 Said Nursi, 'On sincerity', in 'The twentieth flash', in *The Flashes Collection*, (vol. 3 of the *Risale-i Nur*), 1995:208.

wants among Muslims is a greater self-confidence in the arguments for the Islamic faith that enables Muslims to enjoy the pluralist world. Like a much-loved child at home, one can venture into the world unafraid of difference and diversity because one is secure in one's own identity.

Linked to the idea that a committed Muslim is one who can enjoy engaging with other traditions because of the power of his or her arguments, one final comment should be added under this heading. Nursi had plenty of secular critics who were ready to argue that committed Muslims made bad citizens. Again Nursi turns this argument around: instead of sharing the secular assumption that citizenship requires uncommitted religious people, he insists that properly committed Muslims will make model citizens. They are not a threat to the political order; they need not be committed to overthrow of the government. So in *The Damascus Sermon* he explains:

> What we want now is the awakening and attention of believers, for the effect of public attention is undeniable. The aim of the Union and its purpose is to uphold the Word of God, and its way is to wage the 'greater jihad' with one's own soul, and to guide others. Ninety-nine per cent of the endeavors of this blessed society are not political. They are rather turned towards good morals and moderation, which are the opposite of politics, and other lawful aims.[19]

At every point, Nursi handles the challenge of diversity and disagreement not by resorting to the epistemological uncertainty that has shaped many Western apologetics for pluralism, but by insisting on a deeper love of God and a greater understanding of the Qur'an. For Nursi, a faith-commitment, not semi-agnosticism, is the best way of handling diversity.

Comparing Hick and Nursi

There are two key differences between the views of John Hick and Said Nursi. The first is that Hick looks at the problem of religious diversity from the *outside*, while Nursi sees the problem from *within* Islam. Hick is the thinker who is seeking to provide an explanation for the entire phenomenon of religious diversity. He is no longer

---

19 First Addendum, Third Part, 1996:84.

Truth and Toleration 67

committed to the particularities of Christianity.[20] Although he has had a sense of the transcendent in his life, he is content to admit that he is agnostic about the best description of the source. So, as a thinker standing outside traditional Christianity, he offers an account of religious diversity that makes sense of the experience of the divine that many people have. Now John Hick's pluralist hypothesis will appeal to anyone who is in the same place as John Hick. So it is popular in the *New York Times*-reading, liberal, east-coast America and in a post-Christian Europe, but beyond these areas, it does not appeal. Most religious people are not semi-detached from their faith. When people convert and affirm a particular religious narrative, they are prepared to stake their life on the truth of that narrative.

For his part, Said Nursi starts firmly within the Islamic narrative. He is assuming the truth of the particularities of Islam. Nursi's task is to make sense of the fact of diversity from within the perspective of Islam. There are plenty of Christians and Muslims who assume the truth of their traditions and arrive at a place that makes the affirmation of diversity and toleration difficult. Nursi's achievement is that he stands inside a deeply traditional form of Islam and yet affirms the importance of toleration and conversation. Unlike Hick's solution to the problem of truth and toleration in the context of religious commitment, Nursi's approach could, in principle, be affirmed by any traditional Muslim.

The second difference is that John Hick has a highly cultivated English sensitivity to avoiding all forms of potential offensiveness. So, for example, he thinks it is 'offensive' for one tradition to claim that it describes the Transcendent more accurately than any other.[21] For Jews, Christians, and Muslims to claim that God can 'act', 'decide', and 'love' would suggest that a more 'impersonal' Buddhist view of ultimate reality is mistaken. Hick thinks that this would be a conceit that would create a barrier to good interfaith relations. Or, to take another example, he is opposed very strongly to any attempt to 'convert' the other. The religions of the world are simply 'cultural' responses to the Real. In India, the main religious tradition is Hinduism; in America, it is Christianity. For Hick, it does not really

---

20 Hick was editor of *The Myth of God Incarnate*, in which various distinguished scholars explain why they find the traditional doctrine of the Incarnation problematic.
21 To be fair to Hick, he also thinks that such claims are difficult to establish epistemologically.

matter to which religious tradition you happen to belong; indeed, in certain cultures there is just a natural option that fits most people living in that culture.

Although politeness in interfaith relations is a good thing, the commitment to truth in the religious world means that Hick's form of politeness is an unrealistic expectation. Further, as many scholars have pointed out, it is a moot point whether Hick is that polite anyway. His insistence that every religious tradition should deny its distinctiveness and become semi-agnostic is offensive to every traditional believer in every religious tradition – and he wants every traditional believer to 'convert' to his liberal pluralism. It is important to remember that all truth-claims carry implications for the superiority of a certain worldview and a hope that others will adopt it. This is true for the atheist who claims that 'all religions are misguided', for the pluralist who claims that 'all religions are equally valid and lead to the Real', as well as for the Muslim who claims that 'the Qur'an is the final and definitive disclosure of God to humanity'.

Said Nursi believes in the truth of Islam. He accepts that this means that Christianity is fundamentally misguided in certain respects. He also accepts that there is an Islamic duty to present the truth to Christians. Naturally as a Christian I would disagree as to what is 'the truth' in this respect. But Nursi is interesting because he accepts the inevitability of that disagreement; he acknowledges a responsibility to protect my entitlement to worship, and he acknowledges that Christians will coexist in God's providence until the end of the age. Perhaps Said Nursi is not as polite as John Hick, but he is bound to be more influential. Instead of expecting a Hickoid utopia of mutual religious affirmation, Said Nursi arrives at a place where truth is reconciled with toleration.

The Christian taxonomy of 'pluralism', 'inclusivism', and 'exclusivism' does not adapt easily to other faith traditions. The particular Christian question about 'salvation' does not arise in the same way in other religious traditions. However, if we adapt the terminology, perhaps we can place Nursi on the spectrum. Exclusivism can become the view that a symbol-system (i.e. the beliefs and practices that make up a world perspective) is true, and membership of the group affirming that symbol-system is essential. Inclusivism would become the view that a particular symbol-system of a particular group is closer to the truth than the alternatives, but that other groups have a partial understanding of that truth which can be affirmed. Pluralism would be the view that we cannot rank or distinguish between different symbol-systems. Therefore, all groups (which have good ethical expressions) are equally valid.

Interpreting the taxonomy in this way means that Nursi is properly labelled an 'inclusivist'. He is committed to the truth of Islam as disclosed in the Qur'an and the life of the prophet Muhammad. Yet he acknowledges that other traditions have a partial insight into the truth. The real battle in religion is between the inclusivists and the exclusivists. Pluralism will only appeal to the increasingly non-religious. Nursi would understand Karl Rahner. Inclusivism is a space that protects both commitment to truth and toleration.

Conclusion

Those who are familiar with Hebblethwaite's work in the Christian theology of other religions will recognize that his attitude to religious diversity is a Christian mirror of Said Nursi's attitude. Hebblethwaite's own vision of the evolving relationship between Christianity and Islam is a good place to conclude this chapter. He writes:

> The historical rivalry between Christianity and Islam for the allegiance of men and women in many parts of the world has been appallingly ugly and cruel – very much a part of the problem of evil at the heart of the religious world. In some places . . . the urgent need for practical co-operation on issues of race-relations and social justice has been discovered and acted upon by representatives of the various religious communities, including the Christian and the Muslim, with very positive results. This suggests the vision of a future where these different faiths are rivals only in the sense of offering for free acceptance or rejection, entirely in the spirit of tolerance and respect, different comprehensive views of the ultimate context and destiny of human life. The only criteria by which to judge these matters will be the ethical fruitfulness, social as well as personal, of these faiths and the plausibility of their respective claims to truth. And, of course, these two criteria are linked. In Christianity's case, the personal and social ethic that it offers to the world is inextricably bound up with its vision of the triune God and of the grace and love of God manifested in the incarnation.[22]

For Brian Hebblethwaite, it is possible to reconcile religious truth

---

22 *The Essence of Christianity*, 1996:154–5.

with toleration. In this respect, he has created a stronger foundation for dialogue than the practical agnosticism of John Hick. When it comes to religious diversity, I suspect Hebblethwaite's views are likely to triumph in the twenty-first century. Faith does not surrender beliefs easily: and the challenge is to articulate one's beliefs in a way that coexists with tolerance and respect. Brian Hebblethwaite meets this challenge in a way that we should all admire and emulate.

5. Philosophical Presuppositions and Biblical Exegesis

STEPHEN T. DAVIS

The Christian Context

Brian Hebblethwaite's work, especially in Christology and in global philosophy of religion, has been an inspiration and guide to me for many years. I hope we may see many more of his typically sensible, well-argued, and clear books and essays. Let me begin with a terse and typically vigorous quotation from Rudolf Bultmann: 'Every exegesis that is guided by dogmatic prejudices does not hear what the text says, but only lets the latter say what it wants to hear.'[1]

The question of the relationship between philosophical presuppositions and biblical exegesis is a frequently discussed one. It has been analysed from several angles. Some biblical scholars, recognizing as Bultmann did that the presuppositions of certain exegetes have sometimes distorted their interpretations, have argued for the ideal of presuppositionless exegesis. Others, including Bultmann, have argued that this is impossible: we cannot avoid having presuppositions as we approach the Bible or any other text.

Conservative biblical scholars have discussed this issue as well. Their aim has often been to argue that liberal scholars have been blinded by their presuppositions regarding the Bible's message. A great deal of criticism has been heaped on the naturalism or implicit deism of some scholars, especially their acceptance of presuppositions like 'God does not exist', or 'Nature is a closed system of causes and effects', or 'The worldview of the New Testament writers is outmoded and superstitious'. I am going to approach the issue somewhat differently. For it is my view that the holding of certain philosophical positions is *essential* to interpreting the Bible, at least in Christian

---

[1] 'Is exegesis without presuppositions possible?', in *Existence and Faith*, ed. S. M. Ogden, 1964:343.

exegesis.[2] In other words, I think it is crucial for biblical interpreters to have the *correct* presuppositions. I will say what I think they are in due course. Some of them are controversial in philosophical circles.

Let me provide a brief roadmap of where we will be going in this chapter. First, I will define the term 'presupposition', and contrast it with the term 'prejudice'. Second, since I will be using the concept, 'the meaning of the whole of scripture', I need to explain in what sense or senses I consider the Bible to be a unified work that can possess an overall meaning. Finally, I will turn to the task of exploring those philosophical presuppositions that I think are requisite for proper biblical interpretation.

'Presupposition' and 'Prejudice'

What exactly is a 'presupposition'? Philosophers use the word in different ways. I am interested primarily in what are called 'pragmatic presuppositions'. These are claims that a speaker or interpreter takes for granted, i.e. s/he does not state them but takes them to be understood as true. If they are false, the statements made by the speaker or interpreter may well be untoward or inappropriate. If I say, 'The present King of France is bald', it seems that I am presupposing that 'There presently exists a King of France.' If that presupposition is false (as indeed it is), my original statement will be inappropriate. More broadly, then, a presupposition is any unstated premise or background-belief whose truth is necessary to the truth of another statement, or to the soundness of an argument, or to the tenability of a position.

Let me emphasize that a presupposition is a belief for which the believer is normally able to give a principled defence. This does not mean that it must be true. A 'prejudice', on the other hand, is an unstated premise or background-belief for which the believer cannot give a principled defence, and indeed is usually at pains to hide. As Bultmann pointed out, prejudices are often at work in biblical interpretation, as well as elsewhere in life. It is a prejudice when proof-texts are sought out to support a pre-existing and unbiblical doctrine, such as that slavery is divinely sanctioned. It is also a prejudice when modern views are anachronistically read back into the biblical texts,

---

2 I recognize that many scholars are involved in interpreting the Bible who do not see themselves as committed in any sense to Christianity or to the Church, and my suggestions in the present paper have little to do with them.

Philosophical Presuppositions and Biblical Exegesis 73

such as the view of some exegetes in the 1930s and 1940s – ironically, exegetes such as Bultmann himself – that existential philosophy is taught in the New Testament.[3]

On the other hand, we have all heard in recent years that there exists no 'view from nowhere'. And so far as human beings are concerned, that seems to me to be true. There is no such thing as totally neutral, presuppositionless exegesis. Everybody approaches the Bible, or any text, with a network of basic beliefs and attitudes that provides that person's interpretative framework. So, as I say, the task is to approach the Bible with the correct, or most nearly correct, presuppositions. But how do we know what they are? There is no algorithm for finding out. On the present occasion, I will simply suggest a few rules.

1 One's presuppositions must be guided by a thorough knowledge of the history of theology and especially of exegesis.
2 One's presuppositions must be arrived at not on one's own, but in correspondence with the wider Christian and scholarly communities.
3 One's presuppositions must be correctable by the scriptures themselves.

The Unity of the Bible

Before discussing the unity of the Bible, let me say a word about what scholars call the 'hermeneutical' circle. This term can mean different things. I take it to be the following phenomenon: in interpreting the Bible, we need to interpret the whole in terms of the parts and the parts in terms of the whole. The first point is that any defensible opinion about the macro message of the Bible, or the overall message of a part of the Bible, must be informed by and consistent with defensible opinions about the meanings of the various smaller texts and pericopes that it consists in. The second point is that any defensible opinion about the meaning of a smaller biblical text or pericope must be informed by and consistent with defensible opinions about the meaning of the Bible as a whole or of large sections of it in which the text is located.

Yet this comment presupposes something that is deeply controversial today among scripture scholars, namely the very idea that the

---

3 The distinction between 'presupposition' and 'prejudice' is made in a slightly different way by Graham Stanton; see his 'Presuppositions of New Testament Criticism', in I. Howard Marshall (ed.), *New Testament Interpretation*, 1977:61.

Bible is the sort of text that can have a unified meaning. Thus James Barr says, 'The Bible is not a unified writing but a composite body of literature.'[4] In one sense, this is entirely true. The Bible was written over a very long period of time, by many different authors, and its genre-pluralism is staggering. Among other types of literature, the Bible includes: creation stories, historical narratives, law codes, songs, poems, wise sayings, prophetic oracles, parables, letters from one person to another, letters from one person to a group of people, and apocalyptic literature.

Reacting against an uncritical assumption of biblical unity in the so-called 'Biblical Theology' movement of, roughly, 1930–1960, contemporary biblical scholarship has swung mightily in the other direction. Many scholars view the Bible as a literary rather than a unified work. Such critics believe that the Bible does not contain a 'theology' but rather many competing and mutually inconsistent 'theologies'. They seek out discrepancies and contradictions in the Bible with inquisitorial zeal. They view any attempt to harmonize two apparently discrepant texts as laughably unsophisticated. For example, many would consider it uncouth to use a text from the Fourth Gospel to illuminate a Pauline text, or vice versa. At times they give non-canonical texts from the biblical period more weight than canonical ones. It seems to be largely assumed that there is no such thing as 'the biblical view' or even 'the New Testament' view of this or that. It goes without saying that on this view the Bible is incapable of making normative theological statements.

I will argue against such notions and in favour of the unity of the Bible. I will do so in four ways, the fourth of which is the strongest and most important. In none of these four points, however, will I oppose the notion that the Bible is diverse. I will argue for a complex 'unity in diversity' of the Bible. Indeed, I do not rule out *a priori* the possibility that some biblical texts are simply inconsistent with others. However, I must say that the different and logically inconsistent 'theologies' that some contemporary interpreters claim to find in the Bible or even in the New Testament often seem to me to be simply different ways in different contexts of stating similiar or complementary theologies.

It will be helpful to explain the sort of biblical unity for which I am arguing. It is not the sort of uniformity that we would expect to find in

---

4 *The Bible in the Modern World*, 1973:157.

Philosophical Presuppositions and Biblical Exegesis 75

an article in a scholarly journal in mathematics or philosophy. This is the kind of unity that we expect to find where there is one author who has one topic in mind, and who writes in one genre, and all of whose statements are consistent with each other and help contribute to the article's overall aim. Here, as I suppose, the author's intention is the integrating principle of unity. Nor is the Bible's unity the kind that we find in a typical jigsaw puzzle. This is the kind of unity where the various pieces are at first a jumbled muddle rather than a coherent picture, and only after long and patient effort are we able to fit them together and see the picture that was at first hidden. Here the integrating principle of unity is the solution to the puzzle.

I wish to argue for a unity in the Bible that is more like a thematic or organic unity.[5] Thematic unity is involved in cases where a mass of material, even diverse material, in one way or another advances a certain literary or theological theme or series of related themes. Here the integrating principle of unity, as I suppose, is the theme being advanced. A species of thematic unity is what we might call narrative unity. This is involved in cases where a mass of material, even material diverse as to genre and purpose, when taken together is seen as telling one story. Here the integrating principle of unity is the story.

The issue I am raising is this: does the New Testament, or indeed the Bible as a whole, possess sufficient unity for it to be theologically normative for Christians and to support the hermeneutical circle (which talks about the meaning of the *whole*)? Is there enough unity to make 'agreement of our theological statements with scripture' a criterion of theological acceptability? I will argue in four ways that the answer is yes.

Arguments for the Unity of the Bible

1 *The Bible is a book inside a cover*: that is, the Bible is a unity simply in virtue of its being presented as a single book and accepted as such by the Church for nearly two thousand years. This is, of course, a weak sense of unity, and is entirely consistent with views of the Bible as a library like those described above. Nevertheless, this is a unity worth noting. Virtually any writings that have been published together and that have a long tradition of interpretation can be

---

5 As my fourth argument below reveals, however, I do not rule out biblical unity as a function of the intention of one divine author.

considered a unified work in this sense, and discussions about the overall meaning of the book can be quite appropriate.[6]

2 *The Bible is a unity in its basic message*: This is a stronger sense of unity than the first. I am presupposing here the principle that complementary theological claims from various texts of scripture can be fitted together to form coherent wholes. This point was recognized early in the history of the Church: the overall message or meaning of scripture as a whole was called 'the rule of faith'. Accordingly, scripture is the story of the redemptive dealings of the one and only God with human beings. It moves from the creation and the fall of human beings to the choosing of Israel, from the giving of the law to the sending of the prophets, from the birth of the messiah to the salvation of human beings in the life, death and resurrection of Jesus Christ, from the creation of the Church at Pentecost to the final victory of God in the eschaton. It is the story of God's covenant promises, of the universality of sin and human failure to observe God's covenants, and of God's faithfulness in Jesus Christ in fulfilling God's promises.

The unity of the Bible's two Testaments, despite the diversity that we see there, is seen in their complementary views of God, of human nature, of the election of a people of God, and of God's redemptive purposes for humans. It is evidenced further by the consciousness of the writers of the New Testament of being a continuation of the same people of God as the people of the Old Testament, of their acceptance of the Old Testament as sacred scripture fit for Christian proclamation, and of their sense of seeing in Jesus Christ the true meaning and goal of the Old Testament.

The unity of the New Testament, despite the many viewpoints expressed there, is a unity provided by Christology, in particular (as James Dunn convincingly argues) by a shared acceptance of the identity of the earthly Jesus with the now resurrected and exalted Lord and Son of God. The New Testament's unity is also a function of a unified commitment to monotheism, to the Hebrew Bible, to one and the same faith with its promise of forgiveness and salvation, to the

---

6 Let me give an illustration. At my home institution, there is a course called 'Civilization 10' that is required of all first-year undergraduates. The textbook for the course is a made-for-the-course book of readings consisting of selected works (and excerpts from selected works) of history, literature, mathematics, science, the social sciences, philosophy and religion from Genesis until the twentieth century. My point is that questions about its overall meaning can be asked even of a book such as this.

notion that the church both continues and fulfils the role of Israel, to baptism and to common meal rites that eventually solidified as the Lord's Supper, to the experience of the Holy Spirit, to love of neighbour as the hallmark of Christian conduct, and to the hope of Jesus' return.[7]

3 *One potential dire consequence of giving up on the unity of the Bible*: Now this third point can be dismissed as unrelated to the truth of the matter. It is more a pragmatic point about what I see as terrible potential consequences of denying biblical unity. Nevertheless, it is a point I feel deeply. To the extent that interpreters reject both the Old Testament's status as God's word and the firm and unanimous conviction of the New Testament writers of the unity of the two Testaments (among many other texts, see Matt. 21.42–4; Luke 24.25–7, 44; John 5.39–46; Eph. 1.9–10; 1 Tim. 3.16), to that extent the testimony of both Testaments that Israel is the chosen people of God can easily be rejected. The Christian Church can then become severed from its Jewish roots: Jews can come to be viewed as a disposable residuum of biblical times; antisemitism can become attractive, and even genocide can become slightly more thinkable than it was before. Note the alarming case of those German Old Testament scholars who supported National Socialism and raised no voice against its programmes during the Third Reich. Accordingly, in my opinion, Christians must continue to hold that the Old Testament is both divinely inspired and a Christian book. Israel was and is God's chosen people; Christians are shoots grafted on to the branch of the people of God, and Israel has a continuing role to play in the providential plan of God for the human race (Rom. 9–11).

4 *Divine inspiration of the Bible*: This argument for biblical unity – the strongest of the four – has been rejected by many scholars today. But most Christians continue to hold that the books of the Bible, and

---

7 These and other related questions are explored skilfully by James Dunn in his *Unity and Diversity in the New Testament*, 1990: esp. 56–7, 370. I have learned a great deal from Dunn's book, and have no problem with its basic thrust. In particular, I do not hold that only a very narrow range of theological arguments can be said to 'agree with scripture'. And I accept the claim that theological diversity is both present in the New Testament and healthy for the Christian community. I am inclined to believe, however, that many of the competing theologies that Dunn finds in the New Testament are much more complementary than he realizes.

only the books of the Bible, were subject to the inspiration of the Holy Spirit and were brought together by the Church under the influence of the Holy Spirit. This divine inspiration of the books and book writers ceased at the close of the Apostolic age. Thus the Bible is unique among all the books in the world's history in having been produced in some strong sense by God (as well as by its human authors).[8] If the Bible is indeed in some strong sense the product of divine inspiration, its unity as the work of a single, divine author (as well as, of course, its many human authors) is to be expected.

It should also be pointed out here that there is a close relationship between the second and the fourth of my arguments for the unity of the Bible. The fourth may be the best explanation of the second. That is, the striking fact that a book with such diverse origins as the Bible displays the overall organic unity noted in my second argument may well be taken as evidence for some kind of divine providential guidance of its writing. The Bible does possess the very sort of 'unity in diversity' that we might expect from a book that (i) was written in a great variety of historical, cultural, and religious circumstances, and (ii) was intended by God to be a decisive self-revelation, with one message or theme from beginning to end.

My point is that it makes sense to speak of the Bible as a unity, as one work, as the kind of thing that can be said to have a meaning as a whole. Despite its great diversity – of historical content, of authorial concerns, of theological setting, of genre, etc. – the Bible is one book that contains a unified message (along with many different messages). Now it must be stressed that I have not in any serious sense *proved* in this brief excursion that the Bible is a unity. Beside much further consideration of the four arguments that I have raised, this would take detailed exegetical arguments to the effect that various apparently discrepant or unrelated texts actually cohere and help form a unified theological whole. Such a task is beyond my present interests, and perhaps my competence as well. Someone else will have to do the detailed work of sorting out apparent inconsistencies and constructing the macro biblical theology sketched out above.

---

8 Here I disagree with Dunn who says, 'Nor have I said, nor would I want to say, that the NT writings are canonical because they were *more inspired* than other and later Christian writings', 1990:386.

The Bible and Christian Philosophy

It is time that we turned to those presuppositions that I think proper interpretation of the Bible requires. Like all human beings, Christian philosophers want to know what to believe. And on some issues about which we are curious, both philosophy and scripture are possible sources of information. Most Christian philosophers see themselves as living under a methodological obligation to make all their beliefs that are relevant to matters on which the Bible speaks consistent with scripture. I would hold that the Bible is trustworthy and reliable on all matters on which it speaks. Scripture is the source of religious truth above all other sources and the norm or guide to religious truth above all other norms or guides.[9]

If God wants to redeem fallen human beings, it seems sensible to believe that God will communicate the divine method of salvation to those human beings so that they can know and take advantage of it. Christians hold that this is precisely what God has done. Christians affirm that in scripture *God speaks to us*. Accordingly, the Bible is unlike all other books: it is revelatory. Our received tradition is that all proposals on any subject that is relevant to Christian thought and practice are to be judged pre-eminently in the light of scripture.

The Bible says nothing about many issues that are of concern to philosophers. The Bible is not a work of philosophy or even of philosophy of religion. The concerns and questions of the biblical writers are different from those of contemporary philosophers. But there are certain questions with which Christian philosophers are concerned that are also addressed in the Bible:

1 What is the world's origin?
2 What is a human being?
3 How should human beings live?
4 Does God exist?
5 Is there life beyond death?

There are, of course, many others.

Now it would be taken as the height of absurdity by most secular philosophers if anyone were to suggest – as I am suggesting – that the

---

9 For further discussion of this point, see my 'Tradition, Scripture, and Theological Authority', in Stephen T. Davis (ed.), *Philosophy and Theological Discourse*, 1997.

teachings of the Bible and philosophical conclusions can be relevant to each other. We have all heard in recent years, from Alvin Plantinga and others, that we Christian philosophers should not be afraid to allow biblical and Christian teachings to influence our views as philosophers. I entirely agree with that sentiment. But I also believe that it is acceptable for Christian philosophers in certain instances to allow their philosophical opinions to influence how they approach the Bible. They will be poor exegetes, however, if their philosophical views constrain the Bible, if the scriptures are not free to speak, as the Holy Spirit would have them speak.

In this essay, I am not arguing (although I believe it and think I can demonstrate it) that both exegesis and theology require philosophy. Indeed, I think that certain philosophical assumptions and activities are required in order to think coherently about anything at all. Nor will I argue (although I believe it and think I can demonstrate it) that sound exegesis and theology ought not to be tied too closely to any one philosophical system. That this very thing has occurred in the past and still occurs today almost goes without saying. It is possible to find exegetes and theologians in the tradition whose views are, in my opinion, too closely tied to various philosophical schools.

Given what the Fathers of the Church called 'the rule of faith' (as noted above, this is the received and accepted way of interpreting the macro-message of scripture, which was for them synonymous with the Christian message itself), I believe Christian philosophers are allowed to approach the Bible with certain controversial philosophical theses intact. Let me mention seven of them. I am certainly not arguing that no serious Christian exegete or theologian has ever rejected any of them. I am claiming that no serious Christian exegete or theologian *should* do so.

1 *Metaphysical monism is false*: I take metaphysical monism to be the thesis that there is one and only one reality, and accordingly that all differentiation is illusory. Thus ultimately I am the same thing as my pet African Grey parrot, and he and I are both ultimately the same thing as the wall over there, and all of us – parrot, wall, and I – are the same thing as ultimate reality. Metaphysical monism can be found in various places, both in the East and in the West: Advaita Vedanta Hinduism is surely just one example of it. But it seems clear that biblical religion is essentially dualist just in this sense: God is one thing and the world, God's creation, is another. God and the world are, as we might say, different things.

Philosophical Presuppositions and Biblical Exegesis 81

2 *Metaphysical materialism is false*: I take metaphysical materialism to be the thesis that the only reality is matter. The physical universe exhausts reality. Putative immaterial or incorporeal things – whether they be God, angels, human souls, or whatever – simply do not exist. Metaphysical materialism can also be found in various places. Ancient Epicurean philosophy was based on it, and the vast majority of contemporary analytic philosophers accept it as a matter of faith. But it seems clear that biblical religion is essentially committed to the reality of certain spiritual or non-physical things, among them God, angels, demons, and the human soul. Now the last three items on that list – angels, demons, and souls – may be somewhat controversial among Christian thinkers. But the first item – God – is not. God, who is a spirit (John 4.24), alone suffices to show that biblical religion is essentially committed to the falsity of metaphysical materialism. At least one non-physical thing exists: ergo, materialism is false.

3 *Time is linear*: I take the main alternative to the view that 'Time is linear' to be the view that time and history are circular, that history endlessly repeats itself, that there is no novelty or progress, and accordingly that no historical event can have eternal significance. Such views are found in virtually every pre-biblical religious or mythological system and in many such systems existing today. But it seems clear that biblical religion is essentially based on the view that time is linear. That is, history is moving toward a certain goal or *telos*: the kingdom of God. Novelty can and does appear from time to time. Indeed, certain historical events can have eternal significance. Some day things will be different, and infinitely better, than they are now.

4 *Moral values are objective*: I take the claim, 'Moral values are objective' to mean that moral relativism is false. Moral relativism is the view that right and wrong, as well as related notions like duty, obligation, moral goodness, moral evil, etc., depend on individuals or groups. There are no trans-personal or trans-societal truths in morality. What actions are right or wrong depends on who you are or what you believe or what the culture to which you belong holds is right or wrong. Moral objectivism, however, is simply the claim that statements about moral right or wrong are true or false quite apart from what any human individual or group happens to hold. It seems clear that biblical religion is essentially committed to moral objectivism. Certain moral claims are true – ultimately coming, as they

do, from God – quite apart from what any human being might think about them.

5 *Human beings are morally responsible for what they do*: I take the claim, 'Jones is morally responsible for x', to mean that Jones can legitimately be praised or blamed, punished or rewarded, for x. The refrigerator is not morally responsible for keeping the food cold or even (when it malfunctions) for letting it get warm. A person who acts out of legitimate self-defence – so we normally think – is not morally responsible for injuring or maybe even killing someone. Or, better, the person *is* responsible but is excused. Generally, Jones is morally responsible for x if, and only if, (i) Jones did x or caused x to occur; (ii) x is an event or action with moral connotations (like causing pain or pleasure to someone); and (iii) there were no legitimate excuses. Now some philosophers have held that nobody is ever morally responsible; everything we do is brought about by unavoidable causal forces. We are victims of forces beyond our control. But it seems clear that biblical religion is essentially committed to the notion that human beings *are* morally responsible for (at least much of) what they do. Accordingly, God can legitimately hold us morally responsible for our failure to obey God's commands.

6 *Epistemological scepticism is false*: I take epistemological scepticism to be the view that no knowledge-claim can ever be justified, that nothing can ever be known for sure. There are, of course, crudely self-contradictory versions of scepticism (like the view of the person who claims to know that nothing whatever can be known), but there are also much more sophisticated versions. But it seems clear that biblical religion is essentially committed to the view that knowledge is possible, that God created us human beings with the ability to learn certain things on our own, that is with our own cognitive equipment, and that we know certain other things because God has revealed them to us. Human reason is uniquely designed by God for the acquisition of knowledge, and sometimes succeeds in attaining it.

7 *Linguistic realism is true*: 'Linguistic realism' is an expression that I am using technically. I take it as the negation of those extreme postmodern or deconstructionist views that deny the possibility of secure communication between one person and another, claim that texts have no stable meanings, and insist that all thinkers are trapped within the confines of their own perspectives. But I take it that biblical

religion is essentially committed to the view that texts can have stable meanings, that genuine communication between one mind and another is possible,[10] and indeed that it is possible for a divine mind to communicate truth to human minds.

Conclusion

Let me return to the quotation from Bultmann with which we began: 'Every exegesis that is guided by dogmatic prejudices does not hear what the text says, but only lets the latter say what it wants to hear.' I see myself in the present essay as agreeing with Bultmann, although one suspects he would not agree with the spin I have placed on his words. We should not approach the text with prejudices, that is, with preconceptions that cannot rationally be justified. But we cannot approach the text of the Bible without any presuppositions at all (and Bultmann would agree with that), and so we had best approach the Bible with that set of presuppositions that allows the text to speak what it wants to say.

Now I have been describing a method of exegesis for Christians, both philosophers and non-philosophers. I am aware that not every exegete shares Christian assumptions. As noted above, I do not want to be interpreted as ruling out the methods practised by most members of the Society of Biblical Literature, for example, where exegesis is a purely academic discipline and Christian assumptions are not allowed to intrude. I wish such folk well. But I do want to claim explicitly what I think my overall argument in this essay entails, namely that interpreting the Bible Christianly (as the Word of God, as a unity, in conjunction with Christian history), is the correct method of exegesis. It aligns us better with the character the Bible actually has. This does not mean, in specific cases, that Christian exegetes always interpret the Bible better than non-Christian exegetes do. But I do mean that everything else being equal, a Christian 'take' on the Bible is epistemologically superior to all others.

---

10 I once came home from work expecting, as usual, to see my wife. Instead I found a note, in her handwriting. It said, 'Hi Honey, My tooth has been hurting all day. I've gone to see the dentist. See you when I get home. Love, Charis.' Now, no one will deny that (i) the paper with marks on it, and (ii) the meaning of the message, are two different things. Still, I believe I knew, reading that message, exactly what she meant. Thinking about that experience was enough to convince me that texts can have stable meanings and that communication between two minds via a text is possible.

My argument, then, is that it is not only allowable, but in some cases essential, for Christian philosophers to approach the reading of the Bible with these controversial philosophical theses intact. But it is also essential for Christian philosophers to allow the teachings of scripture to influence their philosophical views. Indeed, as noted, I think Christian philosophers are to be encouraged not to fear doing that. It is part of the official view of philosophy's methodology that philosophers accept nothing 'on authority', for example just because the Bible says so, or just because Plato or Quine said so. (Whether philosophers actually follow this rule is another question.) Still, in my opinion, philosophers ought not to imitate the procedure that was apparently followed by a biology professor at a Christian college whom I once met and who told me, 'I keep my faith in one pocket and my science in another.'

We are instead required to do our best to integrate all that we know, our faith and our learning, the teachings of scripture and the results of our research. One of the things that this means concretely is – as Alvin Plantinga has also argued in recent years – 'don't give up too quickly on a given teaching from the Bible or theology just because it seems to conflict with current academic orthodoxy'.[11]

---

11 I would like to thank Alan Padgett, John Stackhouse, and Susan Peppers for their helpful comments on an earlier version of this chapter.

6. A Non-Realist View of God[1]

DON CUPITT

A Historical Perspective

I first put forward a non-realist view of God over twenty years ago, in a book called *Taking Leave of God*.[2] Before it was published I remember trying out the ideas on the Canadian bishops at a retreat house in Canada. They looked *very* dubious. The main argument of the book was that we should see the idea of God as being internal to the religious life. It is used, and has meaning, just within that context. A person's god is an object of the same kind as her Muse, her 'project', her 'dream', her ideal or goal, her ambition or her guiding star. A person's god is a unifying focus of religious aspiration, that towards which, for the sake of which and by which a person lives. But, like *nirvana*, God is not any sort of existent thing. I argued that we should give up the old metaphysical idea of God because it has become so problematic. Nor do people at large any longer invoke God to explain why events in the world have gone the way they have. The proofs of God's objective existence have failed, and the very idea of an objectively existing omniscient and omnipotent Spirit now looks both terrifying and religiously alienating. It is much better to see the God of our own tradition as a guiding spiritual Ideal, a goal to seek, and a symbol of universal love and religious blessedness. The biblical picture of God as always moving ahead of Israel in the wilderness was an old way of indicating that God is not a being, but an ideal that we never quite catch up with.

When we think of God in this new – and also old – 'non-realist' way, we demythologize dogma into spirituality. Like Kierkegaard and the existentialist theologians, we abandon metaphysics and declare that the meaning of a dogma is given by the difference that it makes in

---

1 This is a slightly revised version of a lecture given at the Snowstar Spring Conference, Niagara Falls, March 2002.
2 London, 1980, and subsequent editions/reprints.

your life when you live it out. Thus, to believe in the doctrine of Creation is not to think that the Big Bang occurred when a great cosmic Being snapped his fingers, but simply to treat your own life as a pure gift that is continuously renewed. To believe in the Providence of God is not to think that a hidden divine hand manipulates all world-events, but to trust that if we love life and look in hope to the future, we will come through somehow. So we explain our religious beliefs by showing how in our tradition they work out in our lives.

This non-realist way of looking at religious belief and the religious life was rather similar to what Rudolf Bultmann and his followers had earlier called 'non-objectifying theology'. Others have called it 'Protestantism squared' – faith thoroughly internalized within each person in a way that makes it possible for one to go on constructing a religious way of life in today's radically secular world. The function of doctrine is not to be a mental cage, but to be a lamp unto our feet. God is not a metaphysical fact, but a guiding ideal.

So at least I was arguing back in 1980. A few early readers saw that the book was a continuation of themes opened up in the radical theology of the 1960s, when John A. T. Robinson in his *Honest to God* (1963) had tried to popularize the ideas of Bultmann, Tillich and Dietrich Bonhoeffer. But that consideration did not do me any good, for my book was instantly seen as 'atheism' and denounced as such by the *Church Times* and the then Archbishop of Canterbury. The leading theological journals did not send it out for review, and it was clear to all that I had permanently fallen from grace.[3] My ecclesiastical career and my academic career were over. As the example of John Robinson showed, I would never get any preferment in either sphere. Robinson himself had in his later books made some attempt to back-pedal and work his way back into favour. He did not succeed, but when he died in 1984 he bequeathed his archive to Lambeth Palace Library, as if he were still very keen to secure for himself a permanent place in the tradition that had disowned him – and the bequest was accepted. Other people, however, urged me not to copy Robinson in this. They were disappointed that he had yielded to 'the abominable system of terrorism'[4] by which the Church in every generation breaks its own most adventurous and liberal spirits. Robinson – so these

---

[3] The leading British theological journal (which I need not name) has not reviewed a book by or about me since the mid-1970s!

[4] Benjamin Jowett's phrase, coined in a letter of 15 August 1858, referring to the aims of the group who were preparing *Essays and Reviews*. See my *The Sea of Faith*, BBC, 1984, etc., ch. 4.

A Non-Realist View of God

people said – should have pressed on and developed his ideas further. By itself, *Honest to God* was not clear and substantial enough to make a permanent mark. The ideas needed further work.

I agreed with these critics. I couldn't turn back: I must press on. And so I did, in a series of 23 further books completed with the publication of *Emptiness and Brightness* (2002). It has been a long and complicated personal journey, and I was reminded of how far I have come when *Taking Leave of God* was republished in 2001 as a 'classic', with an introduction by somebody else, as if it now can be assumed that I am safely dead and fixed in the past tense, and my ideas can be presented as museum pieces – interesting, in their day, maybe, but no longer threatening.

Perhaps that is right, for when I look back at *Taking Leave of God* after over twenty years, I see that the person who wrote it is long gone. The book shows the influence, above all, of Kant and Kierkegaard and also (to a lesser extent) of the Young Hegelians of the 1830s and 1840s – people like D. F. Strauss and Feuerbach. It is masculinist, and very committed to belief in the free, autonomous individual – two features of its style that I was to correct within five years, by reconstructing my way of writing, and by abandoning the old, 'strong' idea of the individual, immortal, free and rational human soul.

The 'Non-Realist' Approach

Both *Taking Leave of God* and its author, then, now seem rather dated. In some other respects, however, I still stick to its central argument, and I stick with the awkward, controversial term 'non-realism'. It was right to try to break with the old metaphysical belief in an objective transcendent personal God out there, while yet retaining the idea of God as being like 'the pearl of great price' – a symbol of the magnetically attractive goal of religious aspiration. The non-realist God does not intervene in the world, but he can still 'pull' souls. It was right to try to demythologize dogma into spirituality, and so to take religious thought through into a new post-dogmatic era. We urgently need to repudiate doctrine as a body of objective, *cosmic*, compulsory, unchanging Truth that is to be imposed upon the faithful as a kind of loyalty-test. There are no such Truths, and we don't even *want* any.

At least half of what is in *Taking Leave of God*, then, I still believe, although we are now over twenty years down the line. But I have to admit that even today it remains oddly difficult to explain clearly the nature of the change in religious thinking that I am asking for.

In *Taking Leave of God* I tried to suggest that a traditional realistic theist suffers from what I called a defect of consciousness. One shouldn't 'surrender the apex of one's consciousness' (1980: 9) to a realistically conceived God, I said – a line that has given offence, but which I still insist makes an entirely valid point. For, just as a person who thinks he is possessed by a demon must surely lack clear critical awareness of his own psychological state, so too the realistic theist, the true believer who thinks s/he's got a hotline to God the Father inside her/his own head, is a person who (necessarily) lacks understanding of her/his own faith. Since the rise of modern psychology we can't help knowing that the spirit in your head is always an alienated bit of yourself. If you insist upon theological realism, if for you faith has got to be a way of communing with a great Spirit via a direct hotline inside your head, then for you the religious believer must be a person who lacks a crucial bit of critical self-awareness. Such a believer cannot clearly understand his or her own faith, and conversely, the sympathetic observer who understands what realistic religious faith is and how it works cannot possibly share it.

A philosopher of religion like me cannot be easy about such a disjunction between faith and understanding. I feel bound to seek to reconcile faith and understanding, by finding a way of believing that fully understands and accepts its own status. So I accept that all religious ideas and doctrines are cultural postulates. There are no free-floating gods: on the contrary, every god is *somebody's* god, and as such is sort-of 'real' for that person, and influential in shaping that person's life. A reflective person who stands within a religious tradition can say: 'I fully accept that all my own religious ideas are human, and products of human cultural history. But although I am no longer a realistic believer, it remains true for me that my religious tradition gives me something vital, namely a language to live by. I can show how it works out in life, and you can see for yourself what kind of person and what kind of society it tends to produce. I'm not claiming the old kind of objective, metaphysical truth for any of it. That kind of truth is not to be had. But one can perfectly well see and judge for oneself that one form of religious life is better than another, and that one kind of society is to be preferred to another. Thus a non-realist who has given up the old idea that religious dogmas can be "cosmically" or "literally" true can still make judgements about religious truth, by looking at the way religious ideas work out in life – and that includes one's *own* life.'

The Autonomy of Religion

In this way I tried to show how a self-critical thinking person can still be a religious person, and can still make judgements about religious truth. One advantage of the position I tried to describe is that it allows for religious pluralism. If you take a realist view of the purported meaning and truth of religious doctrines, you are bound to conclude that only *one* major religion, at most, can be true. Thus, if the Holy Qur'an truly contains an objective God's final and definitive revelation to humankind, then Islam is the one true faith. You can allow that Judaism and Christianity were each true *in their day*, and you may therefore treat them with respect as being 'divine religions', as Muslims have traditionally done, but strictly speaking they are now superseded. Conversely, if in Jesus Christ God has become incarnate uniquely and for evermore, then the Christian revelation is final and unsupersedable. In which case the Christian faith is the one true faith. Thus on realist assumptions religious pluralism is impossible: either Islam is the one true faith, or Christianity is, or neither is. On non-realist assumptions, however, we can proceed rather differently. We look at both faiths as whole religious systems. We look at their history, their doctrines, and the forms of religious life and of society that they tend to produce. And then we decide what we think, where we belong and where our loyalty should lie.

A second consequence of the position described in *Taking Leave of God* was that I was implicitly rejecting all traditional ideas of religious authority. Historically, the Church had always insisted that the matter of faith is a set of supernatural dogmas which we must understand in a realist sense, and to which we must give our unconditional assent. As such, revealed truth is 'above reason'. But the Church – or, as Protestants would say, the Bible, and the Bible alone – certifies it to us. Saving faith is, therefore, faith in revealed truth as it is certified to us by the authority of the Bible (and the Church, which is the divinely authorized interpreter of the Bible, as Catholic Christians will add). Acceptance upon authority of truths that are 'above reason' was thus essential to traditional accounts of how one could become a Christian. There was, for Catholics at least, a necessary connection between saving faith and subjection to the authority of the Church. But I am replacing this account of faith as belief upon authority with a new picture of the religious believer as an autonomous person who builds his or her own religious life by freely adopting and using in life symbols and practices chosen from the available tradition. I called this 'the autonomy of religion', on the analogy of Kant's notion of the 'autonomy of ethics'. Kant had argued that in morality mere obedience to authority is not morally commendable: my action is only truly moral when I myself have freely chosen the moral principles on which I act. Now I was applying the same doctrine to religion: acceptance of and loyal submission to religious authority is not, considered simply as such, religiously commendable at all. On the contrary, if I am to live an authentic religious life, I myself must critically examine and freely adopt the 'language' of symbols, doctrines and practices in the terms of which I shape my life.

Thus I was trying to describe religion without prostration – the religion of a free and upright person. Some Quakers saw at once where this must lead me, but it took me many years to see the point clearly. Church-Christianity is Christianity in uniform, seeing the believer as a soldier who must obey orders. But I was evidently looking for the democratic, civilian kind of religion that the original Jesus taught, and that is scheduled to succeed Church-Christianity. This fully adult kind of faith was traditionally expected to arrive in the 'Age of the Spirit' or 'the Kingdom of God', which was to follow the ecclesiastical period, and I was by implication arguing that in our secular liberal democratic societies people are now at last ready for the immediate, ethical and internalized 'Kingdom' kind of religion. Indeed, many people are already practising it, which is why nowadays the word 'spirituality' has become so popular. People aren't interested in religious authority, in dogma, or in 'organized religion'. They are happy to work out for themselves the spirituality or religious lifestyle that suits them – and they are quite right to do so. Nothing any longer comes to us readymade in its final and definitive form, not even religion.

A New 'Body' of Knowledge

I think I have said enough already to show that when, twenty years ago, I abandoned objective theism and sought instead to portray God as a guiding religious ideal, I was opening a Pandora's box. But there is more to be said yet, for I haven't yet described the biggest change of all. We are changing over from an ancient metaphysical and God-centred vision of the world and of life to a new humanistic and language-centred vision of life and of the world. It is an extraordinary change, best described as a change in the nature of knowledge that has been slowly taking place over the five centuries since the end of the Middle Ages, and is only now becoming at last complete.

A Non-Realist View of God

Very roughly, and by way of a first sketch, we are changing over from the traditional conception of knowledge as a fixed, canonical body of truth, communicated to us by tradition, and ultimately, by divine revelation, to a new conception of knowledge as something entirely created by human beings who engage in systematic enquiry, or (as it is called) 'research'. Although it is very powerful, this new human kind of knowledge is at every point disputable, and subject to change. There are no longer any 'absolutes' or fixed points.

In the old world-picture – the picture to which the Church is still utterly committed – all Truth already exists out there in the eternal Divine Mind. The world is seen as a ready-made, ordered and intelligible Cosmos, specially created by God to be our home. The human mind is a finite image of the Divine Mind. Against this background it is clear that human beings do not themselves invent truth. They have to fit themselves into a ready-made divine order of things. Truth already exists in the Mind of God, and God communicates it to us – or at least, he communicates to us all the truth that we need. His Spirit, as the old prayers and hymns still say, illuminates our minds and leads us into all truth. In addition, God also communicates to us the most important of all truths, 'saving truths', by Special Revelation. Against this general background it is clear that truth is essentially divine and unchanging. The job of universities is not to create new truth, but simply to transmit a canonical body of unchanging truth to the next generation. The ideal scholar was not a creative person, but a man of 'learning', somebody who was steeped in the canonical texts and in the languages you had to learn in order to read them. Thus, in religion at least, traditional 'realism' meant not just God out there, but also a ready-made world out there, truth out there, and knowledge as a gift to us from God.

The picture I have so far presented needs of course to be qualified by pointing out that in Greece, at the beginning of the Western cultural tradition, there had lived a number of very great philosophers. Arguably, they had already invented the idea of criticizing existing knowledge, and developing a better account of things by free enquiry and debate. Some of them, perhaps Archimedes, perhaps Aristotle, came near to inventing and implementing the idea of an organized programme of scientific research. While these Greeks were studied there was always the possibility that someone might succeed in breaking out of the closed world of the Middle Ages, but a mass breakout was not achieved until the end of the sixteenth century, when the word 'research' (from the French *recherche*) first came into use, when

Francis Bacon put forward his visionary programme for *The Advancement of Learning* (1607), and when Galileo Galilei made sudden and revolutionary advances in mathematical physics and astronomy. In the next generation René Descartes founded modern philosophy.

The old sacred cosmology was suddenly dead, and scepticism threatened. Philosophy was to be refounded within the individual human subject, who was a free, critical thinker setting out to build all knowledge just out of personal experience and reason. Thus the old divinely given knowledge would be replaced by man-made knowledge. Descartes himself seems confident that the new man-made kind of knowledge can be and will be as clear and as certain as the old divine truth.

All this is very familiar: what is most remarkable about the subsequent story is how very slowly and with what great difficulty we human beings have made the changeover from the old conceptions of knowledge and truth to the new. You might say that over the four centuries after Descartes we repeatedly found that the change is much bigger and more traumatic than we had previously thought.

Under the old regime, there was no research and astonishingly little knowledge, and the common world-picture may in retrospect seem to have been very strange. But because it was backed by all the massive weight of religious authority, it gave people a very strong sense of truth and of reality. They truly had – or so it seemed to them – a real God out there, a real world out there, objective truth out there, and an objective moral law that was built into the fabric of the world. The paradox is that by our standards they knew almost nothing, and yet they had an intense conviction of objective truth and objective value, a confidence, and a sense of being at home in the world, that we entirely lack! We laugh at their ignorance and superstition, but we envy them terribly, for we know almost everything and yet in another sense we have lost everything. We are so much richer, and so much poorer, than they.

At first, during the years of the Enlightenment, people felt able to keep scepticism at bay by calling upon God to underwrite our human knowledge.[5] Our own merely human perspective upon the world was backed up by God's absolute and perspectiveless vision of everything as it truly is. God's function therefore was to guarantee the objectivity of the world and of truth. But then Hume and Kant set out to analyse

---

5 The story is well told by Edward Craig in *The Mind of God and the Works of Man*, 1987.

A Non-Realist View of God

our human knowledge and to demonstrate its objectivity purely from within, and without appealing to any external authority. Can our human knowledge really stand on its own two feet? Can we get across from our own subjectivity to an objective world out there? Hume did not wholly succeed, and ended in a moderate form of scepticism; Kant, more remarkably, found that he could prove that we have objective knowledge of a world only by an argument that also shows that the world becomes an ordered objective world only *in* our knowing of it. There is no real world *prior* to our knowledge: the world only becomes the world *in* our knowledge. In the old world-picture people had thought of the world as having already been turned from Chaos into Cosmos by God, some 6,000 years ago. God ordered the world, got it all ready for us, and then inserted us into it – a home ready-made for us. But in the new world-picture the chaos of experience is getting turned into an ordered world *by us*, now and all the time. Only we *have* a world, and we do not know for sure of anyone else who has an angle upon our world. We are the only makers of our world – and *our* world is the only world we know or can know. Only we *have* a world; we are the only world-builders. The world is built by language: only we have language, and only we, therefore, make the world what it is.

To see how this realization has dawned on people, consider how the use of the word 'perception' has changed during the past thirty years or so. We used to think of the eye as like a camera, and of perception as the passive recording of objectively given sense-data. But in today's English, 'perception' is used to mean 'interpretation', because we now see that everyone's world-view is always already an interpretation. Nietzsche made the point brutally over a century ago by saying that 'there are no facts, only interpretations'.[6] Today his insight has become a commonplace. Today we see that when we use our language to name, describe and order things we are always also putting our own spin on them. Our way of seeing our world is always steeped in our own theories and our values – in short, our own interpretations – and there are no purely objective facts. In a matrimonial dispute, there's her story and there's his story, but there is no accessible objective truth about the relationship, and in a political dispute there's the Israeli account of the situation and there is the Palestinian story, but we will never persuade them to agree by appealing to a supposedly objective account of the situation. They both already know all the facts, and

---

6 See, for example, his *The Will to Power*, 1968, sect. 481, p. 267; see also sect. 604.

they each see all the facts in terms of their own side's dominant story about the conflict. On each side, highly tendentious interpretation goes all the way down and colours everything.[7]

In short, we moderns have created an immense body of knowledge, but, powerful though it undoubtedly is, our knowledge is always shaped by our faculties, our interests, our desires, our plans and (generally) our *language*. Hence the paradox that we have an immensely rich and highly differentiated world; but it is a very unstable world, a world of endlessly conflicting interpretations. We are both far better-off and far worse-off than our predecessors.

The Despair of Fundamentalism

I call this situation 'empty radical humanism'. In a sense the whole world has been appropriated to and by human beings. Everything is bright and comes to a focus in us. In a sense, we make everything, and we know everything, but because everything is only an interpretation, because everything is disputable, changeable and only contingent, we cannot be really sure of *anything*. We don't like this chronic insecurity, and it is not surprising that so many of us are taking refuge in various forms of fundamentalism. I cannot join them, however, because it seems to me, as it probably also seems to you, that the certainty offered by fundamentalism in all its forms is illusory. The reason why fundamentalism is so dangerous and does so much harm is that it is fired by despair. It cannot bring itself to say Yes to life as it is today, our life in its 'emptiness', its transience, its endless uncertainty and disputability – and yet also its extreme beauty. So fundamentalism rejects life.

The desperation of fundamentalism shows that it has some inkling of the enormous change we have been going through, a change now

---

7 Traditional ideas of objectivity still linger, and may give rise to protests at some of what I say. In my own university, Cambridge, the doctrine that the chief business of the university is with 'research', namely the production of new knowledge, and the training of the next generation in the methods of research, has triumphed only in the last century or so. Critical history reached Cambridge only in the 1860s or so, and the research student arrived only in the 1920s or so. The idea that a Ph.D. degree – a qualification in research – is an essential qualification for a university teacher triumphed only very recently. I myself never gained one, and I can recall dons who still saw the university as a place where a fixed, canonical body of knowledge is passed on to the next generation (they were usually classicists or theologians).

nearly complete. We used to have a tradition-directed society, in which the world came ready-made from God and all truth was ultimately grounded in the mind of God. Now it is merely our human language in which the world is all the time being made, disputed and remade. The world is nothing like as 'real' as it used to be. And when we see everything as shaped by human language, naturally we must begin to see religion as human too. There is no truth out there, no ready-made real world out there, no God out there, no persistent and self-identical self in here, and no life after death. There is only the human fray, the passing show, the endless conflict of interpretations, and a world now so completely described and theorized, so fully taken into our language, that it has become achingly, radiantly beautiful. It is all art. In this new context, the non-realist interpretation of religious belief invites each of us to feel free to construct our religious life by choosing and adopting any materials – from the Christian tradition, from Buddhism and from elsewhere – that we may find helpful. We must recognize that all religious ideas are human, with a human history, but the realization that religion and morality are human no more destroys their value and their importance to us than does the parallel realization that art is only human.

There is more that we can say. In our highly aestheticized culture, which is no longer sustained either by the authority of the past or by hope for the future, people find themselves obliged to learn to live for the moment, in the present tense. Some people see us as living in a time of religious dereliction. But I suggest that we may be able to make of it a time of religious fulfilment.

7. The 'Future' of Religion

DOUGLAS HEDLEY

If God's power is to be detected in anything which science can help us to see, it will not be in the way things started, it will be in the way things go.

Austin Farrer

Brian Hebblethwaite has been a key figure within Cambridge and beyond in his work on Truth and Religious Dialogue. And yet he is perhaps best known for his vigorous realist/anti-realist debate with Don Cupitt. I believe that these two concerns are intimately linked. Brian's commitment to dialogue between religions is tied to his conviction in God as a transcendent being. His old friend and colleague Don Cupitt saw the God of theism as discredited by the 'masters of suspicion' Nietzsche, Marx and Freud, and those who inherited the models of these Masters of Suspicion: Lacan, Derrida and Foucault. The Masters of Suspicion were able to subvert the Enlightenment assumptions about religion, subjectivity and language through the recognition of social and unconscious factors within 'rationality' and the Nietzschean tenet that language imposes an arbitrary structure upon 'reality'. According to such a model, 'theism' is a hopelessly naive endeavour which fails to recognize the effects of ideology or the unconscious, gender or politics upon philosophical theology. I wish to argue that the tradition of atheism which Marx, Nietzsche and Freud represent is just as much a metaphysical tradition as that of theism. I wish to question the cosy assumption of the theological avant-garde that their appeals to the Masters of Suspicion evince a superior awareness of the problematic and complex nature of God-talk. Indeed, I wish to propose that the intellectual high ground claimed by those who wish to subvert the philosophy of religion has its foundations in the crude biological obsessions of the nineteenth century, and in particular, the influence of Darwin.

Is Religion a Genuine Category?

Upon arriving in Cambridge I praised the virtues of the great seventeenth-century Cambridge Platonists. I thought it would be most diplomatic to invoke the *genius loci*. I was wrong. Nicholas Lash, the Norris Hulse Professor of Divinity, sniffed in his inimitable manner, and said 'We in Cambridge are rather embarrassed about the Cambridge Platonists.' I was later struck by the widespread conviction within the Faculty of Divinity that religion is not a genuine category – as if it might be an overarching genus with particular religions as species, and in that very year Professor Lash published a book with the programmatic title, *The Beginning and the End of 'Religion'*. The rejection of the category 'religion' which one finds in recent Cambridge writers such as Nicholas Lash or, in a somewhat cruder and more belligerent form, John Milbank (G. D'Costa, 1990:174–91) struck me as rather ironic. After all, the Cambridge Platonists decisively employed the eirenic concept of 'religio' in Nicholas of Cusa and Marsilio Ficino. For Ralph Cudworth (1617–88) heathen gods were 'nothing else but so many several names and notions of that one Numen, divine force and power, which runs through the whole world, multiformly displaying itself therein' (R. Cudworth, 1845: vol. 1, p. 365). Cudworth's own metaphysical work is grounded in an attack upon fatalism, which he saw as serving 'the design of Atheism' and which would 'undermine Christianity, and all religion . . .'. Rather than regarding this as the expression of some lamentable Enlightenment intellectual imperialism, I am inclined to see Cudworth's use of the term *religion* as the expression of a most admirable liberality of spirit which was forged by his experience of some of the fanatical excesses of various parties within the English civil war. It seems a most fruitful paradigm in a pluralist contemporary culture.

Let me isolate what I consider to be misleading about the 'deconstruction' of 'religion'. Two rather weak arguments are often marshalled against 'religion' as a concept. The first is the claim that the term 'religion' is really a product of the Renaissance and Enlightenment, and the second is that 'religion' is hopelessly misleading and vague. The first argument commits the 'no name, no thing' fallacy. It is true that the concept of 'religion' is a relatively modern development; what we refer to as 'religions' are 'secta' for the medieval period. But it is equally true that the medieval period possessed no term for architecture, and the Enlightenment had no term for linguistics or sociology. Yet clearly it is perfectly reasonable to speak of medieval architects or the Enlightened pioneers of contemporary linguistics or sociology. Such genetic arguments about the historical evolution of a term are valid for social but not for natural concepts. There was genuinely no such thing as a 'scrum half' prior to the invention of rugby, and perhaps the proponents of the deconstruction of 'religion' may claim that religion is a social construct, but I want to see it *more Platonico* as a natural concept – the expression of a natural and inherent longing of the soul. Apart from which, 'theologia' is a fairly rare term until the modern period. St Thomas speaks of *sacra doctrina*, but I know that Nicholas Lash does not think that theology is exclusively a modern creation.

Perhaps 'religion' is a woolly or slippery term, in the sense that one cannot provide an *exhaustive* definition, but much of our knowledge is of this rather intuitive kind. It is nevertheless knowledge. The opponents of the term 'religion' are making far too stringent demands. We can talk quite happily about murder being wrong and know that it is wrong without necessarily being clear about whether euthanasia or abortion are murder. The fact that there is no consensus about the definition of 'tragedy' does not mean that it does not really exist.

Lash and Milbank express the widely held postmodern sensibility which rejects 'secular' metanarratives and yet combine this with the old Barthian dislike of 'religion' as a human construct. Religion is seen as subject to Feuerbach's strictures in contradistinction to the God-sent Word of revelation. I do not think we can dismiss the sceptical challenges to religious belief by deconstructing the concept of 'religion' as some monstrous outgrowth of the Enlightenment. I have tried to isolate a tendency among philosophical theologians to employ postmodern attacks upon the Enlightenment in order to subvert the Enlightened attack upon theism as bogus, a product of the false Enlightenment assumptions of universalism and foundationalism. This seems to me a hostage to fortune. The arguments of the Enlightenment were generally not new, especially not the projection theories. But they were reinforced by the huge scientific and social advances of the eighteenth to the twentieth centuries. In the West, the Church lost its grip on education, and scientific work like that of Darwin seemed to upset widely held assumptions about Providence. It was broader cultural factors which made the old sceptical arguments particularly potent.

I prefer the older Cambridge tradition which asserts that religion is grounded in a natural longing of human beings, 'a *Natural Sense* of God' (John Smith), a sense of the sacred domain as a matter of ulti-

The 'Future' of Religion

mate concern with attendant practices of worship and lived adherence to this reality, which is perhaps, though not necessarily, transcendent and personal. Let me qualify my brief further. The question with which I am concerned is one about natural theology and that philosophical theory called theism. Christianity, Judaism and Islam all shared this common inheritance. The *locus classicus* is book 10 of Plato's *Laws*. Projection theories of religion are, of course, ancient. Xenophanes observed that 'the gods of the Ethiopians are black with snub noses, while those of the Thracians are fair, with blue eyes and red hair, and if they were capable of it, animals would depict gods in their image'. I believe that the force of the critiques of Feuerbach, Marx, Nietzsche and Freud are, to a surprising degree, parasitic upon Darwin. Indeed, philosophical interests and obsessions, in particular their rejection of Hegelian rationalism, led all of these writers to seriously underestimate the tradition of natural theology. All of them are convinced that religion is a phase from which mankind will emerge, and as such assume a rather Hegelian evolutionary scheme of relentless development. But perhaps this belief in the future redundancy of religion was itself a dogmatic and unsustainable tenet of faith. The more potent challenge to serious belief in God is to be found in Charles Darwin. And the legacy of Darwin, I believe, shows the persisting relevance of 'First Philosophy' and 'Natural Theology'. I happily concede to Professor Lash 'that religion in abstraction is a non-sense'. 'Divinity is a life rather than a science' is one of the slogans of the Cambridge Platonists. If I may be excused a Kantian pun, natural theology without tradition, experience and revelation is empty, and the faith community without natural theology is blind.

Marx and Promethean Emancipation from Religious Bondage

Lying behind postmodern narratives of 'modernity' and Enlightenment is invariably Hegel. The importance of Hegel for our topic becomes clear when we reflect upon the fact that both Feuerbach and Marx were products of a Hegelian tradition. It is a somewhat denuded Hegelianism because, although it retains the Promethean pathos of German Idealism, in place of the teleology of the Absolute Spirit unfolding itself in history, human history is merely an extension of a materialistically conceived *natural* history. In his doctoral thesis Marx exclaimed: 'Prometheus is the most eminent saint and martyr in the philosophical calendar.' Darwin 'respectfully declined the honour of having the English edition of *Das Kapital* dedicated to him'.[1] Marx seems a classic paradigm of a confidence in 'evolution' between Hegel and Darwin.

The model informing Marx's critique of religion is one of organic development. Religious belief belongs to the period of immaturity, and however strongly some may yearn for the age of childlike dependence and innocence, it is intellectually and morally obsolete. Religious disbelief, by way of contrast, is the expression of the unique maturity of modern humankind. Such theories leave the question of the correctness of theism untouched: they are the fount of the methodological atheism which characterizes the sociological approach to religion from Comte to Durkheim, and the anthropology of the Cambridge School of Robertson Smith, Fraser and Jane Harrison and Lévi-Strauss. The falsity of theism is largely assumed, and theories are developed to explain the genesis of these (false) beliefs.

Thus religion is seen as providing security, but a security which the modern mature mind can recognize as ultimately illusory. For Feuerbach, religion is an imaginary realm which is both a human creation and yet subdues and oppresses humankind. Marx, in his *A Contribution to the Critique of Hegel's Philosophy of Law* of 1844, argues that miserable living conditions create the consolation of religion. It is 'the sigh of the oppressed creature, the heart of a heartless world, just as it is the spirit of spiritless conditions. It is the *opium* of the people.' This, famously, has two related meanings. Religion is a tool by which a ruling class can subjugate and control the masses. It is also an opiate in the sense that it weakens the revolutionary resolve of the oppressed by offering them otherworldly consolations. Such consolations will become otiose when the unjust economic structures have been removed. There are obvious counter examples to Marx's claim. Thomas Clarkson and William Wilberforce came through their religion to the conviction that slavery was evil, despite the fact that many of their 'class' were thought to depend upon the profits of the slave trade. However, what I wish to challenge is the historicism.

'Evolution' is a slippery word. The notion of evolution has its roots in the Judaeo-Christian messianic-apocalyptic tradition. The concept was used in the German tradition to give expression to the idea of the gradual providential progress of the universe, and was often aligned to

---

[1] See Editor's Introduction in C. Darwin, *The Origin of Species by means of Natural Selection or The Preservation of Favoured Races in the Struggle for Life*, ed. J. W. Burrow, 1985:45.

The 'Future' of Religion

a strongly immanentist or pantheistic notion of deity. Lying behind this viewpoint is a secularized utopianism. Christianity developed within a messianic-apocalyptic context, and there are tensions within the Christian legacy between the historical institution of the Church and the idea of the imminent Kingdom of God. The overriding eschatological perspective of the primitive Church was gradually modified and reinterpreted by institutional Christianity whereby the visible Church came to replace the future Kingdom of God. One might speak of a tension between the idea of the established Church (especially identified with Rome or in Protestantism with the Monarch) and hope of a coming Kingdom evolving within the historical process.

Some, especially mystics, have not been content with waiting for this Kingdom to come, but have seen themselves as part of the process of its establishment. Throughout Christian history the eschatological component has, on occasion, exploded – Montanism, Joachimitism, the spiritual Franciscans, the radical Reformers such as Thomas Munzer or the English Millenarians of the Civil War. Hegel, with his roots in Swabian pietism and mysticism, bears the influence of the 'evolutionary' optimism of German spiritualism in Boehme and Oetinger, and Marx inherited this eschatological dimension from Hegel, however strongly modified by his materialism. Hence it is no accident that German Marxists have been traditionally interested in Munzer and English Marxists in the Levellers, and so on.

I do not wish to accuse Marx of being crypto-Christian. I merely wish to make the familiar point that the idea of a progressive evolution in human society in which the class which is the source of productive economic capacity in society emancipates itself from a parasitic class, and whereby the rejection of religion is part of this process of emancipation, presupposes a model of inexorable historical evolution and progression. I wish to counter this organic model of human progressive development with Ralph Cudworth's view. He would have adamantly rejected the view that the issue of religious doubt is a uniquely modern phenomenon. In his *True Intellectual System of the Universe* of 1678, he presents the 'philosophy of religion' as a perennial battle between the Gods and the Giants of Plato's *Sophist*, between theists and atheists. The value of Cudworth at this point is that he makes us aware of the illusion of considering religious beliefs as unquestioned tenets which were firmly held in humankind's childhood and which have to be painfully relinquished by the adult intellect. Cudworth is concerned to show that the criticisms of Hobbes or Spinoza are in a tradition of atheistical thought going back to Anaximander, Strato and Epicurus. Since Cudworth, the critique of theism has become far more widespread and powerful, no doubt, but his point remains pertinent: doubt and scepticism are not uniquely 'modern'. The existence of a tradition of natural theology – which included arguments against theism – means that whatever the nature of popular piety, the highly educated can barely be seen as blissfully untroubled by sceptical queries or doubts about their own faith. Even in the 'dark ages' of medieval Christendom, Thomas Aquinas was aware of the heretical arguments of the *artes* faculty in Paris. It would not have been lost on Cudworth that Marx wrote his doctorate on Democritus and Epicurus.

Nietzsche, Slavish Religion and the Superman

As with Marx, much of Nietzsche's critique of religion is dependent upon Feuerbach. The death of God is intimately linked with the demise of a certain kind of weak slavish character who has produced this God. The masterful Superman who has recognized the fraud of religion places himself in the stead of the Godhead.

In Nietzsche we find the Christian idea of the Superman: the Romantic idea of genius *Sturm und Drang*, Jean Paul and Emerson, including the idealization of Napoleon. But there is also the factor of Darwin: the Superman is not a particular individual genius of the Romantic kind but the development of a novel and superior kind of man. This development is a law of selection. The survival of the fittest is the process by which selection operates. At the end of the *Descent of Man*, Darwin exclaims:

> Man may be excused for feeling some pride at having risen, though not through his own exertions, to the very summit of the organic scale; and the fact of having thus risen, instead of having been aboriginally placed there, may give him hope for a still higher destiny in the distant future. (Darwin, 1998:643)

Nietzsche was almost as rude about Darwin as he was about Christianity and Romanticism: his was the mind of 'respectable, but mediocre Englishmen'. But Darwinism gave Nietzsche an air of scientific credibility and gave his myth of the Superman a particular potency in the late nineteenth and early twentieth centuries (e.g. the novels of Mann, Musil or Doblin). Nietzsche has lately become popular for quite other reasons in postmodernism – on account of his thoughts on language, or via Heidegger's influence, and so forth – but his importance in the first half of the last century was due to the Darwinian toughness of his thought. In his excellent book *Nietzsche, Biology and Metaphor*, Gregory Moore has analysed the evolutionary context of many key Nietzschean ideas such as the 'genealogy' of morals. The standard view of Nietzsche among postmodern thinkers as a genial proto-postmodernist is subjected to a stringent critique. In particular Moore argues persuasively that the epistemological relativism of Nietzsche is the expression of his privileging of biology and a neo-Darwinist obsession with health and sickness.

Hegel's dialectical inversion of the Master–Slave relation in the *Phenomenology of Spirit* is much richer. Here Hegel describes the freedom of the Master who has subjugated the Slave and who uses him as an instrument to enhance his personal being. Yet with this Slave as a tool for his pleasure, the Master can only enjoy the most ephemeral satisfaction. He remains, paradoxically, in bondage to natural laws. It is the Slave who, however modestly, attains through work a higher consciousness than the Master, who merely consumes. And the Master's is an inadequate self-consciousness – not for external reasons of the kind which Marxists espouse, such as the Master's economic dependency upon the Slave, but because the satisfaction of the Master demands recognition, and the recognition he demands from the Slave is inadequate since it is based upon fear and not upon respect for the inherent values of the Master. As such, the response of the Slave cannot sustain the Master's legitimate desire for esteem. Much the same point is expressed when Hegel writes of the 'consummate religion', that

> In friendship and love I give up my abstract personality and thereby win it back as concrete; the truth of personality is found precisely in winning it back through this immersion, this being immersed in the other.[2]

The Slave rebuilds his own identity through work; he finds persisting reflection of his own being in his own handiwork. It is the Slave not the Master who constitutes the paradigm for Hegel. I do not think it is an accident that the Master–Slave dialectic has resonances of the Gospel and Pauline paradoxes of 'gain through loss'.

---

2 G. W. F. Hegel, *Lectures on the Philosophy of Religion*, vol. 3: *The Consummate Religion*, 1998: 286.

Hegel's argument is that the finite agent's identity is suffused and penetrated by the existence of other agents, that personality is not identical with isolated individuality, and this solidarity with others is inextricably related to a deeper reciprocity with the Divine Spirit. That is to say, human beings are not self-sufficient units, but continuously dependent upon others, and ultimately upon God. Nietzsche, by way of contrast, is rehearsing the Epicurean (and Stoic) conviction in human self-sufficiency, greatly heightened by secularized ideas of evolution and the impact of Darwin.

The Master–Slave argument is particularly pertinent against Nietzsche. Self-consciousness seeks recognition in other centres of consciousness – not mere private gratification, but some public ratification is required. The proper identity of self presupposes reciprocal relations of 'my station and its duties'. Not only does the Master fail to gain any freely bestowed recognition from the Slave, but he does not express his freedom in work, as does the Slave. This implies a stark contrast between Nietzsche's vitalistic self-transcendence of superior individuals, and the sophisticated domain which Hegel sees as the realm of Spirit, a public and concrete realm of freedom in which the capacity for rationality can be realized and mediated through mutual recognition and creative work. The interests of the self-conscious moral agent are so closely intertwined with the interests of other agents that Nietzsche's heroic atheism, together with his revolt against the bourgeois morality, seems little more than rhetorical and rather futile self-assertion.

Freud and God the Father

Freud saw Darwin's work as resulting in one of the great humiliations of humankind, yet he envisaged his own work as pursuing the path of Copernicus and Darwin. Like Nietzsche, Freud drew upon late nineteenth-century Darwinistic views of science and reality. The biological idea that human nature consists of various layers in which some are relics of a much earlier phase influenced Freud's psychological picture of the mind as composed of a variety of levels. Another obvious analogy is the centrality of struggle. Freud's model of the pysche is an internalization of the outward struggle which Darwin perceived in nature. The ego is beset by both the irrational and powerful drives of the id and the stringent demands of the super-ego.

Freud is working ostensibly in another tradition of which Nietzsche was rather contemptuous. This is the tradition of the scientific explanation of religion, which we can see in Comte and Durkheim. Freud wishes to explain the evolution of religion in scientific terms. Some of Freud's theories are very peculiar and based upon dubious anthropology. In *Totem and Taboo*, he sees religion as based upon anxiety about incest, while *Moses and Monotheism* contains fascinating but highly questionable historical theses. Perhaps the best place to concentrate on Freud is *The Future of an Illusion*, where the idea of an illusion is distinguished from error.

> When I say that these things are all illusions, I must define the meaning of the word. An illusion is not the same thing as an error; nor is it necessarily an error. Aristotle's belief that vermin are developed out of dung . . . was an error . . . On the other hand, it was an illusion of Columbus's that he had discovered a new sea-route to the Indies. The part played by his wish in this error is very clear . . . What is characteristic of illusions is that they are derived from human wishes. (Freud, 1978:26–7)

It is clear that Freud does not rule out the possibility of the truth of illusions. He uses the example of the illusion of a middle-class girl that she will marry a prince, or the illusion of the alchemist that all metals can be turned into gold. 'Thus we call a belief an illusion when a wish-fulfillment is a prominent factor in its motivation, and in doing so we disregard its relations to reality, just as the illusion sets no store by verification' (ibid.).

Freud has no sense of the intellectually rich and penetrating tradition of natural theology.

> Where questions of religion are concerned, people are guilty of every possible sort of dishonesty and intellectual misdemeanour. Philosophers stretch the meanings of words until they retain scarcely anything of their original sense. They give the name of 'God' to some vague abstraction which they have created for themselves . . . and they can even boast that they have recognized a higher, purer concept of God, notwithstanding that their God is now nothing more than an insubstantial shadow and no longer the mighty personality of religious doctrines. (Freud, 1978:28)

Religion, whatever its dress, is 'wish-fulfilment'. But the great philosophical tradition of a 'First Philosophy' steers a path between avoiding anthropomorphism and apophaticism. Freud dismissively suggests how remarkable it would be if our 'wretched, ignorant and downtrodden ancestors had succeeded in solving all these difficult riddles of the universe' (Freud, 1978:29). The natural theology of the Greeks gives a fine expression of the attempt to climb out of the cave of human images of the divine in order to reach a rigorous vision of God. Plato's 'demiurge' is consciously part of a likely tale; the unmoved mover of Aristotle, 'thought thinking itself', or the One of Plotinus as *'causa sui'* are hardly anthropomorphic, and they played such a powerful and definitive role in the philosophical theologies of the Abrahamic religions because they did not employ naive and crude images of the divine. Hegel's distinction between Imagination (*Vorstellung*) and Concept (*Begriff*) was employed by the *Linkshegelianer* to strip the assets of traditional metaphysical theology, but the distinction itself is rooted in the ancient sense of the tension between *mythos* and *logos* in theology. John Smith writes:

> If the Superstitious man thinks that God is altogether like himself ... the *Atheist* will soon say in his heart *There is no God;* and will judge not without some appearance of reason to be better there were none ...[3]

A critic of religion like Freud presents religion as providing primarily consolation, bolstering the weak ego. I do not doubt that consolation is a component of religion, but it is only a part. Judgement is equally important, and this was clearly why Plato believed that the state could not tolerate atheism because he thought it would lead to moral anarchy. Human frailty dictates that the idea of being watched, as it were, by an all-seeing just God is not a clearly consoling idea; it can be absolutely terrifying and was often perceived as such. Bishop Butler, when walking with his chaplain Dr Foster, was reported to have said: 'I was thinking, doctor, what an awful thing it is for a human being to stand before the great moral governor of the world to give an account of all his actions in this life' (Inge, 1904:179). The Freudian, Nietzschean and Marxian prophecies of the death of God may equally contain a considerable element of wish-fulfilment, the desire to avoid confronting absolute standards, and the remorse connected with indelible shortcoming.

---

[3] *Select Discourses*, 1660: 43.

Darwin's Struggle and the Blind Watchmaker

The metaphysical 'death of God' which Marx, Nietzsche and Freud presuppose is given real substance by Darwinism in the view of the universe as a *blind* watchmaker: the denial of Providence and judgement. 'Darwinism' is the real challenge for modern religious belief. Charles Darwin was himself averse to theological polemic, and his religious opinions were ambivalent and guarded. By 'Darwinism' I mean that theory of natural history which opposes the 'struggle for existence' to divine Providence. Darwin was not a critic of religion; it was T. H. Huxley who was an evangelist for science *against* religion.

Christian teleology seems *prima facie* refuted by Darwin. Human history is just a history of nature, one which needs no recourse to a grand narrative of creation, sin and redemption, but merely the mechanism of natural selection. Yet, as we have seen, the metaphysics of 'evolution' has a strong Christian provenance. There is a strong tradition which argues that Western science has its roots in the theistic and, particularly, the Christian concept of God. Perhaps Christian theism had a propensity for a metaphysics of development rather than the fixity of the Platonic–Aristotelian legacy. Perhaps Christian theism helped encourage the idea that the universe was not an eternal mechanism, but a process of astronomical and biological evolution. Of course, the debt of the Christian concept of creation to Hellenistic ideas is very deep, and the roots of this argument are Pythagorean notions of cosmic harmony, the Platonic idea of the demiurge and creative forms in the mind of God, and those biblical images of God as potter, builder or artist. Yet one very strong difference is the Christian rejection of the eternity of the world. If the world is a limited segment – if it has a history and is contingently dependent upon its sovereign transcendent creative source – one has good reason to develop a metaphysics of development rather than a static ontology. Providence encourages one to think of the creator as being at work in his creation, rather than inferring a remote causal source from static facts. So long as a theologian can accept the idea of the emergence of new forms or species as proper creations within a modified concept of a *creatio continua*, theism has little to fear from this aspect of Darwin's legacy. There were, of course, theistic enthusiasts for evolution long before Teilhard de Chardin.

The first problem which Darwin's theories raised was the discrepancy with the scriptural account of the origin of the species, especially if one held to a version of divine dictation of the texts.

However, the development of biblical criticism since Richard Simon (died 1712) meant that these discrepancies were not entirely surprising. Nineteenth-century scholarship was developing highly subtle methods of interpreting in their context the manifold texts which constitute the Christian canon. Furthermore, this was a necessary prerequisite for any serious reflection about the contemporary meaning of these texts. Let us recall that Genesis presents God acting upon existing materials, and yet this is an idea which is resolutely denied by the idea of *creatio ex nihilo*. We do not have to turn to the most extreme forms of Alexandrine allegory to notice how the philosophical tradition modified the *prima facie* meaning of the scriptural text.

A more serious problem raised by Darwin's thought was in the realm of anthropology vis-à-vis the *unique* position of the human being. This is sometimes conflated with the ludicrous view that the world was made for our convenience, or the more intelligible but still rather optimistic view that human and divine purposes coincide, an idea, however, which is particularly ruthlessly attacked by religious prophets (e.g. Isaiah 55.8–9: 'For my thoughts are not your thoughts, neither are your ways my ways, saith the Lord'). Christianity, though keen to deflate false expectations and hopes, certainly inherited a notion of human separation from the animal kingdom through the doctrine of the *imago Dei* and the Platonic–Aristotelian rationalism which saw the human's capacity for rationality as divine. Perhaps we should distinguish between necessary and sufficient conditions for the emergence of humankind. Perhaps natural selection is a necessary but not a sufficient condition of the 'descent' of human beings. The phenomenon of religion has no obvious analogy in the animal kingdom. The 'naturalist' tries to explain religion in terms of natural instincts such as fear of death or pain, or just general anxiety. The desire for food, shelter and a mate are thus all perfectly intelligible. But religion, like art and science itself, is much harder to explain on the naturalistic model.

Certainly Darwinism has inspired an industry of naturalized epistemology. Yet the problems, questions and ideas which form human cultural life, our second nature, are perhaps different *in kind* from the impulses, motives and behavioural patterns of chimpanzees. Hegel read Proclus and Marx read Hegel. It would be far-fetched to blame the venerable Athenian Neoplatonist, Proclus, for the grotesquely brutal and inhumane 'cultural revolutions' and 'reforms' of Mao or Stalin. The causal story which explains how Marxism

The 'Future' of Religion

became a force in twentieth-century history still looks very different from a strictly scientific explanation.

In ethics too, Darwinism has exerted a powerful, if somewhat subterranean influence. But Darwinism is a theory about nature as a morally neutral domain of blind chance and bitter struggle. It certainly cannot offer any moral guidance. The prevalence of projectivism in ethics is, I think, rooted in Darwin. If everything evolves, so does 'truth', and it depends upon the perspective of the knower.

In short, 'Darwinism' has sown the seeds of a radical disenchantment theory. Whereas Marx, Freud and Nietzsche are parasitic upon some kind of idea of evolution as a progressive tendency, some residual eschatology, and the 'illusion of the future', Darwin grimly reinforced Hume's critique of natural theology. In Hume's *Dialogues on Natural Religion* we read: 'The whole presents nothing but the idea of a blind nature, impregnated by a great vivifying principle, and pouring forth from her lap, without discernment or parental care, her maimed and abortive children' (Hume, 1993:113). 'I believe', Darwin claimed, 'in no law of necessary development' (Darwin, 1887:203). Darwin has less of a theory of evolution than Marx, Nietzsche or Freud.

Prometheus or Sisyphus? Darwin and the Evolution of Natural Theology

I wish to suggest that Darwin is a much more corrosive critic of religion than Feuerbach, Marx, Nietzsche or Freud. All of the latter in their Feuerbachian mode are rhetorical and question-begging in their critiques of religion. A central objection often made against all these writers is that they are guilty of the genetic fallacy. Even if the genesis of religious ideas is accurately conveyed in their narratives, this does not necessarily impugn their validity. In short, they all assume the falsity of religious belief and provide their own, sometimes extremely speculative explanations of religious belief. All, in quite different ways, are fuelled by residual religious elements of their own philosophical inheritance. They all produce some narrative of emancipation from original innocence, and all are subject to the objection that they are basing themselves upon an eschatological illusion of the future. Yet the history of natural theology has been, from its inception, the attempt to temper *mythos* with *logos,* just as the great religious prophets have insisted that human and divine purposes do not easily coincide. In other words, the God made in a human image is an illusion which great religion has sought to combat and not reinforce. What Smith says of Epicureans in a pungent polemic applies to the nineteenth-century projectionists: 'When they would seem to acknowledge a deity, they could not forget their own beloved Image which was always before their eyes . . . So easy is it . . . to slide into a compliance with the *Anthropomorphitae*, and to bring down the Deity to a conformity to their own Image' (Smith, 1660:46).

The power of Marx, Nietzsche and Freud derives to a great extent from what they derive from Darwinism and the metaphysical anti-teleology which they themselves could reinforce. As such they could all present themselves as men of science and facts while indulging in the most speculative fantasies, no little indebted to mystical tradition, namely Marxian Utopianism, Nietzsche drawing upon the image of divinization in his Superman, and Freud drawing upon the sexual mysticism of the Cabbala. This reinforces my initial point that religion constitutes a natural longing in humans, and even religious substitutes bear characteristic 'religious' marks. It was precisely this residual messianic component, a law of necessary development, which was lacking in Darwin's sombre pragmatic and relativistic thought: Nature is a value-free domain and evolution is blind; economy rather than foresight is its motor. The argument from design seems to have been punctured. I am not claiming that evolutionary theory as a scientific account is incompatible with Providence. I am claiming that Darwin, who is popularly thought to have demolished 'natural theology', in fact makes it all the more important for theists to reflect upon and to argue about divine design and action in nature.

Evolutionary theory provides scope for seeing God at work in his creation as opposed to a remote clock-maker. The philosophical tradition ensured the divine making was not envisaged in anthropomorphic terms as the making of a machine which could be left to its own devices. Austin Farrer expresses this point with characteristic pertinence: 'Perhaps it was just this that hurt pious minds so much a century ago, when evolutionary ideas were first taught. It was not that Creation was being taken from them, but that it was being pushed under their noses; so different is fact from fancy' (Farrer, 1966:45).

Theism maintains the essential goodness of the deity, Providence and judgement. I do not think that these tenets are refuted by the scientific data of evolutionary theory, the Mendelian theory of inheritance, or DNA. However, Huxley and, more recently, Dawkins are perfectly justified in exploiting the anti-theistic components in Darwin's thought. Theism cannot retreat into a crude supernaturalistic dualism in which divine activity is perceived at the point where nature stops. As the great and eloquent Cambridge predecessor of Brian Hebblethwaite's own College, the seventeenth-century Fellow of Queens' College, John Smith, observed:

> For though a lawful acquaintance with all the *Events* and *Phaenomena* that shew themselves upon this mundane stage should contribute much to free men's Minds from the slavery of dull *Superstition:* yet would it also breed a sober & amiable Belief of the Deity, as it did in all the Pythagoreans, Platonists and other Sects of Philosophers, if we may believe themselves; and an *ingenuous* knowledge hereof would be as fertile with *Religion,* as the ignorance thereof in *affrighted* and *base* Minds is with Superstition. (Smith, 1660:47)

Indeed, in just this spirit many philosophers of religion appeal to the notion of the 'fine-tuned universe' which makes science possible as evidence of divine Providence, much akin in mode to that later Cambridge Platonist, William Wordsworth:

> How exquisitely the individual Mind
> (And the progressive powers no less
> Of the whole species) to the external World
> Is fitted: and how exquisitely too –
> Theme this but little heard among men –
> The external World is fitted to the Mind. (Wordsworth, 1936:590)

Is such a providential harmony of mind and world undermined by the Darwinian natural selection? Darwin forces us to reconsider those central questions of natural theology which, as Brian Hebblethwaite's *oeuvre* reminds us, remain largely unsolved. Huxley was right to insist that Darwin presents no problem for the 'philosophical Theist' which had not existed 'from the time that philosophers began to think out the logical grounds and logical consequences of Theism' (Darwin, 1887: vol. 2, pp. 179–204). After the efforts of Huxley and his followers the onus is, however, now upon theists to give reasons for their beliefs, to 'save the appearances'. And such modern natural theology is doubtless rather like the work of Sisyphus. Yet if it serves to remind serious critics of religion of the inadequacies of the limits of Promethean atheism of the nineteenth- and twentieth-century kind, it will serve a good purpose.

8. Can Christian Ethics be Universal?
A Focus on War

JOSEPH RUNZO

It is with admiration and pleasure that I write this essay to honour Brian Hebblethwaite: admiration for both his character and his career, and pleasure in both our friendship and our shared sense of the reasons for engaging in philosophy of religion as a Christian. With respect to those shared reasons for engaging in the philosophy of religion, let me mention six important aspects of his body of work. First, Brian Hebblethwaite is an unapologetic 'objective theist', a view he skilfully defends in detail in *The Ocean of Truth*. Second, Hebblethwaite sees ethics as at the heart of the philosophy of religion, and ethics informs all other considerations throughout the broad range of his work. Third, Hebblethwaite insists on the primacy of relationality in matters of value, a view, we shall see, which has important pluralistic implications. I agree with him about all these points concerning the best approach to the philosophy of religion. But there are three further features of his work which I also find attractive: a pluralistic approach to matters of value, an insistence on the importance of considering other world religions when formulating Christian responses to philosophical issues, and, what is an extension of the last two points, a persistent attempt to develop comparative ethics across the world religions.

In this essay I will primarily address this project of comparative ethics, though I will build upon the other aspects I have mentioned of Hebblethwaite's philosophy of religion. Hence, following the spirit of Hebblethwaite's work, I shall first ask if Christian ethics can be universal and, second, I shall attempt to clarify the answer by addressing one of the most comprehensive and surely one of the most recalcitrant of all ethical issues, namely, the problem of war.

Ethical Universality

When we say that an ethical point of view, EPV_1, is 'universal', we might mean at least one of three things. We might mean that:

1 the structure of the universe is such that EPV_1 is 'built into' the universe – that EPV_1 is inherent in the metaphysics of any ethics, whether or not this is recognized by those who subscribe to the various ethical systems of humankind.

Or we might mean that:

2 EPV_1 is, *as a matter of fact*, universally held in the various ethical systems which humans only *as a matter of fact* hold or have recognized, though other ethical systems which do not adhere to EPV_1 could have been held by humans.

Or we might mean that:

3 EPV_1, while not *in fact* universal in sense (2), could *as a matter of fact* become universally recognized.

Sense (1) of 'universality' has prescriptive implications; senses (2) and (3) are descriptive. If one holds (1), that EPV_1 is inherent in the structure of the universe, one might also hold the descriptive thesis (3). But if one holds (1), one will be obliged to hold the prescriptive view that (3) *ought* to be the case. On the other hand, if one holds the descriptive theses (2) or (3), as, say, a historian or a sociologist might, nothing is implied about what *ought* to be the case.

The view of ethical universality encapsulated in (1) is a view typically held by religious ethicists – Christians, Muslims, Jews, Hindus, Buddhists, Jains, Confucians, Baha'is, and so on. Now Christians (assuming objective theism) will hold (1) because they hold that the mind of God and the love of God inform all of creation, and if EPV_1 corresponds, at least in part, to God's divine ethical point of view – let us call it EPV_D – then EPV_1 is, at least partially, literally part of the structure of the universe because EPV_D is essentially part of the structure of the universe. In assessing the question of the universality of Christian ethics, I will focus on comparative ethics among the world religions and only briefly address the further question of whether religious and secular ethics can share a universality.

Uniqueness in Christian Ethics

Part of what it is to take a specific religious point of view and adhere to a religious way of life is to take the moral point of view. Every specific religious point of view has a metaphysics. Since one's metaphysics drives one's ethics, every specific religious point of view inherently provides a metaphysical foundation (this may be implicate and not explicate) which provides resources for reasoning about morality, i.e. for a system of ethics.[1] Thus, Christian views about God, the soul, the meaning of life, and so on, provide the materials for reasoned clarifications and systematic justifications of moral principles. But is Christian ethics unique?

In his essay 'Christian social ethics in a global context', Hebblethwaite argues that the

> distinctiveness of Christian ethics . . . [is] more a matter of specifically Christian motivation, inspiration, and resource than of a unique and incommensurable content . . . On the contrary, Christians have . . . theological reasons based on God's law in creation for expecting and hoping to find such analogies worldwide. (Runzo and Martin, 2001:322)

Hebblethwaite explicates some of those theological considerations for denying the uniqueness of the content of Christian ethics in one of my favourite essays of his, 'The varieties of goodness':

> Christian theological ethics cannot endorse contradictory religious *values,* but can and must welcome other forms of religiously motivated goodness. Here it is a question of recognizing the way in which the Spirit has evoked *conscious* response, and of the forms of life, both personal and communal, that have developed in the different religious cultures. We may well speak of complementary values here. The Christian has no monopoly of the ways of God with humankind. There may well be forms of the religious life that encapsulate and manifest values understressed in the Christian traditions. Christianity's historically dynamic and eschatologically

---

[1] I argue for this in 'Doing ethics and being religious in a global world', in *Ethics in the World Religions*, ed. Joseph Runzo and Nancy M. Martin, 2001:19–37.

Can Christian Ethics be Universal?

oriented moral faith needs to be complemented by Eastern cosmic wisdom.[2]

However, this is not to say that the moral content of Christianity, which is much like that of other world religions, is based on the same metaphysical resources as other traditions. *What* one ought to do is often a shared feature of religious moralities. *Why* one ought to do what one ought to do and *how* one ought to do it – the motivation, inspiration and resource of which Hebblethwaite speaks – is based on the specific religious worldview of a tradition and is less often shared. This is directly indicated in the last passage from Hebblethwaite in his references to the Spirit, God and the eschatological orientation of Christianity, three metaphysical assumptions not shared conjointly with any other single world religion.

A fuller explanation of the underlying metaphysics of Christian ethics intimated here is found in Hebblethwaite's *The Ocean of Truth:*

> The heart of the faith is Christian discernment of the reality of God as the ultimate source of all life and love both here and in eternity. There is an ocean of truth here, in objective theism, to be discovered by all who embark upon the ship of faith and are prepared to use all their faculties, including reason, to chart its course ... the vision of self sacrificial love at the heart of all things, the experience of joy in creation and peace in reconciliation, the promise of healing and liberation for all life's victims, the hope of a perfected new creation in which God's personal creatures will participate for ever – these things more than justify the decision to embark. (1988:143)

So clearly, Christian ethics *in toto* cannot be universal in sense (2) set out above. This is so because Christian ethics does not claim to be merely contingently true, but it is also because the elemental features of the metaphysics of Christianity which undergirds Christian reasoning about morality – such as a creator-God who issues divine commands and the sacrificial love of Christ – are not shared by the ethical reasoning of Hinduism, Buddhism, Islam, etc. But to what extent *could* Christian ethics become universally held in sense (3) of 'universal'?

---

2 'The varieties of goodness', in *Ethics and Religion in a Pluralistic Age*, 1997:61–2.

Universality of Christian Ethics

Hebblethwaite suggests that Christian ethics ought to become universal in sense (3):

> Christian social ethics has three principal areas of concern: first, the form of Christian life in the Christian community itself . . .; secondly, the gradual permeation of the wider society by Christian values . . .; and thirdly, the structures of responsible life in society at large . . . (Runzo and Martin, 2001:321–2)

But he also argues that Christian ethics is universal in sense (1):

> All the great religions of the world, despite their differences, have some claim, at their best, to be fostering love and compassion, service of the neighbour and a concern for the right ordering of society . . . How should exponents of Christian ethics view these facts? On both human and theological grounds, it seems that they should welcome these facts as signs of the universal Spirit of God at work in human religion . . . The ability of the religions to foster goodness and love, like the capacity of secular men and women to manifest the virtues, should, for Christians, be an indication that God revealed in Christ is God of the whole world, the source of all value as of all being.[3]

On Hebblethwaite's view, the divine ethical point of view, EPV_D, is reflected to varying degrees in the various ethical points of view of the world religions, EPV_{R1}, EPV_{R2}, etc., including its fullest reflection in the Christian ethical point(s) of view. But Hebblethwaite finds the presence of God's ethical point of view in secular ethics as well:

> there is a great deal of profound moral worth in the lives of non-Christian individuals from Socrates to Gandhi and in the teachings of non-Christian moralists from Aristotle to Marx (to say nothing of contemporary examples) that is not only quite compatible with Christ and his revelation but which reveals new facets of human goodness and human idealism, from which Christians can only learn with gratitude. (1981:129–31)

---

3 *The Adequacy of Christian Ethics*, 1981:113.

Can Christian Ethics be Universal?

So EPV_D is reflected in both EPV_{R1}, EPV_{R2} ... and in secular views, EPV_{S1}, EPV_{S2}, etc. However, it is important to keep in mind that on Hebblethwaite's inclusivist view, Christian ethics is the final arbiter of the moral life since it is Christian metaphysics which best captures the underlying structure of the universe:

> Such human goodness and such human idealism can be regarded as less or more conscious reflections, in different social and cultural environments, of the goodness of God the Creator ... it is an indispensable aspect of Christian belief to hold that Christ himself is the criterion of all good, and that implicit response to God in Christ will one day be transformed into explicit response ... The ultimate basis for the claim to adequacy on the part of Christian ethics is the fact that the love of which it speaks is, in reality, the source and goal of all there is. (1981:136)

This Christian inclusivist view regarding both religious and secular ethics is summed up in *The Ocean of Truth* as follows:

> If Christ is indeed the incarnation of the 'person' in God, through whom the world was made, it must in reality be none other than the Spirit of Christ that vivifies and sustains morality and spirituality wherever they are to be found. (1988:124)

So Hebblethwaite holds that the Christian metaphysical grounding of Christian morality is universal in sense (1). This is the point of disagreement I have with Hebblethwaite. Non-Christians would not of course accept his proposal of an inclusivist Christian grounding of all morality. While I agree in faith that God's viewpoint is inclusivist, I have argued elsewhere that Christians, and indeed the adherents of all the world religions, should be 'Henofideists'.[4] This would entail a Christian faith in the Christian metaphysical foundations of ethics, but an acceptance of the possibility that there may be other, equally viable metaphysical bases for ethics in Hinduism, Buddhism, Jainism, Islam, and so on.

---

4 *Global Philosophy of Religion*, 2001:37–43.

Relationality

Apart from the question of whether Inclusivism or Henofideism is preferable, since the various religions and the various secular ethical systems do not wholly agree, what feature of ethics could be the trans-ethical feature which all religious and secular systems can share with EPV_D? That is, what trans-ethical feature is it which would make Christian ethics conducive to either Henofideism or Inclusivism vis-à-vis other ethical systems?

To my mind, Hebblethwaite identifies the key for why Christian ethics could be inclusivist, when he declares in 'The varieties of goodness' that:

> Christian ethics has the flexibility to embrace and baptize these varieties [of goodness] just because its key category is not imitation but relation. One of the things that makes each individual person unique is the specific set of interpersonal relations that has gone into the fashioning of his or her life history. (*Ethics and Religion in a Pluralistic Age*, 1997:9)

This is spelled out in some detail in specifically Christian terms in the earlier work *The Ocean of Truth*, where he says that,

> all the facets of Christian existence – our identity, our community, our worships, our ethical ideals (both individual and social), our spirituality – are thoroughly relational in character. We depend on God, we are reconciled by God, we are loved by God and enabled by God to love him in return; our fellowship and our prayers are inspired and empowered by God; and it is the resources of God that both give us our ethical ideals and spiritual vision and also empower what is realized in us and through us of that vision and that ideal. (1988:6)

And to conclude this explication of Hebblethwaite's basic view, we should note that he puts this point about relationality most explicitly in terms of the Christian *Trinitarian* metaphysics, a clear instance of how one's metaphysics drives one's ethics:

> For the driving force of the Christian religion is undoubtedly its conviction of a saving power from beyond . . . it is in the minds of its adherents a religion of grace, a religion that lives by its faith that

Can Christian Ethics be Universal?

man, in his weakness and inability to find from his own resources the way to wholeness and love, is taken out of himself, forgiven and enabled to grow in love by the Spirit of God and of Christ crucified and risen. Christians see their spirituality and ethics as flowing, not from their own strength but from the lived and experienced relation between believers and their Lord. (1988:141)

Hence, one strength of Christianity, as Hebblethwaite understands it, is an encompassing flexibility which comes from the varieties of relatedness at the heart of the human experience of God. Variety allows for universality in the broad scope. Though the specifics of Christian metaphysics do not carry over to other world religions, *relationality*, with its variety, is the trans-ethical feature which would enable Christian ethics to be both inclusivist and universal in senses (1) and (3). But just how much of the specific content of Christian ethics is universal in sense (1)? A comprehensive answer to this question would require a detailed analysis of Christian ethics. Here, in considering the ethics of war as a paradigmatic case, we shall see that variety clearly poses problems for universality when we turn to the variety of positions which are taken on specific ethical issues such as war.

The Varieties of Christian War Ethics

Within the Christian way of life, Hebblethwaite argues against a narrow interpretation of the 'imitation of Christ' on the one hand, and for variety on the other:

Certainly, there are some general features of the Christian life which we shall expect authentic followers of Christ to manifest in their lives. Paul spells these out in terms of the 'fruit of the Spirit' (Gal. 5.22). There will indeed be family resemblances between Christians, both as individuals and in community. But despite these characteristic general features, we should not think of Christian men and women as, ideally, clones of Jesus... (*Ethics and Religion in a Pluralistic Age*, 1997:51-2)

Jesus himself was a pacifist and indeed, historically, Christians have not been, on the whole, 'clones' of the one who said 'Do not resist one who is evil. But if any one strikes you on the right cheek, turn to him the other also' (Matt. 5.39-40, RSV). Hebblethwaite enunciates this moral ambiguity in Christian war ethics with this comparative observation:

> Taken together the religions of the East, at their best, provide deeply pacific spiritual resources against the resort to war . . . But, while Christian pacifism has a long and honoured history, for the greater part of the Christian centuries the Churches have endorsed just war theory, and in fact Christian nations have been extremely bellicose. It is not surprising that, second only to Islam, Christianity has been regarded as a factor making for war rather than for peace. (ibid.:209–10)

Now, on a scale from the most to the least bellicose, with the Hebrew and Islamic traditions among the most bellicose and Jainism and to a lesser extent Buddhism among the least, Christianity and Hinduism tend to be placed in the centre. (Among Chinese traditions, Confucianism is closer to Islam and Taoism closer to Jainism in the ethics of war.) During its earliest centuries, pacifism was the norm for Christianity until the 'Constantinian shift', which began in 311 CE when Christianity was declared a legal religion within the Roman Empire, and reached its apogee by 436 when *only* Christians were allowed to serve in the legions. While it was Aristotle who first introduced the notion of 'just war' in the West, theologians from Augustine to Aquinas refined the idea of *bellum justum* in response to Christendom's active participation in warfare. Yet throughout the Middle Ages, for those whose lives were thought to best exemplify the imitation of Christ – that is, priests and monks – pacifism remained the norm.

It is at the end of this period when Erasmus, the greatest Renaissance humanist, wrote *Querela Pacis*, *Antipolemus*, and *Dulce Bellum Inexpertis*.[5] In 'The education of a Christian prince' he writes:

> Some evils come from one source and others from another, but from war comes the shipwreck of all that is good and from it the sea of all calamities pours out. Then, too, no other misfortune clings so steadfastly. War is sown from war; from the smallest comes the greatest; from one comes two; from a jesting one comes a fierce and bloody one, and the plague arising in one place, spreads to the

---

[5] Albert Marrin (ed.), *War and the Christian Conscience: From Augustine to Martin Luther King, Jr.*, 1971:157.

Can Christian Ethics be Universal?

nearest peoples and is even carried in to the most distant places . . . how disastrous and criminal an affair war is and what a host of all evils it carries in its wake even if it is the most justifiable war – if there really is any war which can be called 'just' . . . Some princes deceive themselves that any war is certainly a just one, that they have a just cause for going to war . . . but who does not think his own cause just?[6]

Thus, historically the Christian ethics of war contains two strands: pacifism and just war theory. If Christian ethics is to be universal in senses (1) and (3), there must be a shared aspect of these pacifist and just war views within Christianity which can be universalized.

Limited War as Total War

Though the historical predictive value of the book of Revelation is questionable (as Luther observed: a revelation ought to be revealing), this last book of the New Testament does offer a chilling revelation of the human condition:

> 'Come!' And out came another horse, bright red; its rider was permitted to take peace from the earth, so that men should slay one another; and he was given a great sword . . . When he opened the fourth seal, I heard the voice of the fourth living creature say, 'Come!' And I saw and behold, a pale horse, and its rider's name was Death, and Hades followed him; and they were given power over a fourth of the earth, to kill with sword and with famine and with pestilence and by wild beasts of the earth. (Rev. 6.3-4, 7-8, RSV)

Wars have always been the scourge of humankind, the greatest horror of the four horsemen of the apocalypse. Indeed, war is a Trojan horse which carries pestilence and famine in its bowels: Erasmus' 'shipwreck of all that is good' pouring out all calamities. But the deepest problem with waging war is not the resultant pain, suffering and death, as horrific as that may be. I submit that the deep problem with engaging in war is the destruction of the soul, both the soul of the individual and the soul of society. The elements of this soul-destruction point in

---

6 Desiderius Erasmus, 'The education of a Christian prince: "On beginning war"', in A. Marrin, 1971:158-9.

opposition to the underlying universal ethic of war which Christianity can share with the other world religions.

War, the eminent British war-historian John Keegan has said, is collective killing for some collective purpose. Though the political status of the 'collective' doing the killing needs careful definition, this broad description alone tells us that wars are bad, yet we are told that they are sometimes necessary as the lesser of two evils. What could be the greater evil which could outweigh the evil of this collective killing, which could make this collective killing a case of *bellum justum*? First, if the occasion and the intensity of war is unlimited, there would be no greater evil. Indeed, we would be left with the sort of soulless approach which Hitler took to warfare as 'the highest form of human endeavour, the greatest expression of life's purposes, the fate of all being: "One creature drinks the blood of another. The death of one nourishes the other. One should not dribble about humane feelings [Hitler said] . . . the struggle goes on."'[7]

Consequently, an attempt is made to limit the evil of war using the theory of just war developed by theologians and then proponents of international law, an attempt which is divided into two levels. At the first level are *jus ad bellum* considerations which are an attempt to limit the number and possibility of wars. Thus, war is to be seen as a last resort, it must be carried out with right intention for a just cause, it must be a proportional response to the injustice being addressed and there must be a formal declaration of war by a proper authority. Once a people engages in war, the second level of *jus in bello* considerations comes into effect. The *in bello* norms are discrimination and proportionality. To be just, warfare must be directed toward the appropriate targets and coupled with the attempt to avoid direct intentional harm to non-combatants, and to be just warfare must be carried out with an intensity which is appropriate to the kind and degree of injustice putatively requiring rectification.

An important contribution to our understanding of these latter *in bello* considerations is that of the sixteenth-century Spanish theologian Francisco de Vitoria. In *De Indis* and *De Jure Belli* he argued against the massacre of and plunder of the lands of Native Americans by the Spanish Conquistadors, asserting that 'the deliberate slaughter of innocents is never lawful in itself, for it is forbidden by natural law . . . The basis of a war is a wrong done. But a wrong is not done by an innocent person. Therefore, war may not be employed against

---

7 See Robert G. L. Waite, *The Psychopathic God: Adolf Hitler*, 1993:77.

Can Christian Ethics be Universal?

him.'[8] The injustice of the slaughter of innocents stays in force even after a war ends, for as James Turner Johnson points out, just war theory includes the notion of 'no Carthaginian peace' (named after the razing of Carthage by the Romans): 'I understand the requirement of 'no Carthaginian peace' already to be implied by the principle of discrimination. After a war is over, all are noncombatants, and ongoing harm to them violates the immunity from harm they should then enjoy.'[9] So the *ad bellum* and *in bello* norms are intended to conjointly delineate *bellum justum* by limiting both the prevalence and the 'collateral damage' of war for the innocents. But in what sense is any 'limited war' which harms the innocent not a total war? Put otherwise, can there be a just war, a war which Christians and/or the adherents of any other world religion could support?

The Hellishness of War

It is easy enough to find 'pacifist' passages in religious literature against waging war – Jesus' 'turn the other cheek', and Buddhist and Jain notions of *ahimsa* – but it is incumbent on us to listen to the practitioners of war themselves. One of the greatest and most thoughtful generals in the history of warfare, William Tecumseh Sherman, is noted for a speech long after the American Civil War in which he said 'There is many a boy here today who looks on war as all glory, but, boys, it is all hell.' This is accurate in a religious sense and not just a symbolic sense.

Why is war hell? As even Sun Tzu, the great Chinese strategist who wrote his definitive *Art of War* some 2,500 years ago observed, the practical problem with war is that 'War is like unto fire; those who will not put aside weapons are themselves consumed by them.'[10] The neat, quick, surgical 'lightning war' becomes protracted, innocents are slaughtered, the land ravaged, and, in any war, casualties of war always include the surviving soldiers themselves, trained to kill and made to suffer the sights and sounds of the horrors of war. Indeed, when we consider the effect of war on the soldiers themselves, we should bear in mind Amnesty International's estimate that presently

---

8 From *De Indis*, in James Bron Scott (ed.), *The Classics of International Law*, 1917: Sect. III 13.171, and III 35.178.

9 James Turner Johnson, *Morality and Contemporary Warfare*, 1999:126.

10 Sun Tzu, 'Waging war', in *The Art of War*, trans. Samuel B. Griffith, 1963:73.

there are about 300,000 children – child-soldiers – bearing arms in conflicts in some 25 countries.[11]

Wars have been putatively justified on all sorts of grounds, but if we eliminate egoism – perhaps the motive of Alexander the Great or Ghengis Khan or Napoleon – as a justification for war, then minimally a just war must be proportional. Proportionality, whether *ad bellum* or *in bello*, is a utilitarian consideration. One of the most important considerations about the utility of war is enunciated by Hugo Grotius, the father of international law. Grotius points out that 'Kings who measure up to the rule of wisdom take account not only of the nation which had been committed to them, but of the whole human race.' But this raises the fundamental practical problem with war: it usually if not always gets out of control, loses proportionality and loses utility.

First there is the staggering loss of life in war, especially in the technologically advanced and prolonged wars of the mid-nineteenth century and beyond. In the First World War, 10 million people died, while in the Second World War, 50 million people lost their lives, the percentage of civilians increasing as war increased its totality. In the First World War, 15 per cent of the fatalities were civilian; in the Second, this proportion rose to a horrific 65 per cent, while in the 'small' wars of the late twentieth century, in Africa and East Timor and what once was Yugoslavia, the rate of civilian casualties became a grotesque 90 per cent. One particularly odious slaughter of defenceless civilians occurred at the start of the Second World War in Nanking. Iris Chang relates the butchering of some 350,000 people in the city within a few weeks this way:

> On Hsiakwan wharves, there was the dark silhouette of a mountain made of dead bodies. About fifty to one hundred people were toiling there, dragging bodies from the mountain of corpses and throwing them into the Yangtze River. The bodies dripped blood, some of them still alive and moaning weakly, their limbs twitching. The laborers were busy working in total silence, as in a pantomime. In the dark one could barely see the opposite bank of the river. On the pier was a field of glistening mud under the moon's dim light. Wow! That's all blood!
>
> After a while, the coolies had done their job of dragging corpses

---

[11] Amnesty International, *In the Firing Line: War and Children's Rights*, 1999:8.

Can Christian Ethics be Universal? 125

and the soldiers lined them up along the river. Rat-tat-tat machine-gun fire could be heard. The coolies fell backwards into the river and were swallowed by the raging currents. The pantomime was over.

A Japanese officer at the scene estimated that 20,000 persons had been executed [at that location].[12]

As we consider a horror like the Rape of Nanking, it is important to remember that both sides shared in targeting civilians in the Pacific War. In the bombing campaign of 1945, the USA destroyed 60 per cent of the ground area of Japan's 60 largest cities, killing more civilians than the atomic bombing of Hiroshima and Nagasaki combined.

The limitations of 'just war' soon give way to total war, seriously undermining the idea that 'proportionality' has any real meaning in war. As the prominent just war theorist James Turner Johnson notes:

> if values are to be defended, there must be justifiable means for defending them; otherwise, we are locked in an unenviable dilemma of either not protecting these values against destruction by others or destroying them ourselves through the use of disproportionate and/or indiscriminate means.[13]

But to cite Thomas Babington Macaulay, in the modern era 'the essence of war is violence, and . . . moderation in war is imbecility',[14] and as the book of Deuteronomy infamously advises:

> When you draw near to a city to fight against it, offer terms of peace to it. And if its answer to you is peace and it opens to you, then all the people who are found in it shall do forced labour for you and shall serve you. But if it makes no peace with you but makes war against you, then you shall besiege it; and when the Lord your God gives it into your hand you shall put all its males to the sword, but the women and the little ones, the cattle, and everything else in the city, all it contains by way of spoil, you shall take as booty for yourselves; and you shall enjoy the spoils of your enemies, which the

---

12 *The Rape of Nanking*, 1997:47–8.
13 *Can Modern War be Just?* 1984:186.
14 Thomas Babington, First Baron Macaulay (1800–59), in his *Essays Contributed to the Edinburgh Review*, vol. 1, 'John Hampden'.

> Lord your God has given you . . . in the cities of these people that the Lord your God gives you for an inheritance, you shall save alive nothing that breathes, but you shall utterly destroy them . . . (20.10–17, RSV)

I call this the violent excess of empire. For, the Godless Greeks followed the same war-making recipe as the God-fearing Hebrews. When Alexander razed Thebes, 6,000 Thebans were killed and 30,000 sold into slavery to finance Alexander's attack on the Persian Empire in his pursuit of world conquest. To effect this destruction of the population, Alexander let his Greek allies loose in the city:

> Greeks were mercilessly slain by Greeks, relatives were butchered by their own relatives, houses plundered, and children and women and aged persons who fled into the temples were torn from sanctuary and subjected to outrage without limit . . . Every corner of the city was piled high with corpses.[15]

Lest we think such slaughter of non-combatants as a violent excess of empire is either limited to ancient barbarian peoples or limited to non-Christian nations, in the same spirit of limited warfare degenerating into total warfare here is a participant in the My Lai massacre in Vietnam:

> That day in My Lai, I was personally responsible for killing about 25 people. Personally. Men, women. From shooting them, to cutting their throats, scalping them, to . . . cutting off their hands and cutting out their tongue. I did it . . . But like I say, after I killed the child, my whole mind just went. It just went. And once you start, it's very easy to keep on. Once you start. The hardest – the part that's hard is to kill, but once you kill, that becomes easier, to kill the next person and the next one and the next one. Because I had no feelings or no emotions or no nothing. No direction. I just killed. It can happen to anyone.[16]

The 'just war' is often justified on the 'humanitarian' grounds that others will be defended from violence. But as Tolstoy observes:

---

15 Victor Davis Hanson, *The Soul of Battle*, 1999:21.
16 Michael Bilton and Kevin Sim, *Four Hours in My Lai*, 1992:7.

Can Christian Ethics be Universal?

apologies for violence used against one's neighbor in defense of another neighbor from greater violence are always untrustworthy, because when force is used against one who has not yet carried out his evil intent, I can never know which would be greater – the evil of my act of violence or of the act I want to prevent.[17]

Similarly, Gandhi argues that while belligerents in war believe that they are in the right and that warfare will definitively achieve their just ends, neither belief can be known to be true with certainty.[18] So, just war theory always faces an enormous epistemic hurdle: we can never know in advance the outcome of this collective killing. Moreover, the *jus in bello* norms of discrimination and proportionality are inevitably abrogated in warfare. And the problem is that the overwhelming disregard for the *jus in bello* norm of discrimination in war is not just a result of rapid-fire weapons, aerial bombardment and even nuclear weapons, it is part of the very fabric of war-making. Indeed, one of the deepest horrors of war is the destruction of the soul of the larger society when it commits to a war. Thich Nhat Hanh says this about the American-initiated Gulf War:

> In the Persian Gulf, many people practiced killing in their minds – Iraqi, American, French, British, and other soldiers. They knew that if they didn't kill, the enemy soldiers would kill them, so they used sandbags to represent their enemy, and holding their bayonets firmly, they ran, shouted, and plunged the bayonets into the sandbags . . . To work for peace is to uproot war from ourselves and from the hearts of men and women. To start a war and give the opportunity to one million men and women to practice killing each other day and night in their hearts is to plant many seeds of war – anger, frustration, and the fear of being killed.[19]

Substituting the State for the Transcendent

From a religious point of view, the mere physical destructiveness of war – as horrific as that may be – is not the most elemental evil of warfare. For one thing, lack of discrimination and proportionality are

---

17 Leo Tolstoy, *The Kingdom of God is Within You*, 1984:35.
18 Bhikhu Parekh, *Gandhi: A Very Short Introduction*, 1997:66.
19 Thich Nhat Hanh, *Love in Action: Writings on Nonviolent Social Change*, 1993:74–5.

utilitarian failures of war, and while religious ethics includes considerations about the greater good, religious ethics is ultimately deontological. The intent of our actions matters, and in particular the intent to be related to others – and this includes relation to God for the monotheisms – matters the most in moral matters. War fundamentally lacks right intent in so far as warfare substitutes the state for the transcendent.

Simone Weil neatly identifies the perpetual state of warfare which the nation-state or empire engenders to justify the defence of the state as the highest good:

> What a country calls its vital economic interests are not the things which enable its citizens to live, but the things which enable it to make war . . . Thus when war is waged it is for the purpose of safeguarding or increasing one's capacity to make war . . . What is called national prestige consists in behaving always in such a way as to demoralize other nations by giving them the impression that, if it comes to war, one would certainly defeat them. What is called national security is an imaginary state of affairs in which one would retain the capacity to make war while depriving all other countries of it. It amounts to this, that a self-respecting nation is ready for anything, including war, except for a renunciation of its option to make war.[20]

Simone Weil's lifetime spanned two world wars fought among a multitude of nation-states, but we can clearly see the same substitution of the state for the transcendent, which Weil saw in the twentieth century, in the transition of the Christian community from its early pacifist stance to its full participation in the militarized Roman Empire:

> Because the early Christians refused to honor or participate in the state religion, Christians were frequently, and ironically, accused of 'atheism.' They did not 'believe in' (as we would say today) the national gods of Rome. They certainly refused to deify and worship the emperor . . . In fact, many of the early Christian martyrs who refused military service did so precisely because participation in military service amounted to participation in a rival religion – a religion which mandated violent activities.[21]

---

20 *The Simone Weil Reader*, ed. George A. Panichas, 1977:273.
21 Daniel Smith-Christopher, 'Political atheism and radical faith: the challenge

Can Christian Ethics be Universal? 129

Ironically, by the late Middle Ages, with the rise of the great Islamic Empires, Christians and Muslims both faced each other 'under God'. At the Turkish siege of Constantinople,

> Both Turks and Christians began to look for omens of heavenly intervention. The Christians were dismayed when a statue of the Virgin fell to the ground during a procession through the streets. An unseasonal cloud of mist settled over the city, and was immediately taken as an omen that God had withdrawn his light from his people. The sultan Mehmed was similarly despondent when he saw a mysterious shaft of sunlight which seemed to suffuse the great church of St Sophia (Aye Sofya) with a golden glow; this he interpreted as a sign of divine intervention on the side of the city . . . the emperor Constantine turned and spoke to his people for the last time: 'The Turks have their artillery, their cavalry, their hordes of soldiers. We have Our God and Savior.'[22]

Similarly and several centuries later, in the American Civil War, the pious Confederate General Stonewall Jackson wrote: 'Our gallant little army is increasing in numbers, and my prayer is that it may be an army of the living God as well as of its country.'[23] Meanwhile the Union army was singing the Battle Hymn of the Republic:

> In the beauty of the lilies Christ was born across the sea,
> With a glory in his bosom that transfigures you and me:

---

of Christian nonviolence in the third millennium', in Daniel Smith-Christopher (ed.), *Subverting Hatred: The Challenge of Nonviolence in Religious Traditions*, 1998:144. With the example of Hippolytus (d. 236 CE), the apostolic tradition and the Canons clearly reveal this Christian attitude by the early third century: 'The soldier who is of inferior rank shall not kill anyone. If ordered to, he shall not carry out the order . . . The believer who wishes to become a soldier shall be dismissed because they have despised God.

Canon 13: Of the magistrate and the soldier: Let them not kill anyone evil if they receive the order to do so.

Canon 14: Let a Christian not become a soldier: A Christian must not become a soldier . . . Let him not take on himself the son of blood' (Daniel Smith-Christopher, 1998:154).

22 Andrew Wheatcroft, 'The fall of Constantinople'. from Andrew Wheatcroft, *The Ottomans: Dissolving Images* (Viking, 1993), in John Keegan, *The Book of War: 25 Centuries of Great War Writing*, Penguin Book, 1999:64–6.

23 George F. R. Henderson, *Stonewall Jackson and the American Civil War*, 1962:189.

As he died to make men holy, let us die to make men free,
While God is marching on.

During the First World War the United States had propaganda posters in which 'Jesus was dressed in khaki and portrayed sighting down a gun barrel . . .', and the Bishop of London 'called on Englishmen to "kill Germans – to kill . . . the good as well as the bad, to kill the young men as well as the old . . . As I have said a thousand times, I look upon it as a war for purity, I look upon everyone who dies in it as a martyr." '[24] In the Second World War, a quintessential example of the substitution of the state for the transcendent was Hitler's Germany:

> Since Hitler saw himself as a Messiah with a divine mission to save Germany from the incarnate evil of 'International Jewry,' it is not surprising that he likened himself to Jesus. On one occasion during the 1920s, as he lashed about him with the whip he habitually carried, he said that 'in driving out the Jews I remind myself of Jesus in the temple.' At another time he said, 'Just like Christ, I have a duty to my own people . . .' 'What Christ began,' he observed, he, Hitler, 'would complete.' And in a speech on 10th February 1933, he parodied the Lord's Prayer in promising that under him a new kingdom would come on earth, and that his would be 'the power and the glory, Amen.' He added that if he did not fulfill his mission, 'you should then crucify me.' (R. Waite, 1993:27)

Now as James Turner Johnson points out, for monotheistic cultures, this substitution is inevitable when a clear relation to the transcendent is lost:

> If God is not the motive force for transforming the world (as Augustine thought), then a contemporary secular entity such as the United Nations, NATO, or even the United States acting alone must take God's place as the motive force in history . . . (1999:17)

Hebblethwaite's response to the sort of danger articulated by Johnson of substituting the state for the transcendent is that:

> the adequacy of Christian ethics rests in part on its ability to inspire

---

[24] Barbara Ehrenreich, *Blood Rites: Origins and History of the Passions of War*, 1997:205.

Can Christian Ethics be Universal?

men and women to establish a just framework for human life on earth – for all human beings, whether or not they call themselves Christians. I deliberately refer to a just framework; for Christian ethics does not make the mistake of idolizing the state as such. (*The Adequacy of Christian Ethics*, 1981:135)

Expanding this point to other world religions, Hebblethwaite says of the 'First Conference on a Global Ethic and Traditional Indian Ethics' in New Delhi in 1997, that:

> Participants observed that ethical principles which refer to and arise from the ethical domain alone may not be sufficient to ensure discharge of ethical responsibilities. It is spirituality, the dynamism of faith, which has through the ages empowered and spurred individuals and groups to live up to ethical standards. We may conclude that, at this basic minimum level of rights and responsibilities, while the need for a global ethic can be perceived and urged across the borders of the religious and the secular, it is the religions that can best provide the motivation and the spiritual resources to sustain it. (in J. Runzo and N. Martin, 2001:328)

I would argue that in addition to motivation and spiritual resources, the world religions provide a vision of our humanity, and the motivation and spiritual resources of religion can help maintain that vision against warfare.

Christianity and a Global Ethic for War

Einstein notes that 'More dreadful even than the destruction, in my opinion, is the humiliating slavery into which war plunges the individual. Is it not a terrible thing to be forced by the community to do things which every individual regards as abominable crime?'[25] Employing the same sort of imagery of the 'slavery of war', *Gaudium et Spes* (The Pastoral Constitution on the Church in the Modern World) from Vatican II states: 'the arms race is an utterly treacherous trap for humanity, and one which injures the poor to an intolerable degree ... Divine Providence urgently demands of us that we free ourselves from the age-old slavery of war.'[26]

---

25 Albert Einstein, *The World As I See It*, trans. Alan Harris, 1998:61.
26 See *The Documents of Vatican II*, ed. Walter M. Abbot SJ, 1966:295.

In opposition to this fundamentally evil 'slavery' of both the individual and of society to war, the world religions have something to add to the moral point of view, something which I call the religious point of view. Just as the obligation to take others into account in one's actions because one respects them as *persons* is a defining feature of the moral point of view,[27] an obligation always to act in a way that respects others *because* they are not only persons but spiritual beings is a defining feature of the commonality among the diverse world religions. Treating all other persons as spiritual beings will mean that one treats all other persons as having the same spiritual value as oneself, as being on the same spiritual quest as oneself, and with the same potential for salvation or liberation.[28] This is what it *is* to take the religious point of view, and this spirit–spirit relationality at the heart of the world religions is manifest in the variety of religious ethics, interconnected through the bond of 'we', not 'I'. Consequently, abstaining from war, because war breaks spirit–spirit relations and does not take all other persons into account equally as spiritual beings, is a *religious* obligation.

Now, any appeal like this to a spiritual commonality among the world religions must take into account that the Hindu *bhakti* conception of *nishkama karma* is not identical to the Christian notion of love,[29] which in turn is not identical to the Confucian emphasis on *ren* (human-heartedness), say, or the Buddhist focus on compassion. Moreover, as Hebblethwaite points out,

> in Christian social ethics, the religious motivation and the spiritual resources making for commitment at the basic level of the rights and responsibilities affirmed in a global ethic will continue to stem not only from beliefs in natural law and human dignity, but also from the Gospel of the Incarnation, the sacramental principle, the social theology of Trinitarian belief, and from specifically Christian

---

[27] I offer a further analysis of the moral point of view in my essay in J. Runzo and N. Martin, 2001:23.

[28] This can also be put in terms of two other features of the religious point of view which parallel the moral point of view: recognizing the spirit of everyone equally, and accepting the universalizability to others of one's own treatment of oneself as spirit.

[29] Julius Lipner argues for strong parallels between notions of Hindu *bhakti* and Christian love in 'The God of love and the love of God in Christian and Hindu traditions', in *Love, Sex and Gender in the World Religions*, ed. Joseph Runzo and Nancy M. Martin, 2000:51–88.

eschatology – the vision of the Kingdom of God in the communion of saints. Again, other religions will have their own, often very different, beliefs and resources by which to motivate and sustain commitment to a global ethic. Agreement on a framework of shared values for politics and economics worldwide does not entail any conflation or homogenization of the beliefs and spiritualities that sustain that agreement. ('Christian social ethics in a global context', 2001:327)

But what the world religions do share is the rejection of self-aggrandizing behaviour and the promotion of other-regarding behaviour – though we must always keep in mind that they ground this religious point of view in divergent metaphysics. Thus, the world religions not only offer a critique of the evils of war, they offer the potential for a universal ethic against warfare and its attendant evils. This is the ethical foundation which could make a universal religious ethics of war (in sense 3) possible, namely, a universal religious ethic against war which, while not currently universally held, could become universally recognized. This is the hope for a humanity freed from the slavery of war.

Gaudium et Spes declares that:

Christians should collaborate willingly and wholeheartedly in establishing an international order involving genuine respect for all freedoms and amicable brotherhood between all men . . . [but] . . . peace is not merely the absence of war. Nor can it be reduced solely to the maintenance of a balance of power between enemies . . . Peace results from that harmony built into human society by its divine Founder, and actualized by men as they thirst after ever greater justice. The common good of men is in its basic sense determined by the eternal law. (W. Abbott, 1966:290)

This idea, without the Christian metaphysics and with a more Buddhist perspective, is echoed by Thich Nhat Hanh's Engaged Buddhism: 'We may think of peace as the absence of war, that if the great powers would reduce their weapons arsenals, we could have peace. But if we look deeply into the weapons, we will see our own minds – our own prejudices, fears and ignorance' (1993:75). Christian pacificists and Christian just war theorists share a deontological commitment to morality, and they share the religious point of view. These other-regarding perspectives are clearly universal features of

Christian ethics in sense (1), and they are features of the religious ethics of every world religion. So while the specific metaphysical tenets of Christianity are not universally shared, Christian ethics shares universal features of religious ethics, and so shares universal features of a more focused ethic of war. And the variety of relationality makes this universality possible.

The Place of Religion in a Global Ethic of War

The religious point of view together with a non-exclusivist view of conflicting religious truth-claims would provide key elements for a universal religious ethic of war. But even if there could be a global *religious* ethic of war, how would such an ethic figure in a global ethic which was neither religious, *per se*, nor anti-religious? The religious point of view and the moral point of view, as an action guide for both religious and non-religious people, are potentially powerful allies in the quest to limit the number and intensity of wars, and to condemn the dishonourable soldier's actions. For a universal ethic (in sense 3) against war can only be developed through the active participation of the religious as well as the secular, the nonviolent person as well as the honourable soldier. As Thich Nhat Hanh says:

> Anyone can practice nonviolence, even soldiers. Some army generals, for example, conduct their operations in ways that avoid killing innocent people; this is a kind of nonviolence ... If we divide reality into two camps – the violent and the nonviolent – and stand in one camp while attacking the other, the world will never have peace. We will always blame and condemn those we feel are responsible for wars and social injustice, without recognizing the degree of violence in ourselves. (1993:65)

In the modern world, groups like the UN are often thought to constitute the administrators of The Hague, Geneva and similar Conventions on warfare. The theoreticians of these Conventions of international law are in some cases influenced by religious traditions, but their role is secular. Yet the majority of humanity is religious, and it is difficult to convince a primarily religious global population that avowed secular theoreticians are comparable to practising religious theoreticians. Thus, the number of people committed with respect to any purely secular declaration of a war ethic is always limited, a resistance based in part not on the moral quality of the proposals but on

Can Christian Ethics be Universal? 135

the perceived final authority of the proposals. The reverse is also true: any attempt at claiming a religious exclusivity for a 'correct' war ethics only makes an enemy of benevolent secular attitudes (see B. Hebblethwaite, 'Christian social ethics in a global context', 2001:319).

To reduce opposition to secular-based international law – thereby increasing the numbers of those committed to these norms – but to also provide vision, motivation and spiritual resources, any universal ethic of war must take account of religious commitments and religious theoreticians.[30] This would not entail a subservience of secular to religious theory but rather the participation of religious theory in the construction of a social ethic which is intended to take account of both the secular and the religious. The goal is to expand the ethically committed to include both those with a religious and those with a secular metaphysics, and the secular and the religious will need to be partners in this enterprise: the secular can provide a constructive voice against the dangers of religious egoism and the religious can add a powerful voice of vision, motivation and spiritual resources to the call to other-regarding action which lies at the heart of both the religious life and the moral life, and is fundamentally opposed to the inherent failure of proportionality in warfare, the violent excesses of empire.

---

30 For an attempt to frame a religious Declaration of Human Rights, see Part III of *Human Rights and Responsibilities in the World Religions*, ed. J. Runzo, N. Martin, and A. Sharma, 2003.

9. Intercultural Christology and Human Values

GEORGE NEWLANDS

Christology's Role in the Modern World

B. F. Westcott in his *Christus Consummator* laid emphasis on the Christian affirmation of the centrality of Jesus Christ to all things. In doing so, he was affirming no less and no more than the tradition affirmed, from Athanasius to Schleiermacher and beyond. If theology is the queen of the sciences, then Christology is the centre of that theological enterprise. The particular branch of the Christological tradition of which Westcott was such a distinguished advocate had dimensions ranging from the meticulous interpretation of the Patristic tradition to the appropriate strategy for mission in deprived areas of the East End of London. Westcott was concerned to explore the best theological interpretation of the person and work of Jesus Christ within the best intellectual paradigms of the day. He searched for the most appropriate interpretation of the Patristic texts in which the doctrine was first articulated. He was also passionately interested in the social implications of the doctrine in particular sections of contemporary society. Here was intercultural theology, seeking explanation and expression within different cultural milieux, past and present. Here was contextual theology, immersed in the cultural norms and expectations of its time. Theology could do much worse than Westcott did, then as now.

I return to the problem of Christological hegemony. We are now much more conscious than Westcott was of the cultural limitations of our own perspectives – though eminent Victorians were not always as insensitive to these matters as we like in our superior way to imagine. We know about the links between knowledge and interests, between description and domination, and we mourn our lost innocence. Suitably chastened, we may well be able to continue Westcott's enterprise with considerable success in the future. Yet other possibilities arise.

The one I want to explore in this essay in honour of Brian Hebblethwaite is the possibility that for Christian faith, theology – and especially Christology – may be more effective, and perhaps more true to theology's natural role, when it plays in the game of further developing human values, not as the 'queen' of the sciences but as a team player on a level playing field with the other players, as a contributor, partner, catalyst. This is not a call for a false humility: false humility comes naturally enough to theologians without further encouragement. It is rather a recommendation of a strategy for the more effective deployment of Christology in a world in which the voice of Christian faith is increasingly either silent, or so shrill that it blends with other postmodern fundamentalisms as an option only for the determinedly irrational.

Christus est Dominus: so, legend has it, the Crusaders chanted as they broke the skulls of their Muslim opponents in the Middle Ages. Sadly, conflicts involving Christians and other religions in contemporary society, not least in the Balkans and in Indonesia, mirror scenes of medieval horror in ways which polite modern society never anticipated. Is Christology always inimical to human rights? If there is a persistent track record of oppression in the name of the highest religious values, beginning from the tragic juxtaposition of the divine love and anti-Judaism in the Fourth Gospel, can we undo the past and offer Christology as a catalyst for human rights? This is the theme of my essay.

Brian Hebblethwaite has written movingly and profoundly of the love of God in incarnation in Jesus Christ. John Hick has given us timely reminders of the havoc once caused by Christian triumphalism. We must note at once, too, that the negative side of Christological advocacy has not impinged only on non-Christian people. Those who have claimed the 'right' Christology have rarely hesitated to anticipate presumed divine displeasure in their treatment of those with whom they disagree. In the name of Christ all sorts of minority groups are persecuted by majorities in every century. Christians have prided themselves on their responsibility for taking a tough line on the role of women, on divorcees, on criminals, on all manner of groups. They have found it less easy to combine such acknowledgement with repentance and attempts at reconciliation and redress.

We may say that as Christians we forgive those wrongs suffered at the hands of enthusiasts for Christ who were too wedded to the cultural norms of their day to listen to the challenge of the gospel. But it is not ours to forgive. Only the damaged and destroyed can forgive.

We may speak of the need to replace the language of conflict in our liturgies and hymns with the language of compassion, mutuality and reciprocity. But the replacement of honest brutality with politically correct sentimentality can only accelerate nausea. The simple liberalism of a gentle Jesus, meek and mild, will not solve our problems either. At least, not by itself.

What has gone wrong? Certainly modern theology can scarcely be accused of failing to attend to the manifold dimensions of Christology. Nineteenth-century theology did not fail to learn from Schleiermacher and from Hegel the importance of Christ. But the religion of *Kulturprotestantismus* tended to blend the God of the nation state with the Christ of the individual heart. Political conservatism was the order of the day at home, and outside Europe non-white people were subordinated to the culture of the white Jesus. Sin was largely conceived within the world of convenient introspection, and the aggression of a hegemonic Christian commercial culture was mainly overlooked. Christian Europe practically committed suicide in 1914. The project of worldwide Christian mission was all but halted in its tracks.

With Karl Barth, the archetypal anti-modern master, the God of religion was replaced by Jesus Christ, the Lord of the universe. Culture was subordinated to Christian community, and a defensive repristination of classical Christian doctrine in the face of Weimar decadence and Nazi fascism was achieved. While in Europe church attendance began to collapse towards the end of the twentieth century, in America God was still reassuringly linked to patriotism, and we remained on his side.

The modern was succeeded by the postmodern and the postmodern in turn deconstructed. In the third millennium we are firmly in the metamodern, the postfoundational. That is to say, we are aware of a variety of intellectual subcultures, which concentrate on different paradigms of thought and action, some more fissiparous, some more holistic. Within these guilds scholars find niches of the likeminded, and live happily ever after. If there is any truth in this sketch, then we shall not expect to find any single Christological argument which will be universally acceptable. But we may still legitimately hope to make a contribution to an ongoing dialogue, a contribution offered to be handled differently by different dialogue partners. This is part of the risk of the contemporary debate. I shall argue that risk and resistance is also, in a different but not totally disanalogous way, part of the Christological contribution to human rights.

Contemporary Christology in a European Context

Christology has been central to some of the most striking attempts to make any sense of talk of God in the modern world. How can we speak effectively – effectively to ourselves and to others – about God today? The enormous modern industry of systematic theology has explored numerous approaches: experiential, kerygmatic, narrative and other. As the deconstruction of the modern has been followed by the deconstruction of the postmodern, some theologians have begun to explore the postfoundational or the metamodern, seeking new combinations of epistemological and hermeneutical paradigms. Others have returned to more traditional paths, finding between the cracks in modern totalizing theories refuges from which to weather the storms of secularism, in Patristic or medieval retrieval. There are things to be learned from all these strategies. My own concern here is to try, with the aid of just a few examples, to distinguish legitimate uses of Christological language in contemporary society.

Some preliminary caveats. There will always be Christian theologians and communities which remain entirely content with the traditional language of Christology – incarnation and atonement, redemption and reconciliation, sacrifice and substitution. But there is an important constituency, especially in Northern Europe and in North America, which remains attracted to Christian faith but which finds its house of language increasingly unusable. Contrary to prevailing opinion, I regard this constituency as important for theology today. If I look to theologians who address this problematic, I find valuable suggestions in the work of David Tracy. In Tracy we find a profound apprehension both of the value of tradition – in worship, thought and action – and at the same time, a keen awareness of the need to recast our language about God in a postmodern framework in which fragments, mystery and silence are often more evocative of the God of Christian faith than the exhaustive schemata of much modern theology. It is with this perception of the plasticity and elasticity of the postmodern turn that I come back to the basis of what is, if I hear rightly, often asked for today – a non-kyriarchal but unsentimental Christology.

Among recent German Christologies, for Moltmann the key to understanding is solidarity with the oppressed, for Jüngel it is the power of the self-authenticating Word, for Dalferth it is the proclamation of resurrection. The presence of this powerful, compelling narrative of solidarity and effective victory is at the heart of all

Christology. Yet we are also called on to find reasons for the faith that is in us. It is only against the background of a cumulative rational case for talk of God as creator and reconciler that any of the kerygma makes sense. But faith is not there to make sense, we immediately recall. Yet unless there is a minimal level of rationality, to enable us to cope with life in the world of everyday reality, then faith alone will not help us. It may have done so in the past. It will do so no more.

I return to the role of an unsentimental Christology in the normal conditions of the postmodern world. In my *Generosity and the Christian Future* (1997), I explored the potentially transformative role of Christology in extreme conditions of discrimination, bigotry, gratuitous violence, namely antisemitism, racism, homophobia. Such people will always be with us, and sadly they will continue to be within as well as outside the churches. Here I want to consider the role of Christology in the working and social lives of European citizens. This may be thought too Eurocentric. Europe's interests do not always coincide with those of other continents – hence the tragic history of recent Africa. Yet Christology is a powerful reminder of the solidarity of all humanity; we are all neighbours in Christ.

European culture is dominated by commerce and industry, banking and technology. Ironically, just as we begin to see the relevance of the black Christ in solidarity with the suffering inhabitant of the southern hemisphere, we are losing any sense of the meaning of Christology for the frequent flyer, the global business traveller. In so far as such people think of Christ, many apparently subscribe to a highly individualist and characteristically Protestant perspective which sees Christ as a kind of therapy, a stress-releasing agent for the busy executive. We have to respect the *particula veri* in all such reflection. Yet the theologian will scarcely be satisfied with such a conclusion.

Because we all live simultaneously in a number of cultural worlds, for some people a particular confessional background will provide a Christological framework which the traveller will deploy in the context of the changing cultures in which he or she works. But are there common features of our contemporary commercial reality to which Christology may make a distinctive and unique contribution?

We are here, I suspect, driven back to the basic features of incarnation. Jesus came into a world which was riven like ours, with the conflicts between cultures, the dominant and the dominated. Like ours, it was strongly orientated towards the cultivation of factors of esteem, wealth and status. Jesus made choices, which led to his death.

Intercultural Christology and Human Values 141

Christians believe that in some mysterious way, to which we shall only gain access eschatologically, God the creator of the universe was uniquely involved in this life and death, and brought an effective transformation out of death, which affected God, and the created order, for ever after. Christian doctrine attempts to clothe this mystery in explanation, and is only partially successful. It is within this overall pattern of divine compassion that all life is lived, and according to which it is encouraged to move. Within this vision faith lives, and has hope. For faith, the conflicts of interest which characterize modern society are to be resolved with reference to this framework, this is the *cantus firmus*, not only of individual human life, but of the entire universe. What happens in the major religions and in all human thought and theoretical reflection is to be related to this point of reference, in order that the recollection of Christ may shed light on every aspect of the created order. But when this vision is to be imposed on society as an authoritarian template, it is entirely corrupted.

Leading observers of the religious scene in the past century have noted significant features, and have evaluated them in different ways. This must be an ongoing process. They have stressed the importance of religious experience, sometimes direct, sometimes indirect. Appeal to direct experience has the merit of intensity and urgency, and the disadvantage of a tendency to intolerance of those who do not share that intensity. Indirect experience is more accommodating of pluralist interpretation, but may fade into vagueness. Appeals to the Word, to narrative, to rationality, have their own pluses and minuses. Alasdair MacIntyre's Benedictine oases of spirituality may light up the world around them, and nurture faith. But they may not communicate beyond the magic circle. MacIntyre recognized this in looking for commonly agreed virtues. But these may not be imposed by the elect communities on the unelect. They need to be negotiated in a context of mutuality. Theology on the edge of these centres may be more open to dialogue and more humble. But it may also lose the central dimension of grace and descend into an intolerant moralism.

Where in the overlapping subcultures of modern society may we expect to find a response to *Christus transformator*? Christians believe that the cosmic Christ is present in all human life. This presence is a hidden presence, not always easily articulated and acknowledged. The worship of the Church will always remain a focus of recollection and recognition of the divine presence. As traditional structures break down, worship becomes an increasingly unfamiliar experience to most Europeans. But as long as it continues, in an open structure as an invitation to the divine hospitality, it provides a vital fragment in the cluster of Christian meaning.

From communities of worship, and sometimes without formal worship, there emerge communities of Christian service. Some are explicitly church-related, like Christian Aid. Others are largely operated by people with Christian beliefs, in Oxfam, Médecins Sans Frontières and so on. Yet others contribute Christian perspectives to ethical and political decision-making in economic, scientific and business enterprises. In this way, different fragments may function at different levels in complex cultures, overlapping and reinforcing each other in often random ways. Such a vision of the pervasive power of fragments of Christian engagement may be utopian. But it does indicate ways in which a non-hegemonic understanding of the influence of Christ in our culture may be developed and acted upon. None of these elements is infallible or free from the possibility of error. Bernstein has spoken of an engaged fallibilistic pluralism in philosophy. We may perhaps see the above sketch as a social application of this model in action. The power which is made effective in this understanding of church is dependent on constancy of commitment rather than organizational hegemony within a given culture.

There are likely to be at least two other factors supportive of Christian goals in such a social context. Even in the most authoritarian or misguided Christian culture there are likely to be exceptions to the rule, and authentic faith and practice keep breaking through. Christians also believe that non-Christians too will have important contributions to make to the discernment of God's will for his creation. Hence they will expect to learn from the otherness of other perspectives, and to share in the human dialogue of values which they believe God wishes to encourage in the direction of his purpose for human fulfilment. In the nature of the case, neither complacency nor panic is appropriate to the contemporary social reality. The grace of God remains prevenient within the created order.

Between the major tyrannies of Culture and the minor tyrannies of culture, often identical in fractal pattern, Christology offers the events concerning Jesus Christ, with their antecedents and consequences, as decisive for the flourishing of human society as its creator intends. The significance of Christ has been expressed through various forms of cultural expression. At different times some of these expressions have been deemed more consonant with faith than others, often with notoriously disastrous results. It would be good to be able to escape into a supracultural domain, where none of this messy experimentation need occur. But none of the suggested escape routes appears to survive an application of hermeneutical suspicion. This suggestion is itself culturally determined. But we cannot say it is entirely culturally determined, without abandoning any sense of rationality.

Christology is committed to the political and the economic. It is concerned with the welfare of real people within actual societies. It may remind culture of its links with natural and social constraints. A culture which floats above the exigencies of everyday living is no more useful for human flourishing than an abstract theology. There may then be an ongoing mutual critique between Christology and culture.

The Critique between Christology and Culture

Christology is committed to the particular. It is also committed to the welfare of all humanity as God's people. It can relinquish neither the subcultures which make up our diverse societies nor the global dimension which is concerned for the welfare of all persons, not only as cosmopolitan consumers but as persons whose dignity is to be fostered. God's concern is for the sinners as well as the saints.

This unconditional compassion may be highlighted effectively in twenty-first-century terms in relation to issues of human rights. This is a complex and much disputed area, in which those who attack human rights have been singularly adept at first criticizing the concept and then pleading it for their own programmes. Human-rights advocacy has not been immune from mistakes. It has caused loss and harm to those who have participated in it. It has generated an effective backlash which has sometimes made oppressive situations worse than they were. But Christian faith, focused on the *eikon* of God in Jesus Christ, will not be unfamiliar with such situations. Faith is not always convenient nor apparently effective. It is in large measure a matter of hope. At the transition of a century in which one hundred million people were killed by their fellow human beings, faith keeps faith with the dead as well as the living, the crushed as well as the successful.

It is all too easy for us to scorn the relation of Christology to the *Kulturprotestantismus* of the nineteenth century. In seeking to relate Christ to the highest cultural values, it attributed finality to its own perceptions and social conventions. It was incorrigibly elitist, and it came to grief in the mutual near-suicide of the European nations in 1914. Yet in finding scapegoats for Christian mistakes, we must be careful not to immunize ourselves against learning. What we Europeans saw as the ultimate sin of 1914 was no worse in principle than the effect on large parts of the world of the myriad mini-wars of commercial rivalry in the preceding colonial period. Our exclusive theologies of revelation might themselves become microcosms of *Kulturprotestantismus* in their ecclesial self-satisfaction. There is a continuing need to relate theology to culture, and there is no highway to an infallible relationship. It is by assessing the similarities as well as the differences in succeeding attempts at dialogue that ways forward may be found.

Christology in Christian faith is not an isolated area. Jesus Christ is significant because of his constitutive relationship to God the creator of the cosmos and to the Spirit of kenotic love throughout human history. The work of the Spirit is grounded in the events concerning Jesus, but does not reproduce these slavishly. Christians understand the Spirit to be active in the Church and in society, in ways which are often hidden and unexpected. This too is a ground of hope, and a challenge not to confine the concerns of faith within the boundaries of the Church. Christology leads through the Spirit to all the human and natural sciences, and also to world religions. There need be no basic incompatibility between theology and religious studies. There will be dialogue and debate.

I am going to choose here for illustration of the task of transcultural theology an example from the field of Christology. In the Christian understanding of God, Jesus Christ is obviously at the centre. Christ is the justification for talk of the vulnerability of God, the identification with otherness, and also, through the link between the Christ stories and the Genesis stories in the biblical narratives and the tradition, for talk of the unity of all humanity. Yet Christianity, precisely in the context of an emphasis on Christ, has often been notoriously dominating, hegemonic, intolerant and exclusive. The Genesis narratives have been used to discriminate against blacks, women and other groups. The language of servanthood often has an immunizing effect on the 'servants'. Of course, the abuse does not take away the proper use, and no supermodel of Christology can be free of the possibility of corruption. But it should be possible to find more and less legitimate means of expression. Let us see how this might be approached.

The Christian understanding of Christ has been built up as a cumulative tradition in innumerable ways. The Gospel narratives, themselves the product of a long cultural history, reflect at different levels the life of a man whose purposes seem most probably to have been directly connected with a commitment to the poor and the marginalized in society, not simply as a social class but as particular

Intercultural Christology and Human Values

individuals. His commitment leads to some sort of public conflict, death by crucifixion, and what his followers were to understand as resurrection. Belief in God, in the Hebrew tradition, is transformed into belief in God through Jesus Christ. God is gradually then understood as the God who is essentially in relationship, in commitment in incarnation, cross and resurrection.

The Gospel narratives speak about faith, and about God as the source of love, peace and justice. Christians have come to faith in God as the personal instantiation of these values. My own preference is for the construal of these central characteristics of the God of Jesus Christ in the models of vulnerability and generosity. Vulnerability and generosity characterize the life of Jesus and are now understood as central to the life of God. From a Christian perspective, the story of Israel, historically hugely complex, is seen theologically as the involvement of a God who is, was and will be a God in all respects both vulnerable and generous.

The Christian Model of God as Vulnerable and Generous

Vulnerability and generosity are not exclusive attributes of a Christian understanding of God. They are certainly not incapable of distortion and abuse. They are not necessarily the most appropriate or the most significant factor in every human situation. But they are intrinsic to the distinctively Christian contribution to dialogue about ultimate value, meaning and truth.

Vulnerability and generosity may be construed in different ways in different contexts. They may be translated practically into hospitality. There will be debate and disagreement about what they mean in different cultures. Other Christians, other religions and other perspectives may wish to advocate different models for the basic understanding of God and of God's purpose for his creation. But in my proposal divine vulnerability and generosity remain central to the Christian contribution to culture at all levels.

Vulnerability and generosity are for theology always open concepts. They are always the vulnerability and generosity of grace. That is to say, they are understood as pointers to the nature of divine action as the source of all that is. God is neither being nor non-being: God is hospitable, vulnerable generosity in Godself.

It may be thought that a moment's glance at either the impersonal cruelties of nature or the highly personal cruelties of history reveal such assertions as nonsense. Yet that is the specificity of the Christian contribution, that there is in the way things are a God who instantiates, invites, and purposes an order of vulnerability and generosity. This divine economy is not a command economy by definition. It operates through spontaneous recognition in human history that this is the nature of the good. It is not always successful, but it is always available.

It must, of course, be acknowledged that the biblical narratives and the Christian tradition have been and can be construed in many different ways. My suggestion is that the direction which is indicated in terms of vulnerability, generosity and hospitality may be legitimately considered to be compatible with the tradition, and is particularly apposite to the particular task which faces the Christian contribution in the contemporary world. I also think that such an emphasis could have been more helpful in the past and may always be in the future.

Vulnerability and generosity are particularly apposite to the dilemmas of concepts of liberty. A 'negative' liberty which is vulnerable and generous will seek to relate its individual freedom to freedom along with others in relationship. It will not regard freedom in isolation as true freedom. A positive liberty which seeks positive emancipation will not seek this at the expense of others, who would then be marginalized. It would seek emancipation which creates mutual enrichment.

Vulnerability, generosity and hospitality are not permanent attributes which can be assumed. They are always capable of subversion and have to be deconstructed, retrieved, transformed. Otherwise, like all concepts, they can have the opposite effect from that originally intended. But they are core concepts which arise out of the centre of the Christian gospel. They are potentially major contributors to any transcultural Christian theology in the future.

The themes of vulnerability and hospitality occur typically in modern and especially in emancipatory theologies. I come in the final section of this essay to their application to the traditional agendas of classical Christology. God for Christian faith is the maker of heaven and earth. God is the ground of all that is; God is also love and goodness. God is absolutely loving and absolutely good. It is a commonplace to say that contemporary theology is more concerned with the ethical than with the ontological. But of course there need be no immutable gulf fixed between fact and value, between the ethical and the metaphysical, the cognitive and the aesthetic. This too is implicit in the classical metaphorology of the wondrous exchange. God is

Intercultural Christology and Human Values 147

involved in suffering and in joy, in the struggle of ethical ambiguity in the centre of incarnation, both in his divine and in his human nature.

I should like to illustrate the importance of an emancipatory approach with reference to the relevance of some aspects of Black Theology in Britain today. Readers familiar with the American development of Black Theology, with its transition from a civil rights-based call for integration to a militant assertion of black power, may be somewhat surprised by the prevailing patterns of Black Theology in Britain. Black Christians in Britain were for a long time practically invisible, and in many areas remain so because they are very few in number, for example in Scotland. But from the 1950s there was a significant influx of black Christians into Britain from the West Indies and especially Jamaica. Their development has been well documented in Roswith Gerloff's two-volume *A Plea for British Black Theologies*. The development of this community was shaped by the experience of exclusion from existing local churches, and by the need to affirm continuity with their heritage in the Caribbean. Roswith Gerloff sees comments by Eric Lincoln on the US situation as an accurate description also of the British scene from 1952 to 1976 at least.

White Western theology has contributed significantly to the involuntary invisibility of black people – to black oblivion. In sum, 'white theology is an entrapment which leaves the black Christian without hope, without recourse and without identity, and leaves White Christians with unrealistic views about themselves' (Gerloff, 1992:1.45). The problem is not persecution but neglect. Gerloff quotes some fairly well-known lines read at an Apostolic Church service in Watford, England (1992:1.75):

When Jesus came to Watford/ They simply passed him by
   They never hurt a hair on him/ They simply let him die
For men had grown more tender/ and would not cause him pain
   They simply shut the door on him/ And left him in the rain.

Despite the long tradition from Augustine to Gadamer, there remains no communication.

This sense of alienation led to the development of independent churches in the charismatic/apostolic tradition, with a great emphasis on holiness and personal piety, notably the Pentecostal Oneness Church, representing Apostolic Pentecostalism. A strong sense of community was reaffirmed in the sphere of charismatic worship. More recently, there has been a greater awareness of the social and political dimensions of the gospel, coupled with a radical stress on issues of justice and poverty. Paul Grant has said this of traditional Christology:

> What is the point of a personal relationship with someone who apparently does not want to understand how and why you live as you do? It is pointless to be freed from 'sin', only to be enslaved by a Saviour who does not live in the backstreets, does not know what it feels like not to have enough cash or can only condemn or patronize those who defend themselves against the incursions of the police and racist attacks. Give me Someone who I can trust.[1]

It might be thought that in this respect the British churches are far behind their American counterparts, in which pietistic community was transformed into black power in the seventies. Yet that would be an inappropriate stereotyping. The reaffirmation of traditional Caribbean worship may itself be an effective means of coping with marginalization, while the 'black power' approach to issues of justice has not always led to progress, and may often have to be supplemented by more assimilative approaches in order to achieve long-term goals. A simple division into 'black' and 'white' theology may well suppress the variety and argument which is intrinsic to a process of engagement with the task of searching for common human goals.

In a new preface to his book *Black Theology and Black Power*,[2] James Cone noted too a curious omission. There was no mention of the widespread oppression of women in black churches: 'Amnesia is an enemy of justice. We must never forget what we once were lest we repeat our evil deeds in new forms. I do not want to forget that I was once silent about the oppression of women in the church and in society. Silence gives support to the powers that be' (p. xi).

Here is another example of the complexity of cultures, in which even apparently radical stances can mask structures of injustice. Eloquent testimony has since been given about the 'triple jeopardy' of those who are women, black, and poor, by Dolores Williams, Jacqueline Grant and others. We might also reflect further on the hermeneutics of the phrase 'amnesia is an enemy of justice'. Contemporary churches are much concerned to present a caring,

---

[1] Paul Grant, 'If it happened to you, tell me, what would you do?' in Paul Grant and Raj Patel (eds), *A Time to Speak: Perspectives of Black Christians in Britain*, 1990:56.
[2] First published in 1969.

Intercultural Christology and Human Values 149

compassionate face to the world. It is important that there should not be a huge gap between public political correctness and private resentments, and that the lasting damage caused by the damning rhetoric of the recent past should be acknowledged.

The whole issue of the role and status of women in theological perspective is another striking case in which awareness of multicultural complexity is vital. Advocates for feminist and womanist thought, and heterosexual and homosexual women's groups, have opened up whole areas in which traditional theology has been silent, usually with an oppressive silence. Alison Webster, in her study *Found Wanting*,[3] has highlighted the ambiguities of notions of the complementarity of men and women, especially in the case of lesbian Christian women for whom the other is also in a sense the same. She argues that 'the logic of imposed complementarity is imposed heterosexuality', and that this applies particularly to common exegesis of the *imago Dei* in terms of the complementarity between man and woman. She quotes from an interviewee, 'Jackie': 'Women in general are seen as dangerous temptresses, with single women being the greater danger since there is no man to control them' (1995:65).

In the lives of Webster's subjects a traditional theological understanding of the role of women will not do: 'With one and the same breath the church invites me – and all others – to journey in discipleship with all its risks and uncertainties – and then warns me that in no way can it partner me on that journey except in safe and restricted terms' (1995:134). It will not do either to class male and female same-sex relations together. 'Lesbians have historically been deprived of a political existence through inclusion: as female versions of male homosexuality' (1995:150). She concludes that 'Mainstream Christianity is in danger of making an idol of heterosexuality', and has excluded many people's experiences, particularly that of women. We need a new sexual ethics which is astute about power and committed to provisionality (1995:195).

Perhaps most commonly, occasions of vulnerability are tied in our contemporary world to poverty.

There is a light that never goes out. They emerge from the stairway into the darkness of the street. Some of them move in a jerky, manic way; noisy and exuberant. Others cruise along silently, like ghosts, hurting inside, yet fearful of the imminence of even greater pain and

---

3 *Found Wanting: Women, Christianity and Sexuality*, 1995.

discomfort. Their destination is a pub which seems to prop up a crumbling tenement set on a side-street between Easter Road and Leith Walk. This street has missed out on the stone-cleaning process its neighbours have enjoyed and the building is the sooty-stone colour of a forty-a-day man's lungs. The night is so dark that it is difficult to establish the outline of the tenement against the sky. It can only be defined through an isolated light glaring from a top floor window or the luminous street-lamp jutting from its side.

'Come hame wi us for a while Danny. Nae drugs or anything. Ah dinnae want tae be ooan ma ain now, Danny. Ken whit ah'm sayin'. Alison looks at him tensely, tearfully, as they lurch along the street. Spud nods, he thinks he knows what she is saying, because he doesn't want to be alone either. He never can be quite sure, though, never ever quite sure. (*Trainspotting*)[4]

In focusing on vulnerability, I have implied kenosis. It may be argued that complete kenosis signals the end of the subject as such, and with this the end of dialogue and of communication. There may be occasions in human life where there is sheer catastrophe, and where then fragments of communication appear only after meltdown. Apocalypse may be a vital reminder of the reality of disaster as such. But faith still hopes for a moment of transcendence and therefore of the possibility of communication and of dialogue, as part of the dynamic of resurrection. The Christian story does not stop with complete disaster, though it enters this experience fully. We may look for a constructive tension between logocentric triumphalism and romantic preoccupation with catastrophe.

Conclusion

Here is the importance of the dimension of mystery of Christology. We may well be suspicious of the notion of mystery, as being merely a polite term for agnosticism. In response we can then easily revert to a positivism which continues a process of 'building high towers which shall not reach to heaven'. But mystery is not always negative or empty. It can also signal participation in constructive relationship at a profound level, in which otherness is respected on all sides, and in which identity is not absorption. For Christian faith, God is construed

---

[4] Irvine Welsh, *Trainspotting*, 1993:262, 272.

Intercultural Christology and Human Values 151

as the ground of the kenotic love in which we participate through Jesus Christ. Here the forms of kenosis which the modern emancipatory theologies mediate to us, the kenosis of the crucified peoples of the earth, may help us to imagine the political, economic and social implications of the divine kenosis.

We should not imagine, however, that the end of the twentieth century has given us *the* definitive Christological model for the Christian future. The crucified peoples have sometimes been sadly blind to their own prejudices. Black male Christians have been notably blind to feminist concerns, African churches have often been insensitive to gay Christians, Asian Christians have not always been conscious of the special problems of black Christians. Antisemitism is no respecter of colour. Some of these problems go back to the colonial legacies of an earlier time. But others are new. Here the whole Christian tradition within its complex and ever-changing cultural contexts, in its continuities and its irruptions, becomes a necessary framework for the understanding of Christology.

The emergence of ever-new forms of discrimination amid communities who have themselves just escaped discrimination is a reminder, if such were necessary, of the fragile nature of our hard-won efforts to achieve common standards of compassion and social justice. Though individuals may feel increasingly self-sufficient, we are still notoriously unable to provide our own social salvation. This does not come as a great surprise to a Christian tradition which is fundamentally committed to human rights but looks beyond these to a transcendent horizon, not as an instrument of social change but simply because in the experience of faith it is there. This dimension has been memorably recalled recently by Charles Taylor in his evocation of catholic modernity.[5]

For Taylor, redemption happens through incarnation, the weaving of God's life into human lives, but these human lives are different . . . Complementarity and identity will both be part of our ultimate oneness. Our great historical temptation has been to forget the complementarity, to go straight for the sameness, making as many people as possible into 'good Catholics' – and in the process failing of catholicity. He tries to look at the Enlightenment as Matteo Ricci looked at Chinese civilization in the sixteenth century. 'The view I'd like to defend, if I can put it in a nutshell, is that in modern, secularist culture there are mingled both authentic developments of the Gospel,

---

5 See Charles Taylor: *A Catholic Modernity?*, 1999.

of an incarnational mode of life, and also a closing off to God that negates the Gospel' (1999:16).

'The Christian conscience experiences a mixture of humility and unease: the humility in realising that the break with Christendom was necessary for this great extension of Gospel-inspired actions; the unease in the sense that the denial of transcendence places this action under threat' (1999:26). There is a revolt against the modern affirmation of life in Nietzsche. This is a turn to violence, which may perhaps only be escaped by a turn to transcendence. We make very high demands for universal solidarity today, but how do we manage it? Self-worth has limitations. Philanthropy may turn to coercion, unless there is unconditional love of the beneficiaries (1999:33). Christian spirituality points in faith to a way out 'either as a love or compassion that is unconditional – or as one based on what you are most profoundly – a being in the image of God'. 'Our being in the image of God is also our standing among others in the stream of love, which is that facet of God's life we try to grasp, very inadequately, in speaking of the Trinity' (1999:35).

It is as we see Christological models emerging from and influenced by different national, political and economic groups that we may appreciate the confident fallibilism which has characterized much classical theology. Of course, we shall never articulate God's own perspective, short of the eschaton. But we may hope by a process of argument, commitment and participation to continue to respond faithfully to the Christ-event. Chastened by the knowledge of the capacity of classical models for domination which emancipatory Christology has brought us, we may hope to benefit again from the whole spectrum of the tradition. God in majesty is also the God who suffers in solidarity. Marilyn McCord Adams has written perceptively of a God who responds to evil in suffering in both natures. 'Divine and human natures in Christ thus make complementary contributions to God's solidarity with creative suffering, with human participation in horrors here below.'[6] The twentieth century, which in one sense made it impossible to speak of God, has in another way opened up the human significance of Christ with startling clarity.

> God has made himself publicly known, more or less everywhere, by this stage of the twentieth century, in the person of a publicly executed victim. The revelation of the forgiving victim is publicly

---

6 *Horrendous Evils and the Goodness of God*, 1999:174.

available more or less everywhere on the face of the planet, and faith comes by this revelation being preached by those for whom it has become something to which they can give witness. (James Alison, *Knowing Jesus*, 1993:105)

Simul justus et peccator. It is the glory of the Christian tradition that it is able to make a unique and life-saving contribution to the whole human future through witness to the political reality of the divine love in society. It is the malaise of the tradition that it documents frequent betrayal of its own foundation, not least when it is at its most pious. Grace is the gift of facing at least occasionally in the right direction.

Christology develops by reinventing itself, making new connections from Christian thought and practice in different eras, breaking up established associations and finding unexpected links in response to contemporary needs. In this ongoing process, Brian Hebblethwaite's Christological studies over the last decades have provided us with remarkable encouragement in a sane direction.

10. Incarnation and Double Agency

EDWARD H. HENDERSON

Introduction

Critics of the high Christology of Christian orthodoxy, as expressed in the Nicene Creed and the Chalcedonian definition, have argued in various ways that incarnational Christology is incoherent and that it leads, anyway, ineluctably to docetism, according to which Jesus only appears to be but is not truly human. Never mind that the Chalcedonian definition explicitly states that Jesus is truly human, thereby explicitly denying docetism. For, say the critics, affirming that Jesus is truly God, which the definition also does, cannot but overwhelm and defeat the affirmation of his humanity. To be both fully God and fully human is to be a metaphysically unique kind of being, one which cannot fit into the natural human world. The God-Man, say the critics, would have to be a supernatural person in whom God miraculously, unilaterally, and coercively cancels the humanity. Inasmuch as Jesus' divinity means that he cannot but know as God knows and do as God wills, his humanity is a sham; the finitude that goes with human nature and the freedom that must struggle with real choices are undone. If Jesus is the incarnation of the eternal Son of God, then Jesus cannot rationally be thought to be truly human. But, continue most critics, it is the humanity we can most reasonably believe; therefore, we must deny the divinity.

I want to join Brian Hebblethwaite in arguing against this line, and I shall do so by bringing Austin Farrer's ideas about double agency to bear on Farrer's Christological comments for I believe the idea of double agency enables us to think a non-docetic incarnation in which both humanity and divinity are maintained.[1]

---

[1] Brian Hebblethwaite has written on both these strains of Farrer's thought, and I am indebted to him on both counts. See especially, 'Austin Farrer's Concept of Divine Providence', *Theology* 73, 1970:541–51; 'Finite and Infinite Freedom in Farrer and von Balthasar', *CTNS Bulletin* 12(1), Winter 1992:10–16; *The*

Double Agency

The idea of double agency is the idea of two agents for one action. Common examples of two creaturely agents for the same action would be, say, an official acting by delegated authority, a parent teaching a child to ride a bicycle, or a student writing a dissertation under the direction of a mentor. In all these cases there is one recognizable action enacted by (at least) two distinct agents. And in all these cases the freedom and independence of one agent is not cancelled by the other. Such creature cases, however, cannot be isomorphic with God's action in the actions of creatures. For God is not a creature, and God's action in the actions of creatures is not the action of one creature in another. In the case of creaturely actions, we can distinguish the two agents clearly and can specify which part of the larger action is done by one and which part by the other. In the case of God's actions in creatures it is impossible to locate the join and impossible to describe how God's action takes effect in creatures' actions. On the other hand, believers will surely say that they can reasonably believe that certain effects in the world of creatures, even their own actions, are at the same time effects of God. Indeed, St Paul said it of the whole life of faith: 'Nevertheless, not I but Christ who lives in me.' Consequently, believers may say that they experience the action of God in the actions of their own lives and that the experience is not the experience of being diminished as persons, of losing their freedom, or of ceasing to be finite human beings, but rather of being enhanced and fulfilled as the very human persons they are. There is no wonder that we cannot explain how God does it, for we have no access to God's action apart from its taking effect in creatures' actions. However, we can say that there is no contradiction involved in saying that God acts in us, for (a) the relation is unique and (b) there are analogues in the actions of creatures with creatures.

Are we appealing to ignorance, saying that because the how of God's acting in creatures cannot be known, we might as well just say whatever we want to say, in this case that it is non-coercive? No, and it is because of experience. Farrer makes use of an idea from process thought to speak of this experience. He likens the action of God in

---

Incarnation: Collected Essays in Christology, 1987; 'Providence and Divine Action', *Religious Studies* 14, 1978:223–36. We also worked together on a conference and a collection of essays on divine action, including an introduction, which included discussion of double agency: *Divine Action: Studies Inspired by the Philosophical Theology of Austin Farrer*, 1990.

creatures to the non-coercive *persuasion* of one creature by another, and uses the persuasion metaphor to carry forward the idea of non-coercive divine agency. The how of God's action in creatures may be hidden, but the experience we have of persuasion as a mode of non-coercive action among creatures assures us that non-coercive causation is not a contradictory idea and that we can think of God's agency as operating like persuasion. Persuasion is a form of active relation between entities that demonstrates the intelligibility of non-coercive causation. If all causation reduced ultimately and completely to coercive transient causation or external efficient causation, then it would be harder to escape coercive determinism among creatures within the world and between God and the world. But our *experience* is that not all relations of influence are coercive. In the persuading that we do and that we undergo there is an influence that preserves freedom and independence. Consequently, there is empirical justification for speaking of non-coercive causation.

Farrer gladly learned this point from Whitehead, agreeing that the process idea of persuasion is helpful but taking it as an image, not as an explanation.[2] He does not think the experience of persuasion gives us the universal form of all non-coercive operation, such that when we understand how human persuasion works we will also understand *how* God's action takes effect in the operations of creatures, or such that we can take God's action in relation to creatures simply as a species of persuasion. But even if all forms of non-coercive relationships could be seen as forms of persuasion, it would remain true that we do not have the experience of God's activity of persuading in the same way that we have the experience of ourselves and other persons persuading. Because one of the effects traditional theists attribute to God is the very existence of any world at all, and because this is an effect that cannot be in a class with intra-mundane effects, we say that God's non-coercive action is not the same as intra-mundane persuasion (or as any other cases of double agency among creatures). We cannot observe how God makes a divine action take effect in creatures' actions, but we can say that we can reasonably think of God as acting non-coercively in creating and redeeming the world and of doing it by acting in and through the actions of creatures, by acting in a way that resembles but is not the same as the persuasion of one creature by another. Now let us bring the notion of double agency to bear on the doctrine of incarnation.

---

2 Austin Farrer, *Saving Belief*, 1964:72–3.

Incarnation

It is clear that Farrer uses the terms of double agency to think about the Incarnation:

> Wherever the eye of faith looks in the created world it perceives two levels of action. There is the creature making itself, and there is God making it make itself. Jesus is not unique in the mere fact that the personal life or act of God underlies his action; for nothing would either be or act if God did not thus underlie it . . . (1964:75)

Taking incarnation as double agency answers the charges of incoherence and unilateral coercion. It means that God's action in Jesus is not so completely different from God's actions in you or me that we must say the two have no common ground. To put it positively, God's action in being incarnate in Jesus is coherent with God's action in you or me: both are by double agency. The Incarnation is not an incoherent surd. Furthermore, inasmuch as we have experience of non-coercive causation among creatures, we need not regard incarnation as a unilateral coercion of the man, Jesus, so that Jesus in fact has no integrity, freedom, or reality as a man.

Nevertheless, it is not an adequate response to objections to the orthodox idea of incarnation only to appeal to our experience of non-coercive relations among creatures and to use the language of double agency. We must also recognize the *difference* between God's action in Jesus of Nazareth and God's action in you and me. If we cannot speak of the difference, we shall be asserting a great-man Christology, reducing Christ's difference from other persons to the degree of his openness to inspiration by the Spirit, thereby denying incarnation.

Returning to the previous quotation, we see that Farrer does speak of the difference - in two ways. The first is by imagining a scale of double agency; the second is by distinguishing the different intentions of God, the different content or substance of God's actions. Let us look at each in turn.

The Scale of Double Agency

In *Saving Belief*, Farrer extends the idea of a scale of operations, which was important in *Finite and Infinite*, to the idea of double agency. God's action underlies everything that is, 'But the underlying is not everywhere the same or (let us rather say) the relation between the underlying act of God and the created energy overlaid upon it, is not everywhere the same relation' (1964:75).

Different kinds of worldly operation are placed at different points on the scale according to the degree of closeness and mutual interpenetration we see God's action to have in them. Farrer distinguishes three among an indefinite number of points on the scale: mere physical forces, rational creatures, and the person of Jesus Christ. There is, of course, an overlapping in that Christ is a rational creature (and rational creatures embody physical forces). By locating Christ at the apex of the scale, we use the idea of double agency to bring him and God's relation to him into intelligible relation with other creatures and God's relations to them. But we do so in a way that recognizes the difference between Christ and every other being on the scale. In Jesus, we say that God's action and the man's action are perfectly united. What Jesus does is what God does in Jesus. What God does in Jesus is what Jesus does. In our own case we know our actions to be by varying degrees at odds with God's will; nevertheless, we can speak of God's acting *within* us in so far as we grasp divine purpose and cooperate with it. In physical forces, God's action is more like that of an external cause. Consequently, while seeing God's action in others as *like* God's action in Jesus, we at the same time distinguish them and say that in Jesus a perfect unity of God and man is realized.

If we assert so thorough a union of God's action with Jesus' action, however, critics would typically say that we thereby imply that Jesus is not truly a human person like us, that his humanity is supernaturally possessed, coerced, cancelled. But if we use the scale of double agency, we need not think so. The possible interpenetration of God's action with the action of creatures increases as we move up the scale from merely physical forces to rational creatures. The greater the interpenetration of divine and creaturely agency, *the greater the freedom and individual integrity*. The more God's actions enter into ours the more free we are and the more we are ourselves.

This is not a bare assertion. It conforms to the experience expressed in that rich and familiar phrase from the ancient prayer: 'whose service is perfect freedom'.[3] For the practitioner of faith finds it to be the most apt description of experience to say that when one acts freely, intentionally, thoughtfully, deliberately to do the Lord's will, it is true both that God is more fully and actively present and that one is at the same time more truly free and more truly oneself than in those times of

---

[3] 'A collect for peace', *The Book of Common Prayer*, 1979:57.

Incarnation and Double Agency 159

forgetting God's will and pressing one's presumed independence. Farrer eloquently expressed the philosophical point in *A Science of God*? Where in the world, he asks, does the personal nature of God obtain expression in the world? Thinking in terms of the scale of double agency, he answers: 'If the highest, most voluntary part of human behaviour is not the act of God, then nowhere in the universe do we directly meet the divine love' (1966:100).

Further, in *Saving Belief* he says that 'God cannot inspire me, by removing me, by pushing me off the saddle and riding in my place. No, *the more I am inspired, the more I am myself: the will God makes me make is my truest and freest creation*' (1964:78, emphasis added). We are talking now about persons other than Jesus and the way in which, according to the apt description of their experience in the adventure of co-operating with grace, they see others and perhaps find themselves most truly themselves and most truly free when they are most obedient to God and God is most active in them. If we see Jesus to be at the topmost point on the scale, then we must surely say that when God acts so completely in Jesus' actions that whatever Jesus does is what God does, Jesus is supremely free and supremely himself. Neither his real humanity nor his particular personal identity are coerced and cancelled by divine action. They are set free and fulfilled: 'And so, without pretending to see the mystery of his being from the inside, we must believe that Jesus is both more human and more fully himself than any man' (1964:79).

Perhaps this interpretation could be translated out of the scheme of the scale of double agency into the process language of persuasion. Farrer certainly applies the language of persuasion to thought about how God non-coercively acts in relation to rational creatures. In that respect, Farrer and the process tradition are not radically at odds. David Griffin, for example, sees Jesus as a man who was, if not to a unique degree at least to an extraordinary degree, sensitive and responsive to the felt and persuasive divine aim. Such sensitivity and responsiveness means for him also greater freedom and fulfilment of personal identity.

If, however, being extraordinarily sensitive and responsive to the divine aim were the most we could mean by 'incarnation', we would have reduced it to the 'great man' idea of Jesus, to the idea that Jesus was simply a man with a peculiar openness to divine inspiration, and we would have emptied out the orthodox belief that Jesus is the incarnation of the eternal Son of God. But we are arguing that the idea of double agency can express the orthodox and stronger view, the view that requires us to talk about the life of God-in-God so as to affirm the identity of Jesus with the eternal Son. We can do this by distinguishing what it is that God does in Jesus from what God does in other persons.

What God Does in the Action of Jesus

God's action in Jesus differs from God's action in us not only by being at the top of a scale, but by being numerically and substantially different from God's action in other faithful persons – in St Peter, say, or in a 'model village carpenter'. Therefore, God's action in Jesus, though it is a case of double agency, enacts a different relation between God and Jesus than God's action in others enacts between God and them. Let me quote and then comment on Farrer's words to develop this point:

> It is not merely that the life of Jesus, being flawlessly good, shows no divergence from the divine will willed concerning it. Were that all, Jesus might have fulfilled his function by remaining a model village carpenter all his days, and dying a natural death at a ripe age. It is that the very action of Jesus is divine action – it is what God does about the salvation of the world. In the common case of a good human life, humanity supplies the pattern and God the grace. In Jesus, divine redemptive action supplies the pattern, and manhood the medium or instrument. A good man helped by Grace may do human things divinely; Christ did divine things humanly. (1964:74–5)

I take the main point of these difficult words to be that the action God does in Jesus is a different action, that it has a different intention and content, from God's action in others.

What God does in the life, crucifixion, and resurrection of Jesus Christ is a particular action. That it is so is unremarkable. All actions are particular and are distinguishable by their content and circumstances. Surely we can speak of God's having different intentions for and doing different things in different people at different times, places, and circumstances. Even if other persons succeeded in being perfectly attuned to the divine intention for them, and even if they were wholly successful in carrying them out, what God intends and what the action of God would thereby accomplish in their actions would be different from the intention God accomplishes in Christ's actions.

Incarnation and Double Agency

God acts in Moses to deliver the Children of Israel from bondage in ancient Egypt and form a covenant with them under the terms of the Decalogue. God acts in Deutero-Isaiah to bring about a new understanding of the Covenant. God acts in Abraham Lincoln to end the legal existence of slavery in the United States. God acts in Martin Luther King, Jr, to eliminate the Jim Crow laws that unconstitutionally continued slavery. And, to take a more ordinary case, God acts in the village carpenter who lives to be a good provider for his family, to make good cabinets for customers who need them, to be a good citizen in the political and economic circumstances in which he lives, and to do all these things through dependence upon divine grace, loving and worshipping the God on whom he depends.

In all these cases the intentions and the actions of the persons performing them have their various roles and scopes. There may be a sense in which, so far as they are all instances in which God makes the creatures make themselves, they belong to one single and all-inclusive perfect act of love whereby God creates, redeems, and sanctifies. For God's actions are one action in that all are pursuant to the eternal divine intention that defines the nature or character of God. Yet God's actions are many in that God has created and is engaged with a multiplicity of distinct entities, some of which are free and all of which comprise a world whose exact course is open and unpredictable. What is peculiar about God's action in Jesus is that in Jesus, God fulfils the universal and eternal intention of divine love to redeem the world.

God's actions in other creatures are not unrelated to this intention, for the same intention of love is fundamentally at work throughout God's creating and relating to the world. Some lives and events, those running from Abraham through Moses, the Exodus, and the prophets, for example, may have a clearer relation to divine redemption than others, though even in this sacred history we see mixtures of motives, confusions of purpose, and failures of faith. In them, God's action appears to us 'as a persuasion of our mixed and foolish aims' (1964:73) toward an end not clearly seen or unconditionally seized. We see these same mixtures, confusion, and failures in the lives of those who lived in contact with Jesus in his time and place – in his followers, the crowds, the established religious people, the officials of government. And we see them also in ourselves and in the lives of all who came after him, both inside and outside the scope of Christendom. But in the ministry, crucifixion, and resurrection of Jesus of Nazareth 'the natural medium – that is to say, the human story – loses all its opaqueness; the life of Christ no more stands between our perception and the action of God, than the lenses of a telescope stand between us and the star on which it focuses' (1964:74). Seeing the difference we judge its meaning: 'the life and person of Jesus is achievement as perfectly divine as it is perfectly human' (1964:73); 'the very action of Jesus is divine action – it is what God does about the salvation of the world' (1964:75).

Conclusion

Orthodox Christianity specifies the particular action of God in Jesus yet more fully by saying that Jesus is the incarnate Son of God because Jesus' life is seen to be the expression within the conditions of human existence of the active love that God is. That is, what we see in Jesus is not divine substance put together with human substance as though two incompatible metaphysical kinds of stuff were emulsified into one person, but the living out in human terms and before our eyes of a perfect and continuous act of love received and love returned. Jesus' life, death, and resurrection are not imperfect images or hints at divine love; they are its clear and present reality. They are love so received that it makes Jesus all that he is and love so returned that it shows Jesus' love to be all that the giver gives and is. What we see in Jesus is identical with the love that constitutes the very life of God-in-God. Jesus is not 'simply the God-who-was-man',[4] but the expression in a particular man of the very relationship of love that is God. Farrer expresses the point thus:

> God cannot live an identically godlike life in eternity and in a human story. But the divine Son can make an identical response to his Father, whether in the love of the blessed Trinity or in the fulfillment of an earthly ministry. All the conditions of action are different on the two levels; the filial response is one. Above, the appropriate response is a co-operation in sovereignty and an interchange of eternal joys. Then the Son gives back to the Father all that the Father is. Below, in the incarnate life, the appropriate response is an obedience to inspiration, a waiting for direction, an acceptance of suffering, a rectitude of choice, a resistance to temptation, a willingness to die. For such things are the stuff of our existence; and it was in this very stuff that Christ worked out the theme of

---

4 Austin Farrer, 'Incarnation', a sermon preached in Keble College Chapel in 1961, and published in *The Brink of Mystery*, ed. Charles C. Conti, 1976:20.

Incarnation and Double Agency 163

heavenly sonship, proving himself on earth the very thing he was in heaven; that is, a continuous perfect act of filial love. (1976:20)

We have explained the second difference between God's relation to Jesus and God's relation to us as the particular action God undertook to reveal the divine love in the divine Son and thereby to redeem the world. Is such a particular action of God an instance of supernatural, unilateral, and coercive causation, which cancels the real humanity of Jesus? No, it is not. It is supernatural in the sense that it elevates the natural man, Jesus, beyond what Jesus had it in himself to be without the effective action of God within him. It is also supernatural in the sense that we do not have the means to know *how* it is that God acts in the life of Jesus. It is, Farrer says, 'the most stupendous paradox' (1976:19).

'Paradox', however, does not mean 'contradiction'. It is paradox because it takes us beyond ordinary belief and understanding and because we cannot give the explanation of *how* God makes the divine action effective in the action by which Jesus is himself. It is not contradiction because, as we have seen, there is good sense in speaking of non-coercive causation, as in the case of persuasion. Furthermore, again as we have seen, 'supernatural' need not mean a unilateral coercive action that cancels the freedom and the integrity of the man, Jesus. It can mean – and Farrer takes it to be what orthodox Christians commonly do mean – an enhancement of the natural that enables it to be more than it ordinarily can be: 'No one who believes in miracles wants to say that God *violates* the natural working of the created order by a dislocating interference. It is rather that he enhances, or extends, the action of his creatures . . .' (1964:82)

Critics of incarnation, on the other hand, are right in thinking that Christians who affirm orthodox faith often seem to think of Jesus as though his freedom and integrity as a man had been, as it were, replaced in the Incarnation by a divinity that is incompatible with the humanity. It is too bad that the otherwise orthodox slip into heresy here. Their Christian understanding and lives would be improved if they did not. To avoid the heresy of thinking about Jesus as only apparently human, it is necessary to affirm the full humanity of the life in which the incarnation of the eternal Son is enacted by double agency. Doing so, Farrer insists, we would see Jesus 'as a Galilean villager of the first century' who so used the 'Jewish ideas he inherited' as 'to *be* the Son of God' (1964:80). We should not see him as one the content of whose mind was simply identical with that of the omniscient Father creator's. Nor should we think that he thought of himself in the terms of the Chalcedonian definition! From Farrer's sermon again:

> What did Jesus know? He knew, initially, what a village boy learnt, who listened to the Rabbis, and made the best of his opportunities. But of this knowledge, scanty as we should think it, he made a divinely perfect use. It became in his head the alphabet of ideas through which the spirit within him spelt out the truth of what he was, and what he had to do. He was not saved from factual errors in matters irrelevant: he was not prevented from supposing that Moses wrote the whole Pentateuch, or that the world had begun five thousand years ago. But he saw in detail day by day with an unerring eye how to be a true Son to his Father, and a true saviour of his people. He walked in factual darkness by spiritual light; where knowledge was not available, love and candour steered him through. He never judged wrong on the evidence he had; he discerned between good and evil, and marked us out the path of life. He started, like the rest of us, from nowhere – from a germ in the womb; he found the whole truth, through death and resurrection. (1976:20–1).

Saying, then, that God acts in Jesus differently from the way God acts in us, because in Jesus he acts to make his eternal Son incarnate, does not entail that Jesus' real humanity is but a sham. As long as we think concretely about the real humanity of Jesus, we can say that both the divine and the human are present in one person, neither excluding the other.

11. Incarnation, the Trinity, and Fellowship with God

VINCENT BRÜMMER

Introduction

In his essays on Christology,[1] Brian Hebblethwaite mounts a detailed attack on the 'non-incarnational Christology' put forward in Britain in recent years, especially by the authors of *The Myth of God Incarnate*.[2] Such a non-incarnational Christology, Hebblethwaite remarks, is 'an attractive option for Christian believers who hold a strong belief in the reality of God, but who feel the force of the intellectual and moral objections to the idea of the divinity of Jesus Christ' (*The Incarnation*, 1987:vii). In response, however, he tries to counter these objections and to argue for an incarnational Christology in which the divinity of Jesus Christ as God incarnate is vigorously defended. Since I share his conviction that Christian believers should hold on to the belief in the divinity of Jesus Christ, I am not only honoured to contribute to this Festschrift but am also pleased at the opportunity to develop some suggestions for strengthening his case in favour of an incarnational Christology.

Hebblethwaite points out that the objections raised against an incarnational Christology are twofold. On the one hand, it is argued that 'we cannot accept the old formulations since it is simply incoherent, self-contradictory, to speak of one who is both God and man' (ibid.:2). To do so is like speaking of a square circle. Hebblethwaite responds that, although we cannot accept logical contradictions, the doctrine of the Incarnation need not be interpreted as such.

Certainly a square circle is a contradiction in terms. The terms 'square' and 'circle' are precisely defined terms, and their logical

---

[1] *The Incarnation: Collected Essays on Christology*, 1987.
[2] Edited by John Hick, 1977.

incompatibility is obvious from the definitions. But 'God' and 'man' are far from being such tightly defined concepts. It is difficult enough to suppose that we have a full and adequate grasp of what it is to be a human being. We certainly have no such grasp of the divine nature. (ibid.:3)

This entails that the doctrine of divine incarnation allows for a range of interpretations, and it is by no means necessary to make a travesty of it by interpreting it as a contradiction in terms (see ibid.:3, 45–7, 64).
The second and more substantial objection is that

what the old formulations were trying to express about the significance of Jesus for us can be rescued from its involvement in [the alleged] incoherence and expressed more simply and more adequately by speaking of God's acts in and through the man Jesus, or of Jesus' peculiar, indeed unique, openness to the divine Spirit. (ibid.:2–3)

To admit that God inspires and illuminates us through the man Jesus does not require us to claim that Jesus himself was God incarnate. In response to this objection Hebblethwaite argues that the significance of Jesus for us is far more than merely his being a vehicle of divine inspiration and illumination. Of course God can and does act *indirectly* in relation to us 'through the awe-inspiring medium of "the holy" or through a prophet' (ibid.:5), and inspiration and illumination are among the things which God can in this way grant us indirectly through a medium or representative. There are, however, also crucial features of God's dealings with us, which require him to come to us directly and in person. 'These things cannot be done through a representative' (ibid.:5). It is Jesus' role in these matters which requires him to be God himself incarnate, and not merely a human representative or medium through or by means of whom God acts indirectly. It is these features of Jesus' significance for us which constitute the 'moral and spiritual force' (ibid.:23, 25) of the doctrine of divine incarnation. In brief: the doctrine of divine incarnation in Jesus Christ is both logically possible, since it need not be interpreted as a contradiction in terms, and *necessary*, in the sense of being 'morally and religiously compelling' (ibid.:63). 'What the old formulas were trying to express about the significance of Jesus for us' cannot therefore be 'expressed more simply and more adequately' in ways which deny his divinity as God incarnate.

Incarnation, Trinity, and Fellowship with God 167

Hebblethwaite refers to two such features of the traditional belief in the significance of Jesus which require him to be God incarnate and not merely a human representative through whom God acts indirectly. The first is the insistence of traditional belief

> on the direct personal encounter between God and man made possible by the Son of God's coming amongst us as one of us . . . Incarnation represents a new and much more direct, face-to-face way of personal encounter this side of the divide between infinite and finite than is envisaged in the modes of inspiration and illumination. (ibid.:4)

The second feature concerns the way in which Christianity claims to meet the problem of evil.

> God in Christ subjected *himself* to the world's evil at its most harsh and cruel, and in so doing both revealed his love and accepted responsibility for the suffering entailed by the creation of an organic self-reproducing world of sentient and free persons . . . [This] depends wholly on the incarnation. In no way can he be supposed to take responsibility for the world's ills through the suffering of a human representative. (ibid.:5–6; see also 23, 36, 64, 159)

I agree wholeheartedly with Hebblethwaite's distinction between looking on Jesus as a human representative through whom God acts indirectly, and looking on Jesus as himself God incarnate in whom God acts directly. In the first case, the actions of Jesus merely represent or communicate the actions of God. In the second, they *are* the actions of God. However, I have some doubts whether Hebblethwaite's two examples suffice to demonstrate the necessity of direct incarnate divine action in Jesus.

Regarding his first example, Hebblethwaite admits that 'spirituality, prophetic inspiration, mystical experience, can all be construed in personal terms, as they are in all the great religions of Semitic origin, and indeed in many of the eastern faiths as well' (ibid.:4). Nevertheless, according to him the encounter with God made possible by the Incarnation is 'more direct, face-to-face and personal'. I am not sure that I can feel the force of this argument. For me the relationship with God expressed in the Psalms is as direct and personal as you can get. Of course, the disciples and contemporaries of Jesus enjoyed a more 'face-to-face' encounter with Jesus than the Psalmist had with God, but as Keith Ward points out, we live two thousand years later and therefore *we* cannot enjoy that kind of face-to-face relationship with Jesus. Hebblethwaite responds to Ward by referring to the experience which believers can now have of the 'personal encounter with God in and through the spiritual and sacramental presence and activity' of Jesus (ibid.:157; see also 24). Quoting C. F. D. Moule, he argues that 'it is conviction of Christ as a living presence, both spiritually and sacramentally, that differentiates specifically Christian awareness of God from all others' (ibid.:37–8). I grant that this does make a difference to the knowledge and understanding we can now have regarding the God with whom we have fellowship, but surely not to the direct and personal nature of this fellowship. I fail to see how the 'spiritual and sacramental' fellowship with Christ that Christians can experience today is any more 'direct and personal' than the fellowship with God expressed in the Psalms.

Hebblethwaite's second example is not only inadequate as it stands, but highly problematical as well. To claim that in Christ God 'accepted responsibility for the suffering entailed by the creation of an organic self-reproducing world of sentient and free persons' implies that God *is* in fact responsible for the suffering and evil in the world he created. This calls for the kind of theodicy that provides good and sufficient reasons why God should create a world containing such suffering and evils. In some way or other God *causes* evil so that good may come of it. This theodicy is both morally insensitive and perverse.[3] Ivan Karamazov was quite right in rejecting the view that it is 'absolutely necessary, and indeed quite inevitable, to torture to death only one tiny creature' in order to erect 'the edifice of human destiny with the aim of making men happy in the end'.[4] This theodicy not only makes God the author of evil but also claims that evil has a point. From the perspective of faith, this is a perverse claim since evil can never have a point in the eyes of a loving God. Indeed, a loving God does have every reason for creating 'an organic self-reproducing world of sentient and free persons' since only such a world can respond freely to his love. Although this entails the *possibility* of evil and suffering, it does not entail its *actuality*. The actuality of evil results not from God's creation of 'sentient and free persons' but from the fact that they abuse their freedom by pointlessly rejecting his love. We have every reason to accept God's offer of love and there can be no

---

3 See V. Brümmer, *Speaking of a Personal God*, 1992: ch. 6.
4 F. Dostoyevsky, *The Brothers Karamazov*, 1982:287.

Incarnation, Trinity, and Fellowship with God 169

imaginable reason for turning our backs on him. The fact that we do so and become sinners who are subject to affliction, is irredeemably pointless. That God shares this affliction on the cross of Christ merely expresses his profound sympathy and compassion with our predicament, but does not redeem the pointlessness of it all. Furthermore, the fact that God shares our affliction in this way does not entail that he also shares our responsibility for it, as Hebblethwaite seems to suggest.

So it seems clear that Hebblethwaite's example is highly problematical. As it stands, however, it is also inadequate as a demonstration of the necessity for divine incarnation. That God is compassionate and reveals his compassion to us does not necessarily require the Incarnation. God does not *become* compassionate with the Incarnation, nor does he express his compassion exclusively in this way. The psalmist knew all about the compassion of God without knowing about the Incarnation in Jesus. In order to demonstrate the necessity of the Incarnation, it is not enough to merely show how God expresses his compassion through the cross of Christ. In fact, Hebblethwaite admits that God can also 'express sympathy and sorrow indirectly through someone else' (*The Incarnation*, 1987:5). What is needed is to show how the Incarnation is necessary for our salvation from sin and from our alienation from God. Hebblethwaite does agree with Austin Farrer that 'the primary purpose of [the] incarnation . . . [is] the making possible for us of genuine personal union with God' (ibid.:114). Surprisingly, however, he fails to show *why* this should be the case. He also concurs with Hodgson's view that the 'universal significance in the Christ event for the reconciliation of man and God requires us to see the Cross of Christ as an act of God incarnate' (ibid.:62), but he fails to provide any argument in support of this view. He argues that St Paul's claim in 2 Corinthians 5.19 that 'God was in Christ reconciling the world to himself' should be given an incarnational and not a functionalist interpretation (ibid.:159; see also 155, 163). I am not sure, however, that these two interpretations exclude each other in the way he suggests. What is needed is that he should show why the Incarnation ('God was in Christ') is necessary in view of its *function* in our salvation (God was 'reconciling the world to himself'). Although he goes to some lengths to provide an incarnational interpretation of the claim that 'God was in Christ', he fails to show how this incarnation has a necessary function to fulfil in the second half of St Paul's claim, namely, that God 'was reconciling the world to himself', unless we should take him to claim that God reconciles the world to himself by 'accepting responsibility' for the suffering of the world? I have already shown that this is a highly dubious claim. What is needed then is that we *first* examine the doctrine of atonement or divine reconciliation and show why and in what sense it functionally requires the doctrine of incarnation.

'Reconciling the World to Himself'

In what sense, as we have seen Hebblethwaite claim with Austin Farrer, is 'the primary purpose of [the] incarnation . . . the making possible for us of genuine personal union with God'? This depends very much on the kind of union with God that we seek to achieve. Hebblethwaite points out that this union has sometimes been thought of as a form of identity (ibid.:64). This was especially the case in the Neoplatonic strand of Christian mysticism where the *unio mystica* was seen as a kind of identity in which the human is merged into the divine.[5] Hebblethwaite resolutely rejects this view of union with God. 'Once we start speaking of ourselves in any sense as *being* God, we have lost touch with Christianity' (ibid.:18). The most serious difficulty with this view is that it eliminates the personal. Persons are by definition independent agents and they lose their independence as persons if they are to merge with each other in this way. Hebblethwaite quite rightly therefore chooses with Farrer, 'genuine personal union with God'. What is the nature of such personal union and why is the Incarnation necessary to achieve it or to restore it to us when it has been lost?

This personal union with God can be understood as analogous to relationships of loving fellowship between human persons. Here two persons do not merge into a single identity but identify with each other by each freely treating the other's interest as his or her own. In serving your interest as my own, I love you as myself (Brümmer, 1993: ch. 7). Owing to human weakness, we are all too often unable to sustain this sort of fellowship consistently. Through selfishness I put my own interests first and intentionally or unintentionally act in ways which are contrary to your interests and thus cause you injury. Irrespective of whether the injury is serious or trivial, I have marred our relationship and given you grounds for resentment. In being resentful, you endorse the fact that our relationship has been damaged, if not broken. Such a breach in our fellowship can only be healed if you refuse to be

---

[5] See V. Brümmer, *The Model of Love*, 1993: ch. 3.

Incarnation, Trinity, and Fellowship with God

resentful, and instead adopt the opposite attitude, i.e. willingness to forgive. You have to consider the breach in our fellowship a greater evil than the injury I have caused you, and therefore be willing to continue identifying with me and treating my interests as your own in spite of what I have done to you. 'The person who has been wronged can accept the wrong done to him: he can absorb as it were in his own suffering the consequences of the wrong that has caused it.'[6]

Such forgiveness can only be both real and effective on certain conditions. Thus it can only be *real* if there is something to forgive. It would make no sense to say that you forgive me unless I really caused you injury by failing to seek your interests as my own. In this respect forgiveness should not be confused with condonation. If you were to *condone* my action, you would thereby *deny* that it is an action which caused you any significant injury, and thus also deny that there is anything to forgive. If, on the other hand, you *forgive* me for what I have done, you claim that my action did cause you injury, but that you would rather bear the injury than abandon the fellowship, which I have marred by my action. 'The power to forgive is not to be obtained for nothing, it must be bought at a price, it must be paid for with the suffering of him who has been sinned against.'[7] One of the basic characteristics of forgiveness is, therefore, that 'the one who forgives is the one who suffers'.[8] Thus forgiveness costs you something whereas condonation is a denial that there are any costs involved.[9]

Further, your forgiveness can only be *effective* in restoring our broken fellowship, on condition that I am sincerely penitent and express both contrition for damaging our fellowship and the desire that it should be restored. Forgiveness is your willingness to identify with me in spite of what I did. But if I do not through penitence renounce the break which I have caused in our fellowship, your identification with me would not restore the relationship but rather entail your acceptance of my breaking of it. It follows that my asking your forgiveness presupposes penitence and a change of heart on my part as well as the expression of these in penitential action. The one would be incoherent without the other.

---

6 John Burnaby, *Christian Words and Christian Meanings*, 1955:90.
7 O. C. Quick, *Essays in Orthodoxy*, 1916:92–3.
8 J. Edwin Orr, *Full Surrender*, 1951:22.
9 On the difference between forgiveness and condonation, see R. S. Downie, 'Forgiveness', *Philosophical Quarterly* 15, 1965, and J. R. Lucas, *Freedom and Grace*, 1976:78 f.

> To ask to be forgiven is in part to acknowledge that the attitude displayed in your actions was such as might properly be resented and in part to repudiate that attitude for the future (or at least for the immediate future); and to forgive is to accept the repudiation and to forswear the resentment.[10]

Although my penitence is in this sense a *necessary* condition for your forgiveness to achieve reconciliation, it is not a condition for your forgiveness as such. Forgiveness can only be freely and unconditionally given. Thus too my attempts to make good the injury I have caused cannot be more than an expression of my penitence or an attempt to put into practice my repudiation of what I have done. They can neither bring about nor earn your forgiveness since that remains up to you as an independent agent to decide. This is what distinguishes penitence and penance from punishment and satisfaction. Through bearing punishment or making satisfaction I can *earn* reinstatement in my rights and duties in relation to you and what I have earned you are obliged to give. Penitence and penance, however, can never *earn* reinstatement in fellowship, and therefore cannot in the same way create obligations. Furthermore, although penitence and penance are a necessary condition for forgiveness to achieve reconciliation, punishment and satisfaction would make forgiveness unnecessary. If full satisfaction has been made or appropriate punishment has been borne, there is nothing left to forgive. 'Forgiveness after satisfaction has been fully made, is no forgiveness at all.'[11] Thus I can never *demand* your forgiveness as a right I have earned. I can only *ask* it as a favour. In asking your forgiveness (as in asking you anything else), I acknowledge my dependence on your free decision as an independent agent for granting my request. I may hope that you will forgive. I might even count on you to forgive me when I am penitent. But my penitence does not entitle me to your forgiveness and, therefore, I may not presume upon it.

If I repudiate the damage I have done to our fellowship by confessing myself in the wrong, and by an act of penance try to demonstrate the sincerity of this repudiation, and if I express my desire for the restoration of our fellowship by asking your forgiveness, and if you, by forgiving me, show your willingness to identify with me again

---

10 P. F. Strawson, *Freedom and Resentment and Other Essays*, 1974:6.
11 G. Lampe, 'The atonement: law and love', in A. R. Vidler (ed.), *Soundings*, 1966:185.

Incarnation, Trinity, and Fellowship with God

in spite of what I did to you, then our fellowship will not only be restored, but might also be deepened and strengthened. As persons we have come to 'know' each other better than before (on this kind of personal knowledge, see Brümmer, 1993:179–81).

> We shall be to one another what we were before, save for one important difference. I know now that you are a person who can forgive, that you prefer to have suffered rather than to resent, and that to keep me as a friend, or to avoid becoming my enemy, is more important to you than to maintain your own rights. And you know that I am a person who is not too proud to acknowledge his fault, and that your goodwill is worth more to me than the maintenance of my own cause . . . Forgiveness does not only forestall or remove enmity: it strengthens love. (Burnaby, 1955:87)

How do these distinctions apply to our understanding of the relationship between God and human persons and of the way it can be restored when it has been damaged? A relationship of fellowship or love is one in which two personal agents mutually identify with each other. Applied to our relationship with God, this means that God identifies with us by making our salvation and eternal happiness his own concern, and we identify with God by making his will our own. Furthermore, this mutual identification is necessarily free in the sense that one partner can neither compel nor oblige the other to reciprocate the fellowship. In this sense we cannot *compel* God to love us. God remains free in his love. Likewise, God cannot compel us to reciprocate his love for us, since then our response would not be love or fellowship. Neither can we *oblige* God to identify with us by somehow earning his love through doing his will. God's love cannot be earned. Not because the price is too high or our efforts too feeble, but because love is by definition unconditional. We simply cannot talk about love or fellowship in terms of rewards, which might or might not be merited. Thus we cannot earn eternal salvation by doing God's will and God does not try to earn our love by his offer of salvation. He wants us to love him because we identify with him, and not for the sake of that which we can receive from him in return. If we love heaven rather than God, then our efforts are directed towards our own interests and we fail to identify ourselves with the will of God.

This is in fact precisely what we do. We disrupt the fellowship with God by trying to pursue our own interests rather than identifying with his will. If, however, in penitence we repudiate the damage we have done to our fellowship with God, and through acts of penance try to demonstrate the sincerity of this repudiation, and if God should grant us our desire for restoration of our fellowship by forgiving us, then we shall be reconciled with him and our fellowship will be restored. Nothing more than this is required. In the words of D. M. Baillie:

> God will freely forgive even the greatest sins, if only the sinners will repent and turn from their evil ways. Nothing else is needed, no expiation, no offerings, for God has everything already. Sincere repentance is enough, and a real turning from sin to God; and then the sinner can count on God's mercy.[12]

This in a nutshell is the view of divine reconciliation that follows if we interpret our relationship with God in terms of loving fellowship. This is indeed a fully *personal* view emphasizing the personal nature of our relationship with God, as well as the fact that we and not God are responsible for the disruption of our fellowship with him.

What are the Christological implications of this view of divine reconciliation, and more especially, its implications for the incarnational Christology which Hebblethwaite seeks to defend? On this view we can show how both the divinity of Christ and the self-revelation of God through the Incarnation are necessary conditions for our reconciliation with God.

The Christological Implications

We have seen that on this view the person who forgives is the person who has to pay the price for reconciliation. This cannot be done by someone else as a representative acting on behalf of the person who forgives. Since in restoring our fellowship with God, it is God who forgives, it is also God himself who has to pay the price and has to absorb into his own suffering the consequences of the wrong that we have done to him. On Calvary God reveals to us the cost of his forgiveness. Furthermore, since forgiveness is by definition unconditional, the suffering of Jesus cannot be seen as merely the condition for God's forgiveness. It is rather the direct expression of this forgiveness and the price God has to pay for it. In this way we can understand Hebblethwaite's categorical statement 'that God's forgiving love does not depend on the death of Christ, but rather is manifested and

---

12 *God was in Christ*, 1961:176.

Incarnation, Trinity, and Fellowship with God 175

enacted in it' (*The Incarnation*, 1987:37). But then Jesus cannot be a being apart from God whose suffering fulfils on our behalf the conditions necessary for God to forgive, nor can he be a representative who pays the price for divine forgiveness on God's behalf. On the contrary, he must be God himself and, as Hebblethwaite correctly points out, 'the suffering and Cross of Jesus can be seen as God's own suffering and Cross in the world' (ibid.:64). For these reasons we cannot claim that the Cross of Jesus is the manifestation and enactment of divine forgiveness without at the same time affirming the divinity of Jesus.

But this is not all. Christ's suffering is not merely the *revelation* of the price for forgiveness which God has to pay. Such a revelation is also a *necessary condition* for this forgiveness to achieve reconciliation. 'The effect of this revelation is to be the transformation of the loveless into the lovely' (ibid.:1). In this respect Christ's suffering on Calvary is a necessary condition for our salvation. Let me explain. Loving fellowship entails knowing each other as persons in the sense of adopting an attitude of mutual trust and open candour in relation to each other (Brümmer, 1993:179–81). If ultimate happiness consists of being in the love of God, it follows that we can only be ultimately happy to the extent that we know God in this way. 'This is eternal life: to know you the only true God, and Jesus Christ whom you have sent' (John 17.3).

Through sin, however, we have become estranged from God. Our lives are not characterized by loving trust and open candour in relation to God. But worse still, this estrangement has led to ignorance. Not only do we not know God; we do not even know who God is nor that he desires our fellowship. For this reason we have lost the ability to seek reconciliation with God. We cannot identify with his will for we do not know what his will is. We cannot seek divine forgiveness, for we do not know whether God is long-suffering enough to forgive. In fact, we cannot repent, for we do not know whom we have offended. And since we are unable to repent, God's forgiveness cannot be effective. In the words of John Burnaby, 'there can be no effective forgiveness unless the wrong-doer repents of his wrong-doing, knows whom he has offended, and comes back to him with a changed mind . . . The tragedy of the human situation lies in the fact that sinful man has lost the knowledge of the God against whom he has sinned and that *this is the punishment* which sin can never escape . . . The sins of men have built their own prison. They *cannot* repent, because they do not know whom they have offended' (1955:94–5). It is therefore a necessary condition for our salvation that we should come to know God anew whom we have offended and to know what his will for us is in order that we may identify with it anew.

However, we can only get to know God to the extent that he makes himself known to us, and we can only know what God wills for us to the extent that he reveals his will to us. This God has brought about through the suffering of Christ. 'This is how he showed his love among us: he sent his only Son into the world that we might have life through him ... Thus we have come to know and believe in the love which God has for us' (1 John 4.9, 16). Clearly then, the paradigmatic revelation of God's forgiving love through the suffering of Christ, is a necessary condition for God's forgiveness to achieve reconciliation with us. 'By the death of his Son, God commends, proves, makes good his love towards us who were his enemies, and thereby reconciles us to himself' (Burnaby, 1955:95). Thus God makes himself known to us through the Incarnation. In the words of Jesus: 'Anyone who has seen me has seen the Father' (John 14.9).

Is it also possible to see the Father without seeing Jesus? Is the revelation of God in Jesus unique, or is it also possible for people of other faiths who do not know Jesus to come to know God? According to Wilfred Cantwell Smith:

> the evidence would seem overwhelming that in fact individual Buddhists, Hindus, Muslims and others have known, and in fact do know, God. I personally have friends from these communities whom it seems to me preposterous to think about in any other way. (If we do not have friends among these communities, we should probably refrain from generalisations about them.) (1980:102)

Two remarks could be made here. First of all, we could agree with Smith that God in his almighty wisdom is able to make himself known in many ways, also to those who adhere to faiths other than Christianity.

> The God whom we have come to know ... reaches out after all men everywhere, and speaks to all who will listen. Both within and without the Church men listen all too dimly. Yet both within and without the Church, so far as we can see, God does somehow enter into men's hearts. (Smith, 1980:107)

Secondly, Christians would nevertheless maintain that it is only possible in the light of our knowledge of God as revealed in Christ, for us to discern that others (and ourselves) inside and outside the Church can be said to 'know God'. In this sense the Christian will still have to claim that the revelation of God's love in Christ is *paradigmatic* and therefore necessary, since it is only in the light of God's self-revelation in Jesus Christ that we can say what it means to 'know God' and be reconciled with him. Thus Smith has to admit that 'because God is what he is, because he is what Christ has shown him to be, *therefore* other men *do* live in his presence. Also, therefore, we (as Christians) know this to be so' (Smith, 1980:106).

In this sense Hebblethwaite is correct in affirming that:

> the specific, particular Incarnation remains the key, the clue, and the criterion both of God's ways with man, and for man's future in God . . . The Incarnation provides a total interpretative key by which all other knowledge of God can be finally illuminated and transformed. (1987:51–2; see also 23, 35, 166)

In this section we have shown how the view of divine reconciliation developed here can provide a basis for two key aspects of Hebblethwaite's incarnational Christology, namely the divinity of Christ and the necessity of God's self-revelation in Christ for our salvation. Let us now turn to the implications of this view for our understanding of the two natures of Christ and of the doctrine of the Trinity.

'Very God and Very Man'

'The character, acts and teaching of Jesus, are seen as God's own revelatory and loving acts for our salvation' (Hebblethwaite, *The Incarnation*, 1987:63). In this way there are two things which God makes known to us in Jesus. First of all, he makes himself known to us as a loving God who desires our fellowship and is willing to pay the price of forgiveness to win it. Anyone who has seen Jesus has seen the Father. In this respect, Jesus is 'very God'. Secondly, God reveals his will to us in order that we may be enabled to identify with him in fellowship by making his will our own and living our lives in accordance with it. Thus 'Christology is not only concerned with Christ as the human face of God, but also with Christ as the pattern of what man was meant to be. The will of God for the world and for man comes to expression in the incarnate one' (ibid.:151). In this respect Jesus is also 'very man'.

Which aspects of 'the character, acts and teaching of Jesus' are manifestations of his divinity and which express his humanity? In the history of theology this question has not always been answered in the same way. Thus in the Patristic period theologians followed Plato in holding that suffering is a sign of imperfection and that therefore God cannot suffer. The doctrine of divine impassibility was generally held to be beyond doubt.[13] It follows that the suffering of Jesus cannot be a manifestation of his divinity but typically expresses his humanity. In contemporary theology, however, 'the rejection of the ancient doctrine of divine impassibility has become a theological commonplace'.[14] We have seen above that Hebblethwaite also departs from the Patristic belief in divine impassibility (ibid.:43, 162), and views 'the Cross of Christ as God's Cross' (ibid.:151). The view on divine reconciliation which we defended above also entails that it is especially in the suffering of Jesus that God reveals himself to us as a personal God who desires our fellowship and is willing to pay the price of forgiveness in order to achieve it.

In early Christianity the divinity of Jesus was usually connected with his miracles and especially with the resurrection. These were taken as signs of the divine omnipotence and omniscience in which he transcended the limitations of earthly existence. The trouble with this view is that it tends to entail a docetism in which the divinity of Jesus excludes his true humanity. In order to be truly human, Jesus must have been subject to the limitations of human existence. It would therefore be incoherent to claim that he is truly human and then to interpret his divinity in ways which contradict this claim. Furthermore, if Jesus is to be for us the revelation of the true humanity on which it is God's will for us to pattern our lives and actions, then we cannot view Jesus as a being whom it is in principle impossible for us, who are subject to the limitations of human existence, to emulate. Hebblethwaite is therefore correct in affirming that:

> in no way do we follow the 'docetic' tendencies of early Christianity, which found it hard to believe, for example, that Jesus shared the limitations of human psychology and cognition. This is to say that for Christian belief the Incarnation involved God's subjecting him-

---

[13] See Marcel Sarot, 'Patripassianism, theopaschitism and the suffering of God: some historical and systematic considerations', *Religious Studies* 26, 1990.

[14] Ronald Goetz, 'The suffering God', *The Christian Century* 103, 1986; see also M. Sarot, *God, Passibility and Corporeality*, 1992.

self to the limitations of real humanity in order to achieve his purposes of revelation and reconciliation. (ibid.:22; see also 164)

This requires us to adopt some form of kenotic Christology in which the divinity of Jesus is understood in ways that are manifested *within* the limits of his true humanity and not contrary to it. Thus Hebblethwaite asserts that 'it lies at the heart of Christianity to suppose that God's omnipotence was both exercised and revealed in his becoming man, subjecting himself to human limitations, and dying a cruel death' (ibid.:66). Furthermore, he concurs with Austin Farrer that 'an omniscient being cannot be very man. But he knew *how* to be the Son of God in the several situations of his gradually unfolding destiny. God the Son on earth is the fullness of holy life within the limits of mortality' (ibid.:67; see also 121).

The limits of humanity to which Jesus was subjected are twofold. First of all, there are the limits which are inherent to finite human existence: limits to what we can do and to what we can know and the limits to life which go with mortality. If Jesus was truly human he must have been subject to these limits. He could not have been omnipotent and omniscient in the sense he was taken to be so in Patristic theology. Second, there are the limits given by the specific historical circumstances of a human life. Thus Jesus was not a human-being-in-general, but a specific human person living at a specific time and place. In the words of Austin Farrer quoted by Hebblethwaite: ' "This was how God's love was shown to be utterly divine – in accepting every circumstance of our manhood. He spared himself nothing. He was not a copybook man-in-general, he was a Galilean carpenter, a free-lance rabbi; and he wove up his life, as each of us must, out of the materials that were to hand" ' (quoted in ibid.:119; see also 30, 66). The divinity of Jesus did not override the limits of his humanity, but manifested itself *within* these limits. 'Whatever degree of kenoticism we accept ... we cannot suppose that the human vehicle of the divine presence totally obscured the real identity of the incarnate one. The divinity, we may say with hindsight, showed itself in the humanity' (ibid.:75).

Furthermore, these limits also did not obscure the fact that Jesus was not only human but also the paradigm of human perfection which God wills that we should emulate. He was not only *really* human, but also *perfectly* human. This was manifested in the moral and spiritual perfection of his life and actions within the limits of human finitude and historical situatedness. In him the perfect union of wills with the Father is manifested. 'The freedom of Jesus, we must suppose, was always exercised in conformity with the Father's will, just because the human freedom was the vehicle of the divine freedom' (ibid.:72).

This determines what it means for us to be followers of Jesus. We are not called upon to emulate him by living the life of a first-century Galilean carpenter and freelance rabbi. *Imitatio Christi* should not be understood as an attempt to imitate the historical details of Jesus' life and actions.[15] On the contrary, we are called upon to identify with the will of God in the way he did and thus to emulate his moral and spiritual perfection within the limits *of our own* finitude and historical situation. In this sense the character, acts and teaching of Jesus manifest the true and ideal humanity which God wills that each of us should emulate in his or her own situation. In revealing this to us through the perfect humanity of Jesus, God enables us to identify with him in loving fellowship and thus to become reconciled with him. But this is not all. God's action in reconciling the world to himself involves all three persons of the Trinity and not only the incarnate Son. In what sense, then, does the view on divine reconciliation defended above entail a Trinitarian theology?

One God in Three Persons

The Trinitarian nature of divine reconciliation can usefully be explained in terms of St Bernard's distinction between three freedoms: *liberum arbitrium* or freedom from compulsion, *liberum concilium* or freedom from sin, and *liberum complacitum* or freedom from misery.[16] According to St Bernard, *liberum arbitrium* or freedom of choice, belongs to our nature as persons and constitutes the image of God in us. Like God, we are autonomous personal agents who freely initiate our own action and can therefore be held responsible for what we choose to do. This kind of freedom cannot be lost, even by our sinful estrangement from God. Even as sinners we remain persons who can freely decide on our actions. Of course, this does not mean that we can choose to do just anything we please. As Jean-Paul Sartre argues, our freedom as personal agents is always a concrete freedom in

---

15 See M. Sarot, 'The Christian ideal of *Imitatio Christi* as a way of making sense of life', in M Sarot and G. van den Brink (eds), *Identity and Change in the Christian Tradition*, 1999.

16 For a detailed exposition, see V. Brümmer, 'Calvin, Bernard and the freedom of the will', *Religious Studies* 30, 1994, and 'On not confusing necessity with compulsion: a reply to Paul Helm', *Religious Studies* 31, 1995.

Incarnation, Trinity, and Fellowship with God 181

the sense that we can only choose between the options which are given to us in our own concrete situation. I am free to choose what I shall do, but this does not mean that I can choose to be the ruler of a kingdom or a famous concert pianist!

Although sin does not deprive me of my freedom of choice as a person (i.e. the *image* of God), it does deprive me of the option to choose for reconciliation with God. In this way, St Bernard argues, we have lost through sin the *likeness* of God, which is given in the other two freedoms, *liberum concilium et complacitum*. Thus I cannot choose to make God's will my own because I do not know what God's will is. Furthermore, even if I were to know God's will, I lack the power or ability to do it by myself. St Bernard states that it is as difficult to do God's will by my own power as it is to stop a raging torrent with my finger. Thus the ability to choose and consistently do God's will (the *liberum concilium*) can only be restored to me if God should grant me the gifts of enlightenment (in order to know God's will), and of power (in order to do it). These gifts enable me to become free from sin and to live my life in accordance with the will of God. However, they do not free me from misery, since I will then still only do God's will because I must and not because I want to or because I delight in doing it. According to St Bernard, we have all from the very creation of the human race lost the gift of 'wisdom' or 'taste for goodness'. Only if God should grant me this gift of wisdom again, shall I be freed from misery and restored to the *liberum complacitum* by which I can achieve the perfect union of wills that is the ultimate happiness of loving fellowship with God. As we have argued above, the gift of *enlightenment* is granted to us in the incarnate Son. The gift of *power* is bestowed on us by the providential care of the Father, while we may receive the gift of *wisdom* through the inspiration of the Holy Spirit. Only by this Trinitarian action are we enabled to respond to the love of God shown to us in the Cross of Christ. Only thus can we be reconciled to God and saved from the estrangement of sin.

The question now arises as to whether this Trinitarian action issues from a single divine personal agent who in 'his' dealings with us manifests himself as Father, Son and Holy Spirit, or from Father, Son and Spirit as three distinct persons who jointly constitute one Godhead. The latter option is characteristic of the so-called social theory of the Trinity made popular in contemporary theology by Jürgen Moltmann. According to Ingolf Dalferth, 'Moltmann so much stresses the personal agency of Father, Son and Spirit, that it becomes difficult to see how it can still be said to be one and the same God,'[17] and Keith Ward comments that 'this view is indistinguishable from a more robust polytheism, and must be rejected by thoroughgoing monotheists, such as Christians are supposed to be'.[18] In this connection, it is significant to note with John Burnaby that 'the main Christian tradition . . . has instinctively avoided speaking of the Trinity by the plural pronoun "they", even when a plural verb was inevitable. The original Latin of the Athanasian Creed manages very skilfully to avoid the use even of a plural verb!'[19] No wonder that Moltmann is often accused of tritheism!

Hebblethwaite's approach to the social theory is more ambiguous. On the one hand, he tries to avoid the charge of tritheism and, with Leonard Hodgson, is 'not concerned to trace three sorts of divine activity in the world and ascribe them to three different sources or "persons" in God' (*The Incarnation*, 1987:15). On the other hand, however, he holds that:

> there can be no doubt that the model of a single individual person does create difficulties for theistic belief. It presents us with the picture of one who, despite his infinite attributes, is unable to enjoy the excellence of personal relations unless he first create an object for his love. Monotheistic faiths have not favoured the idea that creation is necessary to God, but short of postulating personal relations in God, it is difficult to see how they can avoid it. (ibid.:14)

Thus if God were to be a single individual and not three persons in relation, God would be dependent on the creation of persons beyond 'himself' in order not only to enjoy the 'excellence of personal relations', but also 'to enjoy the fullness of being as love' (ibid.:36, 136, 165), and even 'for being personal at all' (p. 134).

Although Hebblethwaite in this way accepts the social model of the Trinity, he tries to avoid its tritheisic implications by stressing that 'the social analogy is an *analogy* . . . [that] has to be qualified precisely at the point where the spectre of tritheism looms' (ibid.:20). This point is where human personal relations are *external*. 'We must not allow the human side of the analogy to dominate our grasp of the divine side. If

---

17 Ingolf U. Dalferth, 'The eschatological roots of the doctrine of the Trinity', in C. Schwöbel (ed.), *Trinitarian Theology Today*, 1995:152.
18 *Rational Theology and the Creativity of God*, 1982:86.
19 J. Burnaby, *The Belief of Christendom: A Commentary on the Nicene Creed*, 1959:210.

Incarnation, Trinity, and Fellowship with God 183

human persons exist in relation only externally, over against other individuals, this is precisely *not* the feature to be extrapolated into God' (ibid.:135). The relations within the Trinity are *internal* relations.

> God himself, in his own being, exists in an internal relationship of love given and love received. That love ... was mirrored in the relationship between Jesus and the Father. That same love [believers] experience in their own lives ... as a relationship in which they too [are] caught up and could come to share ... The very notion of a God who is love requires us to think of an internally differentiated and relational deity. (ibid.:21–2; see also 64)

The mistake with tritheism is that it views the Trinity as 'a number of finite supernatural beings related externally, each existing in a sphere exclusive of the other or others' (p. 20).

I fear that Hebblethwaite's solution faces some serious difficulties. As we have argued above, persons are by definition autonomous agents who freely initiate their own actions. *Liberum arbitrium* belongs to our nature as persons. It follows that personal relations like loving fellowship are by definition external relations since they lack the necessity which belongs to internal relations. Persons cannot logically be internally related. Love can only be freely given and freely received, otherwise it is not love at all. It is therefore a contradiction in terms to speak of 'an internal relationship of love given and love received'.

Of course, God is not like other people since God's goodness, power and knowledge are unlimited. It follows that concepts like 'personhood' and 'love' can only be applied in a qualified sense to God and to 'his' relationship with us.[20] If, however, we are also to apply the analogy to the internal relations within the Trinity, we will have to qualify it further to the point of equivocation. Furthermore, it makes no sense to claim that the internal relations within the Trinity are relations in which we are 'caught up and could come to share'. This can only be done within a unitive mysticism where the human is somehow merged into the divine. As we have seen, Hebblethwaite quite correctly rejects this option. The analogy can indeed be applied to the loving fellowship which Jesus displayed towards the Father, since this reveals to us the perfect fellowship with God on which God desires us

---

20 See V. Brümmer, 1993: ch. 9, for a detailed analysis of these qualifications.

to pattern our lives. But then the fellowship which Jesus displays towards the Father manifests his perfect humanity rather than his divinity. The prayers of Jesus to the Father do not make known to us 'his inner trinitarian relations . . . to the Father' (Hebblethwaite, *The Incarnation*, 1987:24), but rather the perfect divine–human relationship which we are called upon to emulate in our lives.

If we thus reject the application of the social model to the internal relations of the Trinity, how are we to deal with Hebblethwaite's argument that doing so entails that God is dependent on the creation of persons beyond 'himself' in order to enjoy the 'excellence of personal relations' and 'the fullness of being as love', and even 'for being personal at all'? If, on the one hand, persons are autonomous agents who freely initiate their own action, then God cannot be said to be dependent on persons beyond 'himself' 'for being personal at all'. On the other hand, however, if personal relations (including loving fellowship) are only possible between persons who are autonomous agents, then personal relations are by definition external relations. This means that God can indeed only enjoy such relations with persons (both human and angelic) beyond the divine being. It follows that God cannot enjoy loving fellowship 'unless he first create an object for his love'. Of course, this applies to all relational characteristics of God. God can only be a Creator, Sustainer or Redeemer if there is an independent reality beyond God, which God creates, sustains or redeems. Does this mean that God's love is not eternal but is only possible after the creation of persons beyond 'himself'? Maybe we should respond to this question by questioning with St Augustine the legitimacy of speculations about how God was and what God did before the creation of the world (*Confessions* 11.12). After all, we only have to do with God to the extent that God relates to us, and it is not for us to speculate about how God is or what God does apart from this relationship. Faith is an existential and not a speculative enterprise. It has to do with the relationship with God from which our lives and actions derive their meaning and significance, and not with speculative theories about how God is or what God does apart from this relationship.

It is clear that within the doctrine of the Trinity, the term 'person' (*hypostasis, persona*) functions as a technical term not to be confused with its ordinary sense as 'individual centre of conscious life and independent agency' (Burnaby, 1959:202–3). Such confusion would make tritheism unavoidable. The meaning of the term in the doctrine of the Trinity is analogous to the use of the Latin term *persona* for a theatre mask, the *dramatis personae* or different roles which one and the same actor might portray. The one divine Actor fulfils three roles in his dealing with us humans. Thus we can say that:

> the trinitarian perspective makes it possible to distinguish creation, revelation and inspiration as three basic types of action which constitute divine agency without making it necessary to postulate three different agents . . . This analysis of the trinitarian structure of Christian belief in God seems to avoid the danger of tritheism or of conceiving God as some kind of tri-partite being.[21]

The theatrical analogy is useful but at some essential points it is limited. Overlooking these limits could lead to a modalistic theology like that of Sabellius who first used the analogy. First, a theatre mask is something behind which an actor is hidden. In their daily lives actors differ from the roles they play on stage and their true personality is not necessarily revealed in these roles. Second, these roles are fulfilled only briefly on stage. After playing the role the actor takes off the mask. Third, the same actor can play various roles at various times and these roles could also exclude each other so that they cannot be fulfilled together. At these points the analogy does not carry over to Trinitarian theology.

The creating and sustaining Father, the revealing Son and the inspiring Spirit are not masks behind which God hides his true self from us, but 'three basic types of action' in which God manifests his true self in relation to us. Furthermore, they are not temporary and passing roles which God could abandon at any moment, but divine saving acts on which we can always depend for our eternal happiness. Finally, creation, revelation and inspiration are not contradictory roles but essentially interconnected types of divine action:

> Just as without creation there is no revelation, and without revelation no inspiration, so without inspiration there is no awareness of revelation, and without this no awareness of creation. Hence creation, revelation and inspiration neither merely coexist nor coincide in an undifferentiated way. (Dalferth, 1995:161)

---

21 C. Schwöbel, 'Divine agency and providence', *Modern Theology* 3, 1987:240. See also C. Schwöbel, *God, Action and Revelation*, 1992: chs 1 and 4; and I. Dalferth, 1995.

Thus *opera trinitatis ad extra sunt indivisa* even though they remain distinct, while *opera trinitatis ad intra sunt divisa*.[22] In these *opera trinitatis* (works of the Trinity) God manifests his true nature as the One on whose love we can depend for our eternal happiness in the fellowship we may enjoy with God. However, this does not imply that the Godhead consists of three personal agents who eternally love each other. As we have argued, that would either entail some form of tritheism, which contradicts the unity of God or, as in Hebblethwaite's case, restricts the model of love to the point of equivocation.

In this contribution to Brian Hebblethwaite's Festschrift I have tried to lend support to his defence of both an incarnational Christology and a Trinitarian theology, while at the same time developing some suggestions for strengthening his argument and eliminating the weaknesses which I find in it. It is an honour and a pleasure for me to do so.

---

22 'The external works/actions of the Trinity are indivisible,' while 'The internal works/actions of the Trinity are divisible.'

12. Incarnation, Rationality, and Transformative Practices

DAVID F. FORD

Brian Hebblethwaite has been deeply immersed in both the Hellenic and the Hebraic streams feeding into Western civilization, and his own life and thought have been shaped by both. In this he has been part of a rich European tradition and in particular of its English variety. Even more specifically, he has exemplified a Church of England version of it that has been most thoroughly cultivated through the universities of Oxford and Cambridge.

That home territory should not, however, suggest a constriction: it has been a hospitable home, open to many conversations, philosophies and religious traditions, and he has had a specially close relationship with German-speaking continental European philosophy of religion. Yet there has never been any doubt about his basic allegiance to classical Western philosophy rooted in Greece together with the continuing relevance of the Anglo-American analytic tradition. The theological 'home' which that philosophy helps to support rationally is likewise clear: it is Christian faith centred on the incarnation of God in Jesus Christ.

In this essay I will start from his understanding of incarnation, describe its culmination in his recent thought, and comment on it with special reference to the relationship of wisdom to rationality, and of beliefs to practices and their institutional settings.

Incarnation as the Essence of Christianity

Hebblethwaite's advocacy of the rationality of an incarnational understanding of Christian faith became widely known as a result of his response to *The Myth of God Incarnate*, and later through his critiques of the work of Don Cupitt, but even before all that he had developed a clear, philosophically supported incarnational theology.

In an article in *Theology* in March 1977, he answered affirmatively the title question: 'Incarnation – the essence of Christianity?' He wrote:

> There can be no doubt that the doctrine of the Incarnation has been taken during the bulk of Christian history to constitute the very heart of Christianity. Hammered out over five centuries of passionate debate, enshrined in the classical Christian creeds, explored and articulated in the great systematic theologies, the doctrine expresses, so far as human words permit, the central belief of Christians that God himself, without ceasing to be God, has come amongst us, not just in but *as* a particular man, at a particular time and place. The human life lived and the death died have been held quite literally to *be* the human life and death of God himself in one of the modes of his own eternal being. Jesus Christ, it has been firmly held, was truly God as well as being truly man.[1]

Hebblethwaite went on to support this position against the tendencies soon to be given wide publicity in *The Myth of God Incarnate*, and in the decades since he has maintained it in a variety of ways.

A recent exposition of his thought has been given in the Hensley Henson Lectures in Oxford in 2002, entitled 'A Natural Theology of Historical Revelation'. They are the broadest, richest and most sustained exposition so far of his incarnation-centred account of reality. A brief description of them is in order as a basic statement of the Hebblethwaite side of this essay's conversation. What follows the summary in the rest of this essay might be seen as commentary and footnotes on these lectures.[2]

A Cumulative, Historical Argument for Christian Faith

The first of the four lectures, on 'Revelation and Natural Theology', argued for the rational nature of both natural theology (appealing to facts about the world and human life available at any place or time) and revealed theology (appealing to specific strands in world history). Weaving together strands from Bishop Butler, H. H. Farmer, James

---

[1] See Brian Hebblethwaite, *The Incarnation: Collected Essays in Christology*, 1987:2f.

[2] Quotations in this essay are taken from these lectures as originally delivered. They appear in a slightly revised form under the title *In Defence of Christianity*, 2005.

Incarnation, Rationality and Transformative Practices 189

Barr, John Henry Newman, Basil Mitchell, Richard Swinburne and Robert Prevost, Hebblethwaite puts the case for a 'single, rational, cumulative apologetic argument for Christian faith'. Why not combine arguments from nature and from history? He accepts, with Plantinga, that basic beliefs do not depend on the support of rational argument, but nevertheless sees their credibility and commendability strengthened by it. Aquinas and Farrer are seen as rare cases of thinkers who are simultaneously theologically literate philosophers and philosophically literate theologians.

In the culmination of the lecture he describes the sort of rationality that is exemplified by Aquinas, Farrer and others. This key paragraph reads:

> The kind of critical rationality employed in philosophical theology includes the theoretical and the practical within the scope of *judgement* – the topic of Kant's third *Critique* – albeit in a much more embracing sense than Kant envisaged there. The role of judgement in assessing the case for a specific world view was stressed already by Butler in the passage quoted earlier, where he spoke of 'a great number of things so and so disposed, and taken into one view'. This key aspect of rationality was also stressed by Newman in his well-known section on the illative sense – a 'sense' here being a cognitive not just an affective faculty – a power of judgement seen in the good lawyer or historian, as Mitchell shows. Keith Ward, in his *Rational Theology and the Creativity of God*, speaks of 'synoptic rationality', a creative and imaginative facility of judgement and discernment, evaluating all the world's most significant features and fitting them into an overall pattern. Michael Langford, in his recent book, *A Liberal Theology for the Twenty-first Century*, sub-titled 'A passion for reason', develops this understanding of the scope of human reason for the critical evaluation of philosophical and religious world views. Such comprehensive judgement involves not only the logic of deduction and induction, but also the cognitive elements in feeling, imagination, and intuition, the resulting discernments, all of them being subject to critical reflection and debate.

That is what I would call a description of wisdom by someone primarily concerned with cognition. And a great deal hangs on the meaning of 'subject to' in the final clause, to which I will return later.

The second lecture, entitled 'The History of Religions', supports the cumulative case for Christian belief in God by appealing to religious experience (in a broad sense, covering not only 'mystical perception' but also 'the ways in which ordinary believers in all religious contexts feel themselves sustained, addressed, called, rebuked, forgiven, loved'), moral obligation, beauty, and truth. All of these are seen as historical phenomena that fail to fit a neat division between natural and historically revealed theology. The case allows for a good deal of overlap between arguments for Christianity and for other religions: it posits 'different historical channels of divine special revelation', and claims that 'Christian apologetic today is helped, not hindered, by the presence world-wide of the experiential, moral, aesthetic and metaphysical factors to which I have been attending in adverting to axiological arguments for the existence of God.'

After surveying various ways of coping with the diversity of religions (by Hegel, Schleiermacher, Troeltsch, Hick), Hebblethwaite insists that the revelation-claims of the religions often conflict and 'require some "grading" of religions in terms of their finality and universal scope'. He then debates with the American philosophers of religion Alvin Plantinga, William Alston and Robert Adams, in order to support his position that there can be a plausible Christian theology of religion and the religions that fulfils three criteria. It must (a) account for the diversity of religions, (b) (perhaps along the lines of Adams's treatment) it must appreciate the *value* of that diversity, and (c) it must account for the necessary particularity and indispensability of its own key element – namely, the finality of Christ.

An early example of such a theology has, he suggests, been offered by H. H. Farmer in *Revelation and Religion*, which he finds especially attractive because of its 'incarnational soteriology' in the context of the centrality of history. That sets the scene for the last two lectures, but for the sake of my later discussion I want to draw attention to two closely related points in this lecture. The first is the way religious experience, in line with its broad scope mentioned in the summary above, is embedded in traditions of belief and their 'socially established practices of various kinds'. There is an 'interplay and mutual support of experience and belief' which is especially clear in the ethical dimension. The second point follows from this: the scope of special revelation is extended 'to cover the whole field of religious and moral awareness, just because this is nearly always already embedded in social practice'.

The third lecture, 'The Faith of Israel and the Story of Jesus', is the linchpin of the series. How should the appeals to history at the heart

Incarnation, Rationality and Transformative Practices 191

of Christian faith be assessed? On the one hand, Hebblethwaite wants to take seriously 'the empirical facts accessible to the historian *qua* historian', though taking into account the influence of 'background evidence' and 'background assumptions' (such as a theistic perspective). On the other hand, he also adopts Austin Farrer's and Samuel Taylor Coleridge's idea of a divine–human dialogue in all the messiness of human history. About this he says:

> Farrer's view of historically mediated revelation applies, of course, both to the Scriptures themselves and to the events to which the Scriptures bear witness. The idea of divine–human dialogue in and through the fallible media of history, is particularly important for any rational appeal to the Bible. In Christian apologetic, remember, we do not appeal to the Bible simply as an authority. We appeal, in Coleridge's words from *Confessions of an Inquiring Spirit*, to what 'finds me' – that is, to what comes across as ethically and spiritually profound and life-transforming. That sounds a somewhat subjective criterion, but, of course, it is *inter*-subjective; it is a matter of communally-formed doxastic practice, as Adams showed in respect of its ethical connotations.

The dialogue model involves taking into account long processes of growth and development, traditions of intertwined understanding and practice, and complex forms of learning through history (as through acknowledging what God has been revealing through Jewish and Muslim history, or through the development of historical critical methods).

But how does this sort of God-related, cumulative, communal, practice-shaped understanding relate to what 'the historian *qua* historian' can affirm? The critical event is the resurrection of Jesus. With assistance from David Browne and Richard Swinburne, Hebblethwaite makes the case for his core position. On the Resurrection, as on other vital matters of Christian faith, it is important to be able to do apologetics by bringing to bear 'tentative, exploratory, probabilistic, even hypothetical reasonings'. Yet these are not foundational, and Christians do not have to rely on such reasonings in order to believe with integrity. Why? 'Committed participation in the convictional community of the Christian church has its own internal warrant, as Plantinga has shown.' The obvious question, which will be taken up later in this chapter, is what more might be said about the relationship between these two.

The fourth lecture, 'Christianity and the History of the World', is the largest historical canvas ever used by Hebblethwaite, ranging through history and its civilizations. The cumulative argument here is that it is justifiable to 'look for evidence in history for signs of the sanctification of the world'. He makes a case for the providential (if always vulnerable) implementation of 'Kingdom values' such as freedom, mercy, natural right, and openness to free speech being in line with a Christian understanding of history (and in line with that of other religious and secular traditions too). His main argument is with Samuel Huntington's *The Clash of Civilizations*. That vision of a conflict-ridden future in which religions are a key factor is argued to be in contradiction with Huntington's own recognition that religions can foster the common values necessary for world peace. The conclusion is:

> That there is evidence in the gradual, episodic, though hardly 'inexorable', transformations of public consciousness and political order, not only in Christendom, but after Christendom, of the sanctification of the world, seems to me, at least, arguable and at best, quite plausible. So I think we do have further appeals to history to add to the cumulative case for Christian belief. In addition to natural theology and the inner rationale of Christian doctrine, in addition to the history of Christian morality and religion, in addition to the faith of Israel and the story of Jesus, not least his resurrection, in addition to the lives of the saints and the Christian church, insofar as it actually does embody and manifest the fruits of the Spirit, the apologist also appeals to the ways in which the values of the Kingdom can be seen in fact to have penetrated society and made their contribution to the redemption of the world.

That is the 'comprehensive judgement' emerging from the four lectures – and indeed from the whole of Brian Hebblethwaite's philosophy and theology to date. I will now add some comments to it.

Wisdom, Rationality and Human Transformation

Running through the Hensley Henson Lectures and through the rest of Hebblethwaite's work is a tension between what I have called above the 'wisdom' approach typified by the quotation from the final part of the first lecture, integrating in a cumulative way the cognitive, affec-

Incarnation, Rationality and Transformative Practices 193

tive, imaginative and practical dimensions of apprehension, discernment and judgement on the one hand, and, on the other hand, a narrower conception of rationality that seeks justification in more singlemindedly logical, empirical, critical or analytical terms. It is usually a healthy tension, reflecting accountability before different traditions of thought that flourish best when in dialogue with each other. But a condition for its health is constant vigilance and willingness to take the dialogue further. I will begin to attempt to do so from that concluding section of the first lecture.

I have already commented that in the statement, 'Such comprehensive judgement involves not only the logic of deduction and induction, but also the cognitive elements in feeling, imagination, and intuition, the resulting discernments, all of them, being subject to critical reflection and debate', a good deal depends on the meaning of 'subject to'. The sentence following this is crucial for its interpretation:

> In holding that theistic metaphysics and Christian doctrine can and should be discussed openly, for purposes of self-understanding, mutual comprehension, and apologetic, I am siding with Wolfhart Pannenberg, when, against Bernard Lonergan's insistence on conversion as a precondition of theological insight, he pleads for theology 'to be discussed without reservations in the context of critical rationality'.

I wonder whether siding in such a definite way with Pannenberg against Lonergan is in line with keeping a healthy tension. The role of conversion in Lonergan's theological method is fairly clear: it is to do with the human subject's need to undergo certain transformations if he or she is to be able to know and decide in relation to God. God is not like an object open to inspection by anyone. God is even an exception to the maxim *Nihil amatum nisi praecognitum* ('Nothing is loved unless it is first known').[3] Conversion (or conversions – Lonergan talks in terms of intellectual, moral and religious conversions) is an attempt to do justice to the fact of transformations that are the conditions for human beings recognizing and responding to certain realities. Hebblethwaite in later lectures in the series wants to do justice to historical change, to cumulative developments over time, and also to the mutual interplay of experience and belief. Lonergan's concept of conversion affirms this at the level of the individual

---

3 For Lonergan's discussion of this, see his *Method in Theology*, 1972:122–4.

human subject. The question for Hebblethwaite is: why not affirm both Pannenberg *and* Lonergan? Pannenberg's concept of critical rationality seems well suited to that side of Hebblethwaite's apologetics which insists on taking into account generally acknowledged empirical facts and understandings and what can be affirmed by 'the historian *qua* historian'. But can it do full justice to Christian doctrine in relation to 'self-understanding' and 'mutual comprehension'? The side of Hebblethwaite's cumulative argument that is imaginative, affective, intuitive, illative, practical, and in the interests of comprehensive discernment, judgement and living well before God: that must surely allow for Lonergan as well as Pannenberg?

Hebblethwaite claims that Lonergan's insistence on conversion (coupling it in this regard – unhappily, I think – with Torrance and Barth, allegedly 'making the logic of theological rationality internal to the perspective of faith') 'makes theology – natural or revealed – undiscussable, immune to criticism, incapable of hypothetical reflection', and prevents it from remaining 'open to consideration by all in the context of critical rationality'. The 'by all' is the Achilles heel of that criticism. Are we to take it literally – all infants, criminals, those with mental disabilities . . .? There must be some conditions such as the learning of language, the availability of a certain sort of education, the possession of certain desires and abilities, and so on. It is quite possible that without having undergone certain forms of learning requiring transformation (imaginative, intellectual, moral, religious) there cannot be appropriate self-understanding or mutual comprehension in theological matters. This, however, need not rule out discussion, critique or hypothetical reflection. It just means that there can be no normative assumption about what 'all' think or know or have experienced. Each person has been formed in specific historical ways and mutual comprehension cannot be facilitated by requiring those who have undergone certain crucial transformations to bracket these out for the purposes of theological discussion. In certain apologetic situations that might be appropriate, but in the overall context of Hebblethwaite's cumulative argument, with its strong appeal to history, this may be a case of the healthy tension between wisdom and modern critical rationality having been lost. The 'subject to' may have slipped from meaning 'open to' critical reflection and debate or 'thoroughly examined through' it, to meaning something more like 'limited to the terms of' or 'adjudicated by' critical reflection and debate.

Practices, Beliefs, and their Sustaining Contexts

The preceding discussion might appear too individualist in its approach to religious understanding and transformation. Its point about learning and the conditions for comprehensive judgement is strengthened by considering more fully what the second Henson lecture calls 'socially-established practices of various kinds', and the third lecture speaks of as the 'ethically and spiritually profound and life-transforming' reality that is rooted in the inter-subjective realm of 'communally-formed doxastic practice'. Once formative and transformative practices are taken into account we move even further from any notion of a level playing-field for rational discussion on which 'all' can engage in transparent discussion, critique and reflection.

Think of someone who has over many years worshipped and loved God, repented regularly of sin, practised physical, moral and spiritual disciplines and virtues, meditated on and been shaped by Scripture, read widely and thoughtfully on matters relating to their faith, had friendships and discussions with well-educated, mature fellow Christians as well as with those of other faiths and none, followed a demanding vocation in the world, and had their faith tested in a variety of situations, including some involving great suffering. The likelihood is that such a person will have grown into a wisdom which will be very difficult to describe, explain or justify to someone formed very differently.

Hebblethwaite recognizes this in his emphasis on the long-term formation of ordinary Christians and others, and on the interplay of experience and belief. It is, as he sees, deeply implicated in his concepts of history and incarnation. I am interested in exploring what happens if this is followed through more thoroughly. One current example is the Valparaiso Project through which a number of Christians, involved in a wide variety of practices, have over many years tried to think through together how their faith and their practices inform each other. One recent volume, *Practicing Theology: Beliefs and Practices in Christian Life*,[4] is especially helpful in relation to supplementing Hebblethwaite's Hensons. By focusing on theology in relation to the formation of local communities, traditions of prayer, healing, hospitality, discernment, and theological education, it opens up ways of cultivating the 'middle ground' in Hebblethwaite's position. In his concentration on macro-level ideas of religions, morality, beauty,

---

4 Miroslav Volf and Dorothy C. Bass (eds), 2002.

truth, civilizations, 'Kingdom values', and many centuries of history, on the one hand, and, on the other, his concern with the detail of certain arguments and of the life, death and resurrection of Jesus Christ, he understandably leaves a good deal more to be discussed.

At their best, the Valparaiso participants do theology in relation to some of the densities of history (especially those related to ordinary Christian living), engaging with specific cases of the interplay of belief and experience (though they prefer to talk of practices rather than experience).[5] Close attention is paid to specific ways in which beliefs are affected by practices and vice versa. There is plenty of reasoning, but it is reasoning immersed in the particularities of practices, sensitive to their contours, ambiguities, inconsistencies, conflicts, and open-endedness. As Kathryn Tanner says:

> Apart from deliberate efforts to make them so, Christian practices, and many of the beliefs and values that inform them, do not hang together all that well. Rather than reward sharp and focused attention precisely to them, Christian practices seem to be constituted in great part by slippery give-and-take with non-Christian practices; indeed, they are mostly non-Christian practices – eating, meeting, greeting – done differently, born again, to unpredictable effect.[6]

As Tanner goes on to stress, it is just because of this that Christian practices do not work well without critical theological engagement. None of this contradicts Hebblethwaite, but it is a very different way of coming at the implications of incarnation and the realities of history. If space permitted, it would be fruitful to have an extended dialogue between the two, but for now I want to draw just two conclusions in relation to his Hensons.

First, there is the clear distinction he makes between, on the one

---

5 Bass sums up the convergence among participants as follows: 'Several key components of practices are important to every author. First, as meaningful clusters of human activity (including the activity of thinking) that require and engender knowledge on the part of practitioners, *practices resist the separation of thinking from acting*, and thus of Christian doctrine from Christian life. Second, *practices are social, belonging to groups of people across generations* – a feature that undergirds the communal quality of the Christian life. Third, *practices are rooted in the past but are also constantly adapting to changing circumstances*, including new cultural settings. Fourth, *practices articulate wisdom that is in the keeping of practitioners who do not think of themselves as theologians*' (2002:6).

6 'Theological reflection and Christian practices', in Volf and Bass, 2002:230.

hand, basic beliefs and related religious experience, and, on the other hand, the cumulative case for Christian faith that he builds up rationally, empirically, tentatively, hypothetically, and imaginatively. In so far as he is making the point that marshalling a persuasive rational apologetic argument in the face of all alternatives and objections is not foundational (but may be helpful) for the faith of Christian believers, that seems a sensible position. But in the light of the discussions in *Practicing Theology*, it is worth reflecting further on the relationship between the internal warrants for Christian faith and the apologetic arguments for it. One key question might be, for example: if certain practices are deeply related to certain beliefs, what are the appropriate practices that Christian apologetics ought to recommend and facilitate? There are other ways too in which the co-inherence of (as well as tension between) beliefs and practices complexifies the internal/external distinction.[7]

Second, the social nature of practices (in the sense the term is used in the Valparaiso Project, and has been quoted earlier) suggests that Hebblethwaite's apologetic project might pay more attention to the social settings that enable it to flourish. It would be possible to trace concordances between his actual social setting and the shape of his apologetics. This is a position that is both rooted in the heart of traditional Anglican incarnational faith and is also open, conversational and generous in relation to other (including dissident) understandings of Anglicanism and Christianity, to other religious traditions, and to non-religious philosophies.

The immediate setting that has facilitated this combination for most of Hebblethwaite's academic life is Cambridge University, one of its Colleges (Queens'), and its Faculty of Divinity. The religious history of the situation includes the move from Anglican establishment into a complex set of continually renegotiated 'settlements'. The University is largely secular in ethos, but not ideologically 'secularist'. This has enabled it to respond positively to initiatives that enable academic engagements both with Christianity and other religious traditions, and also between those traditions and other disciplines such as the natural and human sciences. It has also made new links with the Cambridge Theological Federation (an integrated set of colleges from the Anglican, Methodist, Orthodox, Roman Catholic and United

---

7 See, in particular, the essays by Amy Plantinga Pauw, Serene Jones, Sarah Coakley, L. Gregory Jones, Kathryn Tanner and Miroslav Volf in Volf and Bass, 2002.

Reformed traditions and including a Centre for Jewish–Christian Relations) in which Hebblethwaite was active for many years. He has been an energetic citizen of the University in various roles (the culminating one as University Proctor), and was the key intermediary in enabling the benefaction of a new established post in theology and natural science. Queens' College is an Anglican foundation with an Anglican chapel, of which Hebblethwaite was Dean for many years, and not least because of his presence it has been a strong base for theology and religious studies. The Faculty of Divinity has during his time and with his active encouragement and participation continued to develop its Christian studies while at the same time adding major dimensions in the study of other religions and various disciplines in relation to the religions. It has also sustained a tradition of combining the study of religious traditions with critical and constructive thought about their truth and practice, and Hebblethwaite himself has exemplified that combination. Not only that, his citizenship in the Faculty during a time of development unprecedented in its history went far beyond the call of duty, above all by leading it as Chairman of the Faculty Board for two vital years as it was reorientating itself in the 1990s.

If this participation in University, College and Faculty were to be described in terms of practices as discussed in the Valparaiso Project, an academic version of 'hospitality' might spring to mind. In particular, there is his openness to other religions. That has not only been a matter of philosophical and theological discussion but has also involved many years of teaching about the relation of Eastern and Western religious traditions, especially with Julius Lipner. But the practice that I see at the heart of that teaching and much else in his life is conversation. It is, of course, a constitutive element in his many forms of hospitality, both literal and in the 'entertainment' of ideas. But it has also run through his various University, College and Faculty roles (every so often I hear of yet another group, committee or dining club in which he has played a significant part), and is at the heart of his teaching. It is no accident that he is best known for his many years of debate with Don Cupitt, an ongoing conversation between deeply differing positions that has been carried on with rigour, with courtesy, and in growing friendship. That exemplary performance of civilized yet deeply committed religious disputation has deep roots in the institutions and communities of Church, University, College and Faculty that have helped shape Hebblethwaite. But those institutions are always fragile and capable of errant development. Those of us who have been privileged to take part in the life of those institutions with Brian Hebblethwaite are deeply grateful for his commitment to the disciplined conversations through which he himself has shaped them for the better through times when without him things might well have gone very differently. Little of what I have just been discussing could be guessed from reading his publications, but the close affinities between his thought and the nature of the settings and practices in which it has flourished might have practical implications for his apologetics – something else to be rolled up into that cumulative case for an incarnation that is itself related to the whole of creation and history.

Two Large Concluding Issues

Yet such considerations, however significant, are at a different level from the themes considered in the Hensons and in most of Hebblethwaite's writings. The 'middle ground' perspective on social practices and institutions, through which I have been regarding his life and work in the previous section, should by no means distract from the large philosophical and theological issues that he considers. On the vast historical canvas of the Hensons two of the largest are the relationship between world faiths and the pivotal event of the resurrection of Jesus Christ. I will in conclusion say something about each of them in order to connect them to what has been said about institutions and practices.

Universities and Interfaith Relations

Hebblethwaite, in his critique of Huntington mentioned above, puts a good deal of emphasis on the resources of the religions for peacemaking on the basis of commonalities. My point about this is brief and simple. As Hebblethwaite himself exemplifies, one of the institutions important for such peacemaking is the university, especially in so far as it realizes the virtues of intellectual and emotional hospitality to those best able to engage in intensive and disciplined conversations concerning questions raised by the religions, about the religions and between the religions.

As one looks around the world, there are very few institutions in a position to host thoughtful study and dialogue aimed at facing the realities of the past and present and also at trying to open up a better future. Each of the major religious traditions has places where there can be study, discussion and teaching in long-term collegial settings, but between the traditions such collegiality is almost non-existent. It makes sense that this should happen in institutions devoted to education and research such as universities. In fact, most universities in most parts of the world are for various reasons not well suited to this. Many are ideologically secularist and unsuited to hosting the study of religions and discussion of religious truth and practice. Those that are explicitly religious are often dedicated to one tradition in a form that, for different reasons, is also unsuited to this. That leaves those institutions, whether officially secular or religious, that are able and willing to host this study and dialogue, and these, in comparison with the number of universities worldwide, are few. The fact, therefore, that Hebblethwaite's rigorously argued, conversation-shaped and peacemaking approach to the relations between religions has been developed in one of those few institutions may be worth noting explicitly and following through practically (for example, by arguing for the importance of such institutions and by taking part in efforts to build them up and multiply them) if his intentions are to be realized in the future.

The Resurrection of Jesus

Finally, there is the event of the resurrection of Jesus, where questions of God, incarnation, history, rationality, empirical fact and religious experience come together. Hebblethwaite's cumulative apologetic gives considerable weight to this, and I will draw on another former student of his, Sarah Coakley, in order to make some connections with what was said in the previous section.

Coakley has participated in the Valparaiso Project, and her essay in *Practicing Theology* is on 'Deepening practices: perspectives from ascetical and mystical theology'. There she puts forward a complex understanding of the relationship of beliefs to practices based on the classical distinctions and relations between the 'purgative', 'illuminative' and 'unitive' ways in Christian life and prayer. She sees a development from belief-led practice to practice-led belief, always allowing for the mutuality of the two. She summarizes her thesis as follows:

> At the first level, that of purgation, specific, external practices in virtue arise from the initial commitment to belief at baptism. Much of the emphasis is on setting one's life in a direction different from that of the world. For this reason, the rhetoric may be largely oppo-

sitional, and the practices remain somewhat legalistically construed: Christian *ethike* is being established. At the second level, practices start inversely to shape (or re-shape) belief, as a form of identification with Christ begins to flower and to unsettle the extrinsicism of the approach of the first stage. Finally, at the third stage, more arcane theological insights become available that are only the prerogative of those transformed by lengthy and painful practice. (2002:84)

In another essay, 'The Resurrection and the "spiritual senses": On Wittgenstein, epistemology and the Risen',[8] Coakley takes this further in relation to the resurrection of Jesus, enquiring into the meaning of the language of encounter with the risen Christ. She says that 'the reception of religious truth does not occur *on a flat plane*: even within the ranks of "believers" the understanding or perception of the "risen Christ" will have variations of depth' (ibid.:132). She then criticizes those, including Wolfhart Pannenberg and Richard Swinburne (both of whom are favourably reviewed by Hebblethwaite in relation to the Resurrection), whose approach to the historicity of the Resurrection is in line with Lockean probabilism and who 'are propelled by a fundamentally *apologetic* conviction: that the resurrection of Jesus, if it is to be rationally believable, must be subject to the *same* level of critical scrutiny that we would accord to any (secular) "historical" event' (ibid.:133). Their 'flat plane' cannot do justice, Coakley claims, to important features of the New Testament texts, such as their testimony to changes in epistemological response to the risen Christ, and their indication of 'the possibility of simultaneous and different responses to the same event (such that some vital shift is again required for recognition of the risen Christ to take place)' (ibid.:135).

Her own suggestion is that, in line with classic spirituality, we take seriously the spiritual senses or 'faculties of the heart', with their possibility of 'transformed sense knowledge' (ibid.:137). She finds this tradition, with its subtle, multi-levelled approach to perception and understanding, and its insistence that spiritual practices affect our knowing, neglected as a current epistemological option, though she gathers much from the later Wittgenstein to support her case for pursuing it. This challenges the broad tradition of Christian philosophical apologetics to which Hebblethwaite belongs to correct,

---

8 In Sarah Coakley, *Powers and Submissions: Spirituality, Philosophy and Gender*, 2002:130–52.

enrich and expand its epistemology (and in particular to allow more for 'the progressive nature of the epistemological undertaking': ibid.:146) in dialogue with this sort of spirituality and biblical interpretation. Coakley finds in Wittgenstein 'a view of faith profoundly sensitive to its differing "levels" of intensity, perceptual/tactile response, and spiritual and moral maturity' (ibid.:148), and she complements this with insights from feminist epistemologists.

I find this a convincing start in supplementing Hebblethwaite's impressive cumulative case for Christian faith. It also relativizes and complexifies his distinction between the internal warrants of the believer's faith and the probabilistic apologetics directed mostly towards unbelievers. Coakley says:

> We have focused too much in the era of 'secularism', I shall argue, on the great gulf apparently fixed between the 'believer' and the 'non-believer' (and even some of Wittgenstein's conversations seem to get stuck here); yet epistemic and religious transformation surely does not stop with conversion or baptism, and we need to be able to give an account of this. (ibid.:132)

I see this sentiment in harmony with Hebblethwaite's relativizing of other great gulfs, especially those between the religions, and as carrying forward his fundamental concern for a wisdom that unites the theoretical and the practical in arriving at a quality of comprehensive judgement fed by feeling, imagination, and intuition as well as critical reflection.

Publications of B. L. Hebblethwaite

1967

'Doctrinal Criticism: G. F. Woods as a Theological Teacher', *Theology*, 70 (1967), pp. 402–5.

1968

Review of *Christ for us Today*, ed. Norman Pittenger, and *We Believe In God*, ed. Rupert E. Davies, *Theology*, 71 (1968), pp. 516–17.

1969

Review of *The Function of Theology* by Martin Thornton, and *Truths that Compelled: Contemporary Implications of Biblical Theology* by Stewart Lawton, *Theology*, 72 (1969), pp. 88–9.
Review of John Hick and Arthur McGill (eds), *The Many-Faced Argument*, Alvin Plantinga (ed.), *The Ontological Argument*, and *Living Questions to Dead Gods* by Jacques Durandeaux, *Theology*, 72 (1969), pp. 275–6.
'Theology Today', review of *Systematic and Philosophical Theology* by William Nichols, *Cambridge Review*, 91(1969), pp. 26–7.

1970

Review of *Faith under Challenge* by Heinrich Fries, and *Living with Questions: Investigations into the Theory and Practice of Belief in God* by David E. Jenkins, *Theology*, 73 (1970), pp. 425–6.
Review of *Der Pantokrator: Ontologie als Grundlage der Lehre von Gott* by Fritz Buri, *Journal of Theological Studies*, 21 (1970), pp. 521–5.
'Bonhoeffer', review of *Dietrich Bonhoeffer: A Biography* by Eberhard Bethge, *Cambridge Review*, October 1970, pp. 33–4.
'Austin Farrer's Concept of Divine Providence', *Theology*, 73 (1970), pp. 541–51.

1971

'On Understanding what one Believes', *New Fire*, 1 (1971/2), pp. 11–15.
'Rudolf Bultmann', review of *The Gospel of John: A Commentary* by Rudolf Bultmann, *Cambridge Review*, November 1971, pp. 57–8.

1972

'Growing Points in Theology', *The Times Higher Education Supplement*, 19 May 1972.
'Authority and Conscience', *The Franciscan*, 14 (1972), pp. 137–41.
Review of *The Absolute and the Atonement* by Dom Illtyd Trethowan, *Theology*, 75 (1972), pp. 327–9.
'Radical and Liberal Theology: The Bible', *The Modern Churchman*, 15 (1972), pp. 236–8.
'God and the World – One Reality or Two?: A Comment', *Theology*, 75 (1972), pp. 403–5.
Review of *Humanism and Christianity* by Martin D'Arcy, *Journal of Theological Studies*, 23 (1972), p. 59.
'The Appeal to Experience in Christology' in S. W. Sykes and J. P. Clayton (eds), *Christ, Faith and History: Cambridge Studies in Christology*, Cambridge: Cambridge University Press 1972, pp. 263–78.
Theology and Religious Studies: Degree Course Guide 1972/3, CRAC 1972.

1973

Review of *The Study of Religious Language* by Anders Jeffner, and *Language and Belief* by Jean Ladrière, *Theology*, 76 (1973), pp. 267–8.
Review of *Reflective Faith: Essays in Philosophical Theology* by Austin Farrer, *New Fire*, 2 (1973/4), pp. 264–5.
Review of *Contemporary Critiques of Religion* by Kai Nielsen, and *The Faith of the People of God: A Lay Theology* by John Macquarrie, *Journal of Theological Studies*, 24 (1973), pp. 635–8, 649.
'The Philosophical Theology of I. T. Ramsey: Some Further Reflections', *Theology*, 76 (1973), pp. 638–45.

1974

Review of *Models for Divine Activity* by I. T. Ramsey, *Theology*, 77 (1974), p. 159.
'The Writer Shut In', review of *A Common Sky: Philosophy and the Literary Imagination* by A. D. Nuttall, *The Times Higher Education Supplement*, 5 April 1974.
'Becket's Frenzied Solipsism', review of Ian Gregor and Walter Stein (eds), *The Prose for God: Religious and Anti-Religious Aspects of Imaginative Literature*, *The Times Higher Education Supplement*, 17 May 1974.
Review of *God and the Universe of Faiths* by John Hick, and *Falsification and Belief* by Alastair McKinnon, *Theology*, 77 (1974), pp. 315–17.
Theology and Religious Studies: Degree Course Guide 1974/5, CRAC 1974.

1975

Review of *Glaube und Mythos: Eine kritische, religionsphilosophisch-Theologische Untersuchung des Mythos-Begriffe Bei Karl Jaspers* by Aloys Klein, and *Paul Tillich: An Essay on the Role of Ontology in his Philosophical*

Publications of B. L. Hebblethwaite

Theology by Alister M. Macleod, *Journal of Theological Studies*, 26 (1975), pp. 228–30, 230–1.
'Cast out the Devil Myths', *News of the World*, 27 April 1975.
Review of *Christian Empiricism* by Ian Ramsey, *Theology*, 78 (1975), pp. 270–1.
'Exorcism', *South African Outlook*, 105 (1975), pp. 74, 78.
Review of *But Deliver Us from Evil: An Introduction to the Demonic Dimension in Pastoral Care* by John Richards, *Theology*, 78 (1975), pp. 434–5.
'Exorcism and Religion', *Contemporary Review*, October 1975, pp. 188–93.

1976

Review of *The Ministry of Healing in the Church of England: An Ecumenical-Liturgical Study* by Charles W. Gusmer, and *Sacrifice and the Death of Christ* by Frances M. Young, *Journal of Theological Studies*, 27 (1976), pp. 268, 276.
Review of John Hick (ed.), *Truth and Dialogue: The Relationship Between World Religions*, *Theology*, 79 (1976), pp. 242–3.
Theology and Religious Studies: Degree Course Guide 1976/7, CRAC 1976.
Review of *Jesus the Christ* by H. E. W. Turner, *Epworth Review*, 3 (1976), pp. 114–15.
Evil, Suffering and Religion, London: Sheldon Press 1976 (American edition: New York: Hawthorn Books 1976).

1977

'Incarnation: The Essence of Christianity?' *Theology*, 80 (1977), pp. 85–91.
Review of *My Affair with the Church* by Joseph McCulloch, *Theology*, 80 (1977), pp. 141–3.
Review of Vilmos Vajta (ed.), *The Gospel as History*, *Journal of Theological Studies*, 28 (1977), p. 262.
'Philosophy of Religion 1971–1976', *Epworth Review*, 4 (1977), pp. 110–14.
'Perichoresis: Reflections on the Doctrine of the Trinity', *Theology*, 80 (1977), pp. 255–61.
Review of *Karl Barth: His Life from Letters and Autobiogaphical Texts*, and *Suffering* by Dorothee Soelle, *Epworth Review*, 4 (1977), pp. 116–18, 149–50.
'The Doctrine of the Incarnation in the Thought of Austin Farrer', *New Fire*, 4 (1977/8), pp. 460–8.

1978

'The Religions of India' and 'The Buddhist Faith', in The Reader's Digest Association (ed.), *The Reader's Digest Library of Modern Knowledge*, vol. 2, London: Readers Digest Publications 1978, pp. 704–7.
Review of *Faith and Reality* by Wolfhart Pannenberg, *Epworth Review*, 5 (1978), pp. 127–8.
Review of *Religion, Truth and Language-Games* by Patrick Sherry, *Theology*, 81 (1978), pp. 131–3.
'Providence and Divine Action', *Religious Studies*, 14 (1978), pp. 223–36.

1979

'Time and Eternity and Life "after" Death' and 'A Further Comment on Life "after" Death', *Heythrop Journal*, 20 (1979), pp. 57–62, 187–8.
Review of *The Ethics of Freedom* by Jacques Ellul, *The Franciscan*, 21 (1979), pp. 110–11.
'The Myth and Christian Faith', 'The Incarnation and Modern Theology', 'The Moral and Religious Value of the Incarnation' and 'The Uniqueness of the Incarnation', in Michael Goulder (ed.), *Incarnation and Myth: The Debate Continued*, London: SCM Press 1979, pp. 15–16, 27–8, 87–100, 189–91.
'Die Angemessenheit des Inkarnationsbegriffe als Möglichkeit, Christus zu interpretieren', in Klaus Kremkau (ed.), *Christus Allein – allein das Christentum: Vorträge der vierten Theologischen Konferenz zwischen Vertretern der Evangelischen Kirche in Deutschland und der Kirche von England*, Beiheft Zur Ökumenischen Rundschau Nr. 36, Frankfurt am Main: Verlag Otto Lembeck 1979, pp. 36–56.
Review of *Christian Hope* by John Macquarrie, *Theology*, 82 (1979), pp. 452–3.
Review of *Reason and Religion* by S. C. Brown, *Journal of Theological Studies*, 30 (1979), p. 599.
'Some Reflections on Predestination, Providence and Divine Foreknowledge', *Religious Studies*, 15 (1979), pp. 433–48.
Review of *Atheism and Theism* by Errol E. Harris, *Journal of Theological Studies*, 15 (1979), pp. 558–9.
Review of *A Reason to Hope* by David Edwards, *Journal of Theological Studies*, 15 (1979), pp. 561–2.

1980

Edited (with John Hick), *Christianity and Other Religions: Selected Readings*, Glasgow: William Collins Sons (Fount Paperbacks) 1980.
'Recent British Theology', in Peter Toon and James D. Spiceland (eds), *One God in Trinity: An Analysis of the Primary Dogma of Christianity*, London: Samuel Bagster 1980, pp. 158–71.
Review of *Persons and Life After Death* by H. D. Lewis, *Heythrop Journal*, 21 (1980), pp. 228–9.
'The Propriety of the Doctrine of the Incarnation as a Way of Interpreting Christ', *Scottish Journal of Theology*, 33 (1980), pp. 201–22.
Review of *Shadows and the Dark: The Problems of Suffering and Evil* by John Cowburn, SJ, *British Journal of Religious Education*, 3 (1980), p. 158.
Review of *Multiple Echo* by Cornelius Ernst, OP, *Theology*, 83 (1980), pp. 374–5.
The Problems of Theology, Cambridge: Cambridge University Press 1980.
'Religionsphilosophie in Grossbritannien in der siebziger Jahre', *Kerygma und Dogma*, 26 (1980), pp. 303–16.

1981

Review of C. S. Duthie (ed.), *Resurrection and Immortality: A Selection from the Drew Lectures on Immortality*, *Heythrop Journal*, 22 (1981), pp. 224–5.

Review of *After Death: Life in God* by Norman Pittenger, *Heythrop Journal*, 22 (1981), p. 344.
Review of *Does God Exist? An Answer for Today* by Hans Küng, *Theology*, 84 (1981), pp. 367–9.
Review of John A. Howard (ed.), *Belief, Faith and Reason, The Expository Times*, 92 (1980/1), p. 380.
The Adequacy of Christian Ethics, Basingstoke: Marshall Morgan & Scott 1981 (American edition: *Christian Ethics in the Modern Age*, Philadelphia: Westminster Press 1982).

1982

(With David Galilee) 'Farrer's Concept of Double Agency: A Reply', *Theology*, 85 (1982), pp. 7–10.
Edited (with Stewart Sutherland), *The Philosophical Frontiers of Christian Theology: Essays presented to D. M. MacKinnon*, Cambridge: Cambridge University Press 1982.
Review of *The Ground and Grammar of Theology* by Thomas F. Torrance, *Heythrop Journal*, 24 (1982), pp. 194–5.
Review of G. W. Bromiley (ed.), *Karl Barth: Letters 1961–1968*, *Epworth Review*, 9 (1982), pp. 102–3.
'Can there be Genuine Dialogue between the Believer and the Unbeliever?', in Henning Schröer and Gerhard Müller (eds), *Vom Amt des Laien in Kirche und Theologie: Festschrift für Gerhard Krause zum 70. Geburtstag*, Berlin: Walter de Gruyter 1982, pp. 246–55.
Review of D. Stacey (ed.), *Is Christianity Credible?*, *Epworth Review*, 9 (1982), pp. 93–4.
Review of *Christian Faith: An Introduction to the Study of the Faith* by Hendrikus Berkhof, *Religious Studies*, 18 (1982), pp. 523–5.

1983

Review of *Holding Fast to God* by Keith Ward, *New Fire*, 7 (1983/4), p. 299.
Review of *La Création: Essai sur la liberté et la nécessité, l'histoire et la loi, l'homme, le mal et Dieu* by Pierre Gisel, *Journal of Theological Studies*, 19 (1983), pp. 399–400.
'The Experiential Verification of Religious Belief in the Theology of Austin Farrer', in Jeffrey C. Eaton and Ann Loades (eds), *For God and Clarity: New Essays in Honor of Austin Farrer*, Allison Park, Pennsylvania: Pickwick Publications 1983, pp. 163–76.
'Farrer as Theologian', *New Fire*, 7 (1983), pp. 390–5.
'Anthropomorphism', 'Apologetics', 'Epistemology', 'Incarnation', 'Mediator' and 'Omnipotence', in Alan Richardson and John Bowden (eds), *A New Dictionary of Christian Theology*, London: SCM Press 1983, pp. 26–7, 31–2, 182–3, 289–91, 254–5, 413–14.
'Incarnation', in Gordon S. Wakefield (ed.), *A Dictionary of Christian Spirituality*, London: SCM Press 1983, pp. 275–7.
Review of *The Flight from Authority: Religion, Morality and the Quest For Autonomy* by Jeffrey Stout, *Theology*, 86 (1983), pp. 452–3.

1984

Review of David Tracy and Nicholas Lash (eds), *Cosmology and Theology (Concilium, June 1983)*, Theology, 87 (1984), pp. 291–2.
'Religious Truth and Dialogue', *Scottish Journal of Religious Studies*, 5 (1984), pp. 3–17.
The Christian Hope, Basingstoke: Marshall Morgan & Scott 1984 (American edition: Grand Rapids, Michigan: William B. Eerdmans 1984).
Review of *Does God Answer Prayer?* by Peter Baelz, *Heythrop Journal*, 35 (1984), p. 501.
Review of *In Search of Humanity: A Theological and Philosophical Approach* by John Macquarrie, *Journal of Theological Studies*, 20 (1984), pp. 577–9.
Review of *Religious Belief and Religious Skepticism* by Gary Gutting, *Philosophy*, 69 (1984), pp. 544–5.
Review of *Christians and Religious Pluralism: Patterns in the Christian Theology of Religions* by Alan Race, *Religious Studies*, 20 (1984), pp. 515–16.

1985

Review of *Begotten or Made* by Oliver O'Donovan, *Modern Theology*, (1984/5), pp. 163–4.
Review of *God's World, God's Body* by Grace Jantzen, *Theology*, 88 (1985), pp. 236–7.
'Freedom, Evil and Farrer', *New Blackfriars*, 66 (1985), pp. 178–87.
Review of *Faith and Reason* by Anthony Kenny, *Journal of Theological Studies*, 21 (1985), pp. 265–7.
Review of *Why Doctrines?* by Charles Hefling, *Theology*, 88 (1985), pp. 398–9.
Preaching through the Christian Year 10: Sermons from Queens' College, London and Oxford: A. R. Mowbray 1985.
Review of *Christian Theism: A Study in its Basic Principles* by Huw Parry Owen, *Journal of Theological Studies*, 21 (1985), pp. 546–7.
Review of *Theism* by Clement Dore, *Religious Studies*, 21 (1985), pp. 614–15.

1986

Review of A. Phillips Griffiths (ed.), *Philosophy and Practice*, Royal Institute of Philosophy Lecture Series: 18, *Modern Churchman*, 28 (1986), pp. 69–70.
Review of *Metaphor and Religious Language* by Janet Martin Soskice, *Heythrop Journal*, 27 (1986), pp. 225–6.
Review of *God of Chance* by David J. Bartholomew, *Journal of Theological Studies*, 22 (1986), p. 285
'Dialectic', 'Meaning/Meaninglessness' and 'Transcendence', in James F. Childress and John Macquarrie (eds), *A New Dictionary of Christian Ethics*, London: SCM Press 1986, pp. 155, 373, 631.
Review of *Freedom and Alienation* by Hywel D. Lewis, *The Forum*, Autumn 1986, pp. 31–3.
'Höchstes Gut', *Theologische Realenzyklopädie*, vol. 15, Berlin: Verlag de Gruyter 1986, pp. 435–41.
Review of *Metaphoric Process: The Creation of Scientific and Religious Under-*

standing by Mary Gerhart and Allan Russell, *Religious Studies*, 22 (1987), pp. 282–3.
'Mellor's "Bridge-Hand" Argument', *Religious Studies*, 22 (1986), pp. 473–9.

1987

Review of *Beyond Theism: A Grammar of God-Language* by Theodore W. Jennings Jr, *Theology*, 90 (1987), pp. 60–1.
The Incarnation: Collected Essays in Christology, Cambridge: Cambridge University Press 1987.
'Religious Language and Religious Pluralism', *Anvil*, 4 (1987), pp. 101–11.
Review of *Theology and the Problem of Evil* by Kenneth Surin, *The Tablet*, 7 November 1987.

1988

'The Theologian and Philosophy', in Peter Eaton (ed.), *The Trial of Faith*, Worthing: Churchman Publishing 1988, pp. 195–207.
'Philosophy of Religion', in Paul Avis (ed.), *The Threshold of Theology*, Basingstoke: Marshall Pickering 1988, pp. 85–104.
The Ocean of Truth: A Defence of Objective Theism, Cambridge: Cambridge University Press 1988.
Review of *The Evolution of the Soul* by Richard Swinburne, *Journal of Theological Studies*, 39 (1988), pp. 344–6.
Review of Gerard J. Hughes (ed.), *The Philosophical Assessment of Theology: Essays in Honour of Frederick C. Copleston*, Brian Davies (ed.), *Language, Meaning and God: Essays in Honour of Herbert McCabe O.P.*, and *God Matters* by Herbert McCabe, *Heythrop Journal*, 29 (1988), pp. 468–70.
'Fairness' and 'Utilitarismus', in Volker Drehsen *et al.* (eds), *Wörterbuch des Christentums* (Gütersloh: Gütersloher Verlagshaus Mohn) 1988, pp. 337–8, 1303–4.
'The Problem of Evil', in Geoffrey Wainwright (ed.), *Keeping the Faith: Essays to Mark the Centenary of Lux Mundi*, Philadephia: Fortress Press 1988, pp. 54–77.

1989

Review of *God's Action in the World* by Maurice Wiles, *Modern Theology*, 5 (1988/9), pp. 187–90.
'The Jewishness of Jesus from the Perspective of Christian Doctrine', *Scottish Journal of Theology*, 42 (1989), pp. 27–44.
Review of Eric James (ed.), *God's Truth: Essays to Celebrate the Twenty-Fifth Anniversary of* Honest to God, *Epworth Review*, 16 (1989), pp. 94–5.
'MacKinnon and the Problem of Evil', in Kenneth Surin (ed.), *Christ, Ethics and Tragedy: Essays in Honour of Donald MacKinnon*, Cambridge: Cambridge University Press 1989, pp. 131–45.
Review of *Partial Knowledge: Philosophical Studies in Paul* by Paul Gooch, *Philosophy*, 64 (1989), pp. 268–9.

Review of *Anselmian Explorations: Essays in Philosophical Theology* by Thomas V. Morris, *Religious Studies*, 25 (1989), pp. 137–8.
Review of *New Perspectives on Old-Time Religion* by George N. Schlesinger, *Journal of Theological Studies*, 25 (1989), pp. 709–10.
'Kirk, Kenneth Escott', *Theologische Realenzyklopädie*, vol. 19, Berlin Verlag de Gruyter 1989, pp. 213–17.

1990

'Reply to Michael Diamond', *Modern Theology*, 6 (1989/90), pp. 295–6.
Review of *The First Coming: How the Kingdom of God Became Christianity* by Thomas Sheenan, *Journal of Ecclesiastical History*, 41 (1990), pp. 275–6.
Review of *God, Jesus and Life in the Spirit* by David Jenkins, *New Blackfriars*, 71 (1990), pp. 261–2.
Edited (with Edward Henderson), *Divine Action: Studies Inspired by the Philosophical Theology of Austin Farrer*, Edinburgh: T & T Clark 1990.
'Inductive Theology?', *The Modern Churchman*, 32 (1990), p. 100.
Review of *Theology Today*, by Jürgen Moltmann, *Epworth Review*, 17 (1990), pp. 100–1.
Review of *Eternal God* by Paul Helm, *Journal of Theological Studies*, 41 (1990), pp. 790–2.

1991

'Divine and Human Goodness', in D. W. Hardy and P. H. Sedgwick (eds), *The Weight of Glory: A Vision and Practice for Christian Faith: The Future of Liberal Theology: Essays for Peter Baelz*, Edinburgh: T & T Clark 1991, pp. 91–9.
Review of *An Interpretation of Religion: Human Responses to the Transcendent* by John Hick, *Zygon*, 26 (1991), pp. 328–33.
Review of *Divine Nature and Human Language: Essays in Philosophical Theology* by William P. Alston, *Heythrop Journal*, 32 (1991), pp. 554–5.

1992

Review of *Metaphysics and the Idea of God* by Wolfhart Pannenberg, *Epworth Review*, 19 (1992), pp. 99–101.
Review of *The Recovery of Virtue: The Relevance of Aquinas for Christian Ethics*, by Jean Porter, *Studies in Christian Ethics*, 5 (1992), pp. 87–90.
Review of *Probability and Theistic Explanation* by Robert Prevost, *Journal of Theological Studies*, 43 (1992), pp. 341–3.
'Finite and Infinite Freedom in Farrer and von Balthasar', *CTNS Bulletin*, 12 (1992), pp. 10–16.
'Butler on Conscience and Virtue', in Christopher Cunliffe (ed.), *Joseph Butler's Moral and Religious Thought*, Oxford: Clarendon Press 1992, pp. 197–207.
'Incarnation', in Donald W. Musser and Joseph L. Price (eds), *A New Handbook of Christian Theology*, Nashville: Abingdon Press 1992, pp. 250–4.
'The Doctrine of the Atonement: Does It Make Moral Sense?', *Epworth Review*, 19 (1992), pp. 63–74.

Publications of B. L. Hebblethwaite

'The Varieties of Goodness', in Joseph Runzo (ed.), *Ethics, Religion and the Good Society*, Louisville, Kentucky: Westminster/John Knox Press 1992, pp. 3–16.
'Derrida non placet', *The Cambridge Review*, 114 (1992), pp. 109–11.

1993

Review of *Divine Action* by Keith Ward, *Heythrop Journal*, 69 (1993), pp. 100–1.
'John Hick and the Question of Truth in Religion', in Arvind Sharma (ed.), *God, Truth and Reality*, London: Macmillan 1993, pp. 124–34.
'A Critique of Don Cupitt's Christian Buddhism' and 'Reflections on Realism vs Non-Realism', in Joseph Runzo (ed.), *Is God Real?* Macmillan 1993, pp. 135–48, 209–11.
'The Resurrection and the Incarnation', in Paul Avis (ed.), *The Resurrection of Jesus Christ*, London: Darton, Longman & Todd 1993, pp. 155–70.
'The Ontological Implications of Existentialist Theology', in Klaus Held and Jochem Hennigfeld (eds), *Kategorien der Existenz: Festschrift für Wolfgang Janke*, Würzburg: Königshausen & Neumann 1993, pp. 505–16.

1994

Review of *Perceiving God* by William Alston, *Modern Theology*, 10 (1994), pp. 116–19.
'God and Truth', *Kerygma und Dogma* 40 (1994), pp. 2–19.
Review of *Systematic Theology*, vol. 1 by Wolfhart Pannenberg, *Epworth Review*, 21 (1994), pp. 114–16.
Reviews of *God, Action and Revelation* by Christoph Schwöbel, and Christoph Schwöbel and Colin Gunton (eds), *Persons, Divine and Human*, *Heythrop Journal*, 70 (1994), pp. 465–6.
'The Communication of Divine Revelation', in Alan Padgett (ed.), *Reason and the Christian Religion*, Oxford: Clarendon Press 1994, pp. 143–59.

1995

Review of Karl-Josef Kuschel and Hermann Häring (eds), *Hans Küng: New Horizons for Faith and Thought*, *Epworth Review* 22 (1995), pp. 117–18.
Review of *The Providence of God* by Paul Helm, *Religious Studies* 31 (1995), pp. 401–3.
Review of *Spirit and Beauty: An Introduction to Theological Aesthetics* by Patrick Sherry, *Scottish Journal of Theology*, 48 (1995), pp. 273–5.
'Jesus Christ – God and Man: The Myth and Truth Debate', in William R. Farmer (ed.), *Crisis in Christology*, Livonia, Michigan: Truth Inc. 1995, pp. 1–11.
Review of *A Vision to Pursue* by Keith Ward, *Scottish Journal of Theology*, 48 (1995), pp. 126–30.

1996

Review of *Beyond Death: Theological and Philosophical Reflections on Life after Death*, ed. D. Cohn-Sherbok and C. Lewis, *Theology*, 99 (1996), pp. 328–9.
The Essence of Christianity: A Fresh Look at the Nicene Creed, London: SPCK 1996.

Review of *Reported Miracles: A Critique of Hume* by J. Houston, *Journal of Theological Studies*, 47 (1996), pp. 790–2.
'The Anglican Tradition' in Philip Quinn and Charles Taliaferro (eds), *A Companion to Philosophy of Religion*, Oxford: Blackwell 1996, pp. 171–8.
'A Modern/Post-Modern Portrait of God', in Vernon White (ed.), *The Changing Face of God*, Lincoln: Lincoln Cathedral Publications 1996, pp. 42–59.
Review of *A Brief Theology of Revelation* by Colin Gunton, *Modern Believing*, 37 (1996), pp. 56–8.

1997

Review of *Revelation and Reconciliation: A Window on Modernity* by Stephen Williams, *Theology* 100 (1997), pp. 124–5.
Ethics and Religion in a Pluralistic Age: Collected Essays, Edinburgh: T & T Clark 1997.
'Apologetics' and 'Pannenberg, Wolfhart', in E. A. Livingstone (ed.), *The Oxford Dictionary of the Christian Church* (3rd edition), Oxford: Oxford University Press 1997, pp. 87, 1214.
The Problem of Evil, Farmington Paper E13, Oxford: Farmington Institute 1997.
'Rashdall, Hastings', *Theologische Realenzyklopädie*, vol. 28 (1997), pp. 138–41.
'Er gudfraedi til?' (Icelandic trans. of ch. 1 of *The Problems of Theology*), in Gunnar Hardarson (ed.), *Hvad er gudfraedi?*, Reykjavik: Haskolautgafan 1997, pp. 20–47.
Religious Pluralism (Farmington Paper No MT8), Oxford: Farmington Institute 1997.

1998

'The Believer's Reasons', in Eric Springsted (ed.), *Spirituality and Theology: Essays in Honor of Diogenes Allen*, Louisville, Kentucky: Westminster/John Knox Press 1998, pp. 37–48.
Review of *Religion and Creation* by Keith Ward, *Journal of Theological Studies*, 49 (1998), pp. 506–9.
Review of *God's Ways with the World: Thinking and Practising Christian Faith* by Daniel W. Hardy, *Epworth Review*, 25 (1998), pp. 108–9.
'Vive la Différence', *Christian*, Summer 1998, p. 3.
'A New Kind of Fundamentalism?', review of *The Religion of Being* by Don Cupitt, *Christian*, Christmastide 1998, pp. 15–16.

1999

Review of *A Global Ethic for Global Politics and Economics* by Hans Küng, *Studies in Christian Ethics*, 12 (1999), pp. 112–16.
Review of *Systematic Theology*, vol. 1: *The Triune God* by Robert Jenson, *Theology*, 102 (1999), pp. 451–4.
'A Defence of Dualism', *Christian*, Winter 1999/2000, p. 12.
'Finite and Infinite Freedom in Farrer and von Balthasar', in F. Michael McLain and W. Mark Richardson (eds), *Human and Divine Agency: Anglican, Catholic and Lutheran Perspectives*, Lanham: University Press of America 1999, pp. 83–96.

2000

'Sidgwick, Henry', 'Sklaverei VI', 'Social Gospel', 'Sozialethik', 'Sozialismus III' and 'Spencer, Herbert', in *Theologische Realenzyklopädie*, vol. 31, Berlin: Verlag de Gruyter 2000, pp. 247–50, 394–6, 409–19, 497–527, 550–6, 649–52.

Evil, Suffering and Religion (revised edition), London: SPCK 2000.

Review of *Thomas F. Torrance: An Intellectual Biography* by Alister McGrath, *Scottish Journal of Theology*, 50 (2000), pp. 239–42.

Review of *God, Reason and Theistic Proofs* by Stephen T. Davis, *Journal of Theological Studies*, 51 (2000), pp. 792–3.

'Immortality' and 'Soul', in Adrian Hastings (ed.), *The Oxford Companion to Christian Thought*, Oxford: Oxford University Press 2000, pp. 320–1, 681–3.

2001

'Kirk, Kenneth' and 'Rashdall, Hastings', in Trevor A. Hart (ed.), *The Dictionary of Historical Theology*, Grand Rapids, Michigan: William B. Eerdmans, and Carlisle: Paternoster Press 2001, pp. 303–4, 455–6.

'Christian Social Ethics in a Global Context', in Joseph Runzo and Nancy Martin (eds), *Ethics in the World Religions*, Oxford: Oneworld 2001, pp. 309–29.

Edited (with John Hick), *Christianity and Other Religions: Selected Readings* (revised edition), Oneworld 2001.

'The Impossibility of Multiple Incarnations', *Theology*, 104 (2001), pp. 323–34.

2003

'The Nature and Limits of Metaphysical Understanding' and 'The Nature and Limits of Theological Understanding', in Anthony J. Sanford (ed.), *The Nature and Limits of Human Understanding*, London: T & T Clark 2003, pp. 212–59.

2004

'Mascall, Eric Lionel (1905–1993)', in *The Oxford Dictionary of National Biography*, vol. 37, Oxford: Oxford University Press 2004, pp. 136–8.

Philosophical Theology and Christian Doctrine, Oxford: Blackwell 2004.

2005

'Farrer, Austin Marsden', in F. L. Cross and E. A. Livingstone (eds), *The Oxford Dictionary of the Christian Church* (3rd edition revised), Oxford: Oxford University Press, 2005, p. 602.

In Defence of Christianity, Oxford: Oxford University Press 2005.

Bibliography

Abbot, Walter M. (ed.): *The Documents of Vatican II*, American Press, 1966.
Adams, Marilyn McCord: *Horrendous Evils and the Goodness of God*, Cornell University Press, New York and London, 1999.
Alison, James: *Knowing Jesus*, SPCK, London, 1993.
Amnesty International: *In the Firing Line: War and Children's Rights*, Amnesty International UK, London, 1999.
Anderson, E. Byron and Morrill, Bruce T., SJ (eds): *Liturgy and the Moral Self: Humanity at Full Stretch Before God*, Liturgical Press, Collegeville, MN, 1998.
Armstrong, A. H.: *St Augustine and Christian Platonism*, Villanova University Press, Villanova, 1976.
——*Plotinian and Christian Studies*, Variorum Reprints, London, 1979.
Astley, J., Hone, T., and Savage, M. (eds): *Creative Chords: Studies in Music, Theology and Christian Formation*, Gracewing, Leominster, 2000.

Baillie, D. M.: *God was in Christ*, Faber & Faber, London, 1961.
Bandyopadhyay, S. and C. Mignon, SJ (trans.): *Mangalbarta Bible*, Xavier Press, Calcutta, 1984.
Barr, James: *The Bible in the Modern World*, SCM Press, London, 1973.
Barton, Stephen and Stanton, Graham (eds): *Resurrection*, SPCK, London, 1994.
Begbie, Jeremy: *Theology, Music and Time*, Cambridge University Press, Cambridge, 2000.
Beki, Niyazi: 'The Qur'an and its method of guidance', in *International Symposium on Bediuzzaman Said Nursi: A Contemporary Approach to Understanding the Qur'an: The Example of the 'Risale-i Nur'*, Sözler Nesriyat Ticaret ve Sanayi A.S., Istanbul, 2000.
Bhaktivedanta, Swami A. C.: *The Bhagavad Gita*, Penguin Books, 1962.
Bilton, Michael and Sim, Kevin: *Four Hours in My Lai*, Penguin Books, New York, 1992.
Bjarnhall, Dag: 'Pa vag mot en kristen religionsteologi', Ph.D. thesis, Uppsala, 1999.
The Book of Common Prayer, Seabury Press, New York, 1979.
Bourdieu, Pierre and Coleman, James S. (eds): *Social Theory for a Changing Society*, Russell Sage Foundation, Boulder, CO, 1991.
Bowden John: 'Resurrection in music', in S. Barton and G. Stanton (eds), *Resurrection*, 1994.
Brown, David and Loades, Ann (eds): *Christ: The Sacramental Word*, SPCK, London, 1996.

Bibliography

Brown, Peter: *Augustine of Hippo: A Biography*, Faber & Faber, London, 1967.
Brümmer, Vincent: *Speaking of a Personal God*, Cambridge University Press, Cambridge, 1992.
—— *The Model of Love*, Cambridge University Press, Cambridge, 1993.
—— 'Calvin, Bernard and the freedom of the will', *Religious Studies* 30, 1994.
—— 'On not confusing necessity with compulsion: a reply to Paul Helm', *Religious Studies* 31, 1995.
Bultmann, Rudolf: 'Is exegesis without presuppositions possible?', in *Existence and Faith*, ed. S. M. Ogden, SCM Press, London, 1964.
Burleigh, J. H. S. (trans.): *St Augustine's On True Religion*, Introduction by L. O. Mink, Regnery/Gateway, South Bend, IN, 1953.
Burnaby, John: *Christian Words and Christian Meanings*, Hodder & Stoughton, London, 1955.
—— *The Belief of Christendom: A Commentary on the Nicene Creed*, SPCK, London, 1959.

Chadwick, H. (trans.): St Augustine, *The Confessions*, Oxford University Press, Oxford, 1991.
Chang, Iris: *The Rape of Nanking: The Forgotten Holocaust of World War II*, Penguin Books, New York, 1997.
Chaudhuri, Sukanta: *Translation and Understanding*, Oxford University Press, New Delhi, 1999.
Cilaci, Osman: 'Comments on the Holy Bible in the *Risale-i Nur*', in *A Contemporary Approach to Understanding the Qur'an: The Example of the 'Risale-i Nur'*, Sözler Nesriyat Ticaret ve Sanayi A.S., Istanbul, 2000.
Coakley, Sarah: 'Deepening practices: perspectives from ascetical and mystical theology', in Miroslav Volf and Dorothy Bass (eds), *Practicing Theology*, 2002.
—— *Powers and Submissions: Spirituality, Philosophy and Gender*, Blackwell, Oxford, 2002.
Cone, James H.: *Black Theology and Black Power*, Seabury Press, New York, 1969.
Conti, Charles C. (ed.): *The Brink of Mystery*, SPCK, London, 1976.
Craig, Edward: *The Mind of God and the Works of Man*, Cambridge University Press, Cambridge, 1987.
Cudworth, Ralph: *The True Intellectual System of the Universe*, trans. J. Harrison, T. Tegg, London, 1845.
Cupitt, Don: *Taking Leave of God*, SCM Press, London, 1980; Crossroad, New York, 1981. Reprint: SCM Press, 1993; SCM Classics, 2001.
—— *Emptiness and Brightness*, Polebridge Press, Santa Rosa, 2002.

Dalferth, Ingolf U.: 'The eschatological roots of the doctrine of the Trinity', in C. Schwöbel (ed.), *Trinitarian Theology Today*, 1995.
Darwin, Charles: *The Origin of Species by means of Natural Selection or The Preservation of Favoured Races in the Struggle for Life*, ed. J. W. Burrow, Penguin, Harmondsworth, 1985.
—— *The Descent of Man*, Prometheus, New York, 1998.
Darwin, Francis (ed.): *The Life and Letters of Charles Darwin*, 3 vols, John Murray, London, 1887.

Bibliography

Davies, Coral: 'Music in general education', in J. Astley *et al.*, *Creative Chords*, 2000.
Davis, Stephen T. (ed.): *Philosophy and Theological Discourse*, Macmillan, London, 1997.
Day, Thomas: 'Twentieth-century church music: an elusive modernity', *Communio* 6(3), 1979.
D'Costa, Gavin (ed.): *Christian Uniqueness Reconsidered: The Myth of a Pluralistic Theology of Religions*, Orbis Books, New York, 1990.
de Lange, Nicholas: 'Reflections of a translator', The Sixteenth Annual Rabbi Louis Feinberg Memorial Lecture in Judaic Studies, Judaic Studies Program, University of Cincinnati, 1993.
Derrida, Jacques: *Writing and Difference*, translated with an Introduction and Additional Notes by Alan Bass, University of Chicago Press, Chicago, 1978.
Dillard, Annie: *Living by Fiction*, Harper, San Francisco, 1982.
Dostoyevsky, Fyodor: *The Brothers Karamazov*, Penguin Books, Harmondsworth, 1982.
Downey, Michael: 'Worship between the Holocausts', *Theology Today* 43, 1986.
Downie, R. S.: 'Forgiveness', *Philosophical Quarterly* 15, 1965.
Dunn, James: *Unity and Diversity in the New Testament*, 2nd edn, SCM Press, London, 1990.

Ehrenreich, Barbara: *Blood Rites: Origins and History of the Passions of War*, Virago, London, 1997.
Einstein, Albert: *The World As I See It*, trans. Alan Harris, Carol Publishing Group, New York, 1998.
Erasmus, Desiderius: 'The Education of a Christian Prince', in Albert Marrin (ed.) *War and the Christian Conscience*, 1971.

Farrer, Austin: *Saving Belief*, Hodder & Stoughton, London, 1964.
—— *A Science of God?* Geoffrey Bles, London, 1966.
—— 'Incarnation', in Charles C. Conti (ed.), *The Brink of Mystery*, 1976.
Fishbane, Michael: *The Exegetical Imagination: On Jewish Thought and Theology*, Harvard University Press, Cambridge MA, 1998.
Fitzgerald, A. D. (ed.): *Augustine Through the Ages: An Encyclopedia*, Eerdmans, Grand Rapids, 1999.
Freud, Sigmund: *The Future of an Illusion*, Hogarth Press, London, 1978.

Gerloff, Roswith I. H.: *A Plea for British Black Theologies*, 2 vols, P. Lang, Frankfurt am Main and New York, 1992.
Gilson, Etienne: *The Christian Philosophy of St Augustine*, Random House, New York, 1960.
Goetz, Ronald: 'The suffering God', *The Christian Century* 103, 1986.
Goodman, Nelson: *Ways of Worldmaking*, Harvester Press, Hassocks, 1978.
Goulder, Michael (ed.): *Incarnation and Myth: The Debate Continued*, SCM Press, London, 1979.
Grant, Paul, and Patel, Raj (eds): *A Time to Speak: Perspectives of Black Christians in Britain*, Racial Justice/Black Theology Working Group, Birmingham, 1990.

Green, Michael (ed.): *The Truth of God Incarnate*, Hodder & Stoughton, London, 1977.

Hällström, Gunnar af: *Fides Simpliciorum according to Origen of Alexandria*, Societas Scientiarum Fennica, Helsinki, 1984.
Hanh, Thich Nhat: *Love in Action: Writings on Nonviolent Social Change*, Parallax Press, Berkeley, 1993.
Hankey, Wayne: 'Ratio, reason, rationalism', in A. D. Fitzgerald (ed.), *Augustine Through the Ages*, 1999.
Hanson, Victor Davis: *The Soul of Battle*, Anchor Books, New York, 1999.
Hawes, Clement (ed.): *Christopher Smart and the Enlightenment*, St Martin's Press, New York, 2000.
Hebblethwaite, Brian: see Publications of B. L. Hebblethwaite.
Hebblethwaite, B. and Henderson E. H. (eds): *Divine Action: Studies Inspired by the Philosophical Theology of Austin Farrer*, T & T Clark, Edinburgh, 1990.
Hegel, Georg W. F.: *Lectures on the Philosophy of Religion*, vol. 3: *The Consummate Religion*, ed. Peter C. Hodgson, University of California, Berkeley, 1998.
Henderson, George F. R.: *Stonewall Jackson and the American Civil War*, Fawcett, Greenwich, CT, 1962.
Hick, John (ed.): *Truth and Dialogue*, Sheldon Press, London, 1974.
—— (ed.): *The Myth of God Incarnate*, SCM Press, London, 1977 (2nd edn, 1993).
—— *An Interpretation of Religion: Human Responses to the Transcendent*, Macmillan, Basingstoke, 1989 (2nd edn, 2004).
—— *The Metaphor of God Incarnate*, SCM Press, London; Westminster/John Knox Press, Louisville, 1993.
Hick, John and Hebblethwaite, Brian (eds): *Christianity and Other Religions*, 2nd edn, Oneworld, Oxford, 2000 (1st edn, Collins, Glasgow, 1980).
Hill, W. D. P.: *The Bhagavadgītā: Translated from the Sanskrit with an Introduction, an Argument and a Commentary*, Oxford University Press, Oxford, 1928.
Hume, David: *Dialogues Concerning Natural Religion*, ed. J. C. A. Gaskin, Oxford University Press, Oxford, 1993.

Impastato, David (ed.): *Upholding Mystery*, Oxford University Press, Oxford, 1997.
Inden, R. B.: *Imagining India*, Hurst, London, 1990, 2000.
Inge, W. R.: *Faith and Knowledge*, Edinburgh, T & T Clark, 1904.

Jackson, Robert: *The Lincoln Psalter*, Carcanet, Manchester, 1997.
Jean-Marie, Brother: 'Prayer and song in Taizé: opening the doors to an inner life', *Ecumenism* 124, 1996.
Jeffner, Anders: *Six Cartesian Meditations*, Kok, Kampen, 1993.
—— *Biology and Religion as Interpreting Patterns of Human Life*, Harris Manchester College, Oxford, 1999.
—— *Kriterien christlicher Glaubenslehre*, Almquist & Wiksell, Stockholm, 1976.
Johnson, James Turner: *Can Modern War Be Just?* Yale University Press, New

Haven and London, 1984.
Johnson, James Turner: *Morality and Contemporary Warfare*, Yale University Press, New Haven, 1999.
Johnson, W. J.: *The Bhagavad Gita*, Oxford University Press, 1994.
Jones, Gareth (ed.): *The Blackwell Companion to Modern Theology*, Blackwell, Oxford, 2004.

Kaviraj, Sudipta: *The Unhappy Consciousness: Bankimchandra Chattopadhyay and the Formation of Nationalist Discourse in India*, Oxford University Press, Delhi, 1995.
Kerr, Fergus: 'The Trinity and Christian life', *Priests and People* 7(6), 1993.
Knox, Ronald: *Literary Distractions*, Sheed & Ward, London, 1958.
Kumbier, William: 'Benjamin Britten's *Rejoice in the Lamb*: Figural invention, "impression" and the open text', in Clement Hawes (ed.), *Christopher Smart and the Enlightenment*, 2000.

Lampe, Geoffrey: 'The atonement: law and love', in A. R. Vidler (ed.), *Soundings*, 1996.
Lash, Nicholas: *The Beginning and the End of 'Religion'*, Cambridge University Press, Cambridge, 1996.
Lawless, G.: 'Augustine of Hippo and his critics', in J. T. Lienhard *et al.* (eds), *Collectanea Augustiniana*, 1993.
Lienhard, J. T., Muller E. C., and Teske, R. J. (eds): *Collectanea Augustiniana: Augustine Presbyter Factus Sum*, Peter Lang, New York, 1993.
Lipner, Julius: *The Face of Truth: A Study of Meaning and Metaphysics in the Vedāntic Theology of Rāmānuja*, Macmillan, London, 1986.
—— 'The God of love and the love of God in Christian and Hindu traditions', in J. Runzo and N. Martin (eds), *Love, Sex and Gender in the World Religions*, 2000.
Lonergan, Bernard, SJ: *Method in Theology*, Darton, Longman & Todd, London, 1972.
Lucas, J. R.: *Freedom and Grace*, SPCK, London, 1976.
Luckmann, Thomas: 'The new and old religion', in P. Bourdieu and J. Coleman (eds), *Social Theory for a Changing Society*, 1991.

MacCormack, Sabine: *The Shadows of Poetry: Vergil in the Mind of Augustine*, University of California Press, Berkeley, 1998.
MacDiarmid, Hugh: *Complete Poems 1920–1976*, vol. 2, ed. M. Grieve and W. R. Aitken, Martin Brian and O'Keefe, London, 1978.
Markham, Ian: *Truth and the Reality of God*, T & T Clark, Edinburgh, 1999.
—— 'Christianity and other religions', in Gareth Jones (ed.), *The Blackwell Companion to Modern Theology*, 2004.
Marrin, Albert (ed.): *War and the Christian Conscience: From Augustine to Martin Luther King, Jr.*, Henry Regnery Company, Chicago, 1971.
Marshall, I. Howard (ed.): *New Testament Interpretation*, Eerdmans, Grand Rapids, 1977.
Mascaro, Juan: *The Bhagavad Gita*, Penguin Books, Harmondsworth, 1962.
Matthews, A. W.: *The Development of St Augustine from Neoplatonism to*

Bibliography

Christianity 386–391 A.D., University Press of America, Washington, 1980.

Michel, Thomas.: 'Muslim–Christian dialogue and co-operation in Bediuzzaman's thought', in *A Contemporary Approach to Understanding the Qur'an: The Example of the 'Risale-i Nur'*, Sözler, Istanbul, 2000.

Midgley, Mary: *Beast and Man*, Harvester Press, Hassocks, 1979.

Milbank, John: 'The end of dialogue', in G. D'Costa (ed.), *Christian Uniqueness Reconsidered*, 1990.

Miller, James: *Measures of Wisdom: The Cosmic Dance in Classical and Christian Antiquity*, University of Toronto Press, Toronto, 1986.

Moore, Gregory: *Nietzsche, Biology and Metaphor*, Cambridge University Press, Cambridge, 2002.

Nietzsche, F.: *The Will to Power*, ed. W Kaufmann, Vintage Books, New York, 1968.

Newlands, George: *Generosity and the Christian Future*, SPCK, London, 1997.

Norris, Kathleen: *The Cloister Walk*, Riverhead, New York, 1996.

Nursi, Bediuzzaman Said: *Isârâtü'l-I'câz*, Enuar Nesriyat, Istanbul, 1995.

—— *The Flashes Collection*, Sözler, Istanbul, 1995.

—— *The Damascus Sermon*, Sözler, Istanbul, 1996.

—— *Letters*, Sözler, Istanbul, 1997.

—— *The Words*, Sözler, Istanbul, 1999.

Ogden, S. M. (ed.): *Existence and Faith*, SCM Press, London, 1964.

O'Meara, John J.: *Understanding Augustine*, Four Courts Press, Dublin, 1997.

Orr, J. Edwin: *Full Surrender*, Marshall, Morgan & Scott, Edinburgh, 1951.

Parckh, Bhikhu: *Gandhi: A Very Short Introduction*, Oxford University Press, Oxford, 1997.

Pine-Coffin, R. S. (trans.): St Augustine, *The Confessions*, Penguin, Harmondsworth, 1961.

Primavesi, Anne: *From Genesis to Apocalypse*, Burns & Oates, Tunbridge Wells, 1991.

Quick, O. C.: *Essays in Orthodoxy*, Macmillan, London, 1916.

Race, Alan: *Christians and Religious Pluralism*, SCM Press, London, 1983.

Rahner, Karl: *Theological Investigations*, vol. 19, Darton, Longman & Todd, London, 1984.

Rist, John: *Augustine*, Cambridge University Press, Cambridge, 1994.

Runzo, Joseph: *Global Philosophy of Religion*, Oneworld, Oxford, 2001.

Runzo, Joseph and Martin, Nancy M. (eds): *Love, Sex and Gender in the World Religions*, Oneworld, Oxford, 2000.

—— *Ethics in the World Religions*, Oneworld, Oxford, 2001.

Runzo, Joseph, Martin, Nancy, and Sharma, Arvind (eds): *Human Rights and Responsibilities in the World Religions*, Oneworld, Oxford, 2003.

Saliers, Don E.: 'The integrity of sung prayer', *Worship* 55(4), 1981.

—— 'Singing our lives', in Dorothy C. Bass *et al.*, *Practicing Our Faith*, Jossey-

Bass, San Francisco, 1998.
Sambur, B.: 'Is Interfaith prayer possible?' *World Faiths Encounter* 23, July 1990.
Sargeant, Winthrop (trans.): *The Bhagavad Gītā*, State University of New York Press, Albany, 1984.
Sarot, Marcel: 'Patripassianism, theopaschitism and the suffering of God: some historical and systematic considerations', *Religious Studies* 26, 1990.
—— *God, Possibility and Corporeality*, Kok, Kampen, 1992.
Sarot, M. and van den Brink, G. (eds): *Identity and Change in the Christian Tradition*, Peter Lang, Frankfurt am Main, 1999.
Schalk, Carl: *Music in Early Lutheranism*, Concordia, St Louis, 2001.
Schwöbel, Christoph (ed.): 'Divine agency and providence', *Modern Theology* 3, 1987.
—— *God, Action and Revelation*, Kok, Kampen, 1992.
—— *Trinitarian Theology Today*, T & T Clark, Edinburgh, 1995.
Scott, James Bron (ed.): *The Classics of International Law*, Carnegie Institute of Washington, Washington DC, 1917.
Sharpe, Eric: *Nathan Söderblom and the Study of Religion*, University of North Carolina Press, Chapel Hill, 1990.
Smith, John: *Select Discourses*, printed by J. Fletcher for W. Modern, Cambridge, 1660.
Smith, Wilfred Cantwell: 'The Christian in a religiously plural world', in John Hick and Brian Hebblethwaite (eds), *Christianity and Other Religions*, 1980.
Smith-Christopher, D.: *Subverting Hatred: The Challenge of Nonviolence in Religious Traditions*, Boston Research Center for the 21st Century, Boston, 1998.
Stanton, Graham: 'Presuppositions of New Testament Criticism', in I. Howard Marshall (ed.), *New Testament Interpretation*, Eerdmans, Grand Rapids, 1977.
Steiner, George: *After Babel: Aspects of Language and Translation*, Oxford University Press, Oxford, 1975.
Strawson, P. F.: *Freedom and Resentment and Other Essays*, Methuen, London, 1974.
Sudnow, David: *Ways of the Hand: The Organization of Improvised Conduct*, Routledge & Kegan Paul, London, 1978.
—— *Talk's Body: A Meditation between Two Keyboards*, Penguin, Harmondsworth, 1979.
Sullivan, Lawrence E. (ed.): *Enchanting Power: Music in the World's Religions*, Harvard University Press, Cambridge, MA, 1997.
Summit, Jeffrey A.: *The Lord's Song in a Strange Land: Music and Identity in Contemporary Jewish Worship*, Oxford University Press, Oxford, 2000.
Sun Tzu: *The Art of War*, trans. Samuel B. Griffith, Oxford University Press, Oxford, 1963.

Tanner, Kathryn: 'Theological reflection and Christian practices', in Miroslav Volf and Dorothy Bass (eds), *Practicing Theology*, 2002.
Talbot, John Michael: *The Music of Creation: Foundations of a Christian Life*, Penguin Putnam, New York, 1999.
Taylor, Charles: *A Catholic Modernity?* Oxford University Press, Oxford and New York, 1999.

Tolstoy, Leo: *The Kingdom of God is Within You*, University of Nebraska Press, Lincoln and London, 1984.

Vahide, Sükran: *The Author of the Risale-i Nur: Bediuzzaman Said Nursi*, Sözler, Istanbul, 1992.

Vidler, A. R. (ed.): *Soundings*, Cambridge University Press, Cambridge, 1966.

Volf, Miroslav and Bass, Dorothy C. (eds): *Practicing Theology: Beliefs and Practices in Christian Life*, Eerdmans, Grand Rapids and Cambridge, 2002.

Waite, Robert G. L.: *The Psychopathic God: Adolf Hitler*, DeCapo Press, New York, 1993.

Walter, Johann: 'Lob und Preis der loblichen Kunst Musica', trans. Samuel Jantztow, in Carl Schalk, *Music in Early Lutheranism*, 2001.

Ward, Keith: *Rational Theology and the Creativity of God*, Blackwell, Oxford, 1982.

Webster, Alison: *Found Wanting: Women, Christianity and Sexuality*, Cassell, London, 1995.

Weil, Simone: *The Simone Weil Reader*, ed. George A. Panichas, Moyer Bell, New York, 1977.

Welsh, Irvine: *Trainspotting*, Secker & Warburg, London, 1993.

Wheatcroft, Andrew: 'The fall of Constantinople', from Andrew Wheatcroft, *The Ottomans: Dissolving Images*, Viking, London, 1993, in John Keegan (ed.), *The Book of War: 25 Centuries of Great War Writing*, Penguin, London, 1999.

Williams, Rowan: 'The paradoxes of self-knowledge in the *De trinitate*', in J. T. Lienhard *et al.* (eds), *Collectanea Augustiniana*, 1993.

Winter, T. J.: 'Qur'ān: Translations', in the *Concise Encyclopedia of Language and Religion*, cd. John F. A. Sawyer and J. M. Y. Simpson, Pergamon, Oxford, 2001.

Wordsworth, William: *Complete Poetical Works*, ed. Thomas Hutchinson, rev. Ernest de Selincourt, Oxford University Press, Oxford, 1936.

Index

Advaita 80
agency (double-) 154–63
Aquinas, Thomas 98, 102, 120, 189
atheism (-ist) 68, 86, 97, 101–2, 104, 106, 111, 128
atonement (Christian doctrine of) 52, 170
Augustine, Saint 16, 120, 130, 147
authority (in religion) 89–90, 92

Barr, James 74, 189
Begbie, Jeremy 33–4
Bengali (language) 18–19
Bhagavadgītā 20–3
bhakti 132
Bhaktivedanta, Swami 22–3
Bible xv, 11, 19, 50, 59, 60n12, 71–4, 77–80, 83–4, 89, 191
  unity of 73–8
Brümmer, Vincent ix, xviii
Buddhist (Buddhism) 57, 67, 95, 115, 120, 132–3, 176
Bultmann, Rudolf 47, 71–3, 83, 86
Burnaby, John 173, 175, 182, 184

Chaudhuri, Sukanta 14–15, 17
Christ (*also see* Jesus) 11, 28, 30, 33, 35–6, 56–7, 76, 89, 115–17, 119, 129–30, 136, 138, 140–4, 158, 167–9, 174–8, 181, 190, 201
Christian(-ity) *passim* ch.2, 46–7, 51–2, 56, 61–3, 67–9, 77, 79–81, 83–4, 90, 95, 99, 101–2, 107–8, 113, 118–20, 128–9, 133, 137–8, 141–2, 144, 146, 151, 153, 162–3, 165, 167–8, 176, 178–9, 182, 188, 190–2, 195–7
Christology 76, 136–40, 142–4, 148, 150, 152–4, 165, 174, 177, 179
Coakley, Sarah 200–2
'conversion', in Lonergan 193–4
creation 52, 76, 86, 107–8, 110, 115, 168, 182, 185
Cudworth, Ralph 97, 101–2
Cupitt, Don ix, xv–xvi, 54, 96, 187, 198

Dalferth, Ingolf 139, 181, 185
Darwin, Charles 96, 98–100, 102–4, 107–11
Davis, S. T. ix, xv
Day, Thomas 27
D'Costa, Gavin 39
de Lange, N. 12–14
Derrida, Jacques 4–5, 96
Descartes, René 4–5, 42, 92
dharma 20–3

Index

dialogue (inter-religious) 39, 42, 44, 49–52, 54, 56, 67–8, 141, 144, 176, 191, 195, 198–200
doctrine 48, 52, 56, 86, 88–90, 192–3
Dryden 12
Dudley-Smith, T. 30
Duke Ellington 38
Dunn, James 76, 77n7, 78n8

English (language) 18–19
Enlightenment, the 92, 96–8
ethics 113–14, 116, 118, 131–2, 134
 Christian 114–19, 130–2, 134
 of war 120–2, 128
evil, problem of 167–9
evolution 45, 100–1, 107–10

faith 35, 60–1, 70, 76, 80, 84, 86, 88–90, 99, 115, 117, 131, 139 41, 143, 145, 191, 195–7, 202
 'basic' 42, 49, 53
 'religious' 46, 49, 51
Farrer, Austin 110, 154–60, 163–4, 169–70, 179, 189, 191
Feuerbach, Ludwig A. 87, 98–100, 102, 109
Ford, David ix, xviii
forgiveness, virtue of 171–5, 177–8
freedom, kinds of 180–1, 183
Freud, Sigmund 96, 99, 104–7, 109–10

Gandhi, M. K. 116, 127
generosity (as a Christian virtue) 145–6
Gerloff, Roswith 147

God 9–11, 26–8, 32–4, 36–7, 47, 56–8, 62–3, 65–6, 76, 78–82, 85–93, 95–6, 99, 102, 105–7, 110, 113–19, 126, 129–30, 137–46, 152, 154–70, 173–86, 188, 190–1, 193
Grant, Paul 148

Hanh, Thich Nhat 127, 133–4
Hebblethwaite, Brian xiii, xiv, xv–xix, 1, 3, 8, 24–5, 38, 54–5, 58, 69–70, 96, 111–12, 114–19, 130–2, 137, 154, 165–70, 174–5, 177–9, 182–4, 186–8, 190–202
Hedley, Douglas x, xvi
Hegel, G. W. F. 87, 99, 100–1, 103–4, 106, 108, 138, 190
Heidegger, Martin 103
Henderson, E. H. x, xvii
Hick, John xiv–xv, 39, 51n13, 54–7, 60–1, 65–8, 70, 137, 190
Hindu(-ism) 10, 20–1, 49, 67, 115, 120, 176
Hitler, Adolf 122, 130
Holy Spirit, 30, 52, 77–8, 80, 91, 114–17, 119, 144, 166, 181
Hume, David 44, 92–3, 109

Incarnation (of Jesus Christ) 33, 57–8, 69, 89, 117, 132, 137, 140, 145, 151, *passim* chs.10, 11, 188, 195
Inden, R. 6n5
Islam 52, 58–61, 63, 65, 67, 69, 89, 99, 115, 120

Jeffner, Anders x, xiv

Jesus (*also see* Christ) 11, 19, 28, 35–6, 56, 58, 62–3, 76, 89–90, 119, 130, 138, 140, 144–5, 147, 154, 157–68, 174–80, 183–4, 188, 191–2, 200–1
Jew(s) 28, 36, 47, 63, 67, 77, 130, 191
Johnson, James Turner 123, 125, 130
Judaism 58, 61, 89, 99

Kālidāsa 4, 16
Kant, Immanuel 40–1, 45, 57, 87, 90, 92–3, 189
Kaviraj, Sudipta 18
kenosis 144, 150–1, 179
Kierkegaard, Søren 85, 87
Knox, Ronald 12, 15, 19

language 4–8, 47, 82, 90, 93–6
 in religion 47–8
Lash, Nicholas 97–9
Levertov, Denise 26
Lipner, Julius x, 132n29, 198
liturgy 27–9, 31–2, 35, 38, 48, 138
Loades, Ann xi, xiii, 9n9
Lonergan, Bernard 193–4
love 61, 64, 67, 103, 115, 117–18, 132, 144, 146, 151–3, 159, 161–3, 168, 170–1, 173–5, 177, 179, 181, 183–4, 186
Luckmann, Thomas 44–5

MacDiarmid, Hugh 31
MacIntyre, Alasdair 61, 141
madness 4–6
Markham, Ian xi, xiv

Marx, Karl 96, 99–102, 107–10, 116
Mascaro, Juan 22–3
Michel, Thomas 62
Midgley, Mary 30–1, 33
Milbank, John 97–8
moral(ity) 43, 45, 52, 81–2, 90, 104, 114–15, 117, 132n28, 133, 192
Muhammad, Prophet 59, 64–5, 69
music
 temporality of 33–5
 as worship 25–9, 32, 36–7
Muslim(s) 47, 55, 57–8, 62, 64–7, 129, 176, 191
mysticism 40, 43, 101, 170

Newbigin, Lesslie 39
Newlands, George xi, xvii
Nietzsche, Friedrich 93, 96, 99, 102–4, 107, 109–10, 152
non-realism 85, 87–8
Nursi, Bediuzzaman Said *passim* ch.4

pacifism 119–21, 123, 128, 133
Pannenberg, Wolfhart 193–4, 201
persuasion (moral concept of) 156, 159, 161, 163
Plantinga, Alvin 80, 84, 189–91
Plato 4, 84, 99, 106, 178
postmodern(ism) 41–2, 82, 98, 103, 138–40
practice (Christian) in relation to belief 195–7, 200–1
Providence 86, 98, 107, 110–11, 131, 192

Quran 9–11, 57–61, 63–4, 68–9, 89

Index

Queens' College, Cambridge 111, 197–8

Rahner, Karl 29, 56, 61, 69
reason 40–1, 51, 65, 92, 104, 189, 193–4, 197, 201
religion (as a category) 97–8, 100, 102, 105–10, 116, 132–4, 190, 199
Resurrection (of Jesus Christ) 36, 76, 145, 160–2, 178, 191–2, 199–201
revelation 40–1, 46–7, 49, 57, 89, 91, 99, 175–7, 180, 185, 190
Rice, Tim 29
Robinson, J. A. T. 86
Runzo, Joseph xi, xvi

sacred text (*see also* *Bhagavadgītā*, Bible, Quran, Torah, Vedas) 50–2, 58, 63, 84, 108, 191, 201
Sambur, Bilal 56n7
Sargeant, Winthrop 21
Schleiermacher, Friedrich 40, 138, 190
science 41–2, 44, 52, 96, 104, 107
sense-experience 41, 44–5
Smith, John 98, 106, 110–11
Smith, Wilfred C. 176–7
Söderblom, Nathan 40–1, 45–6
Stanton, Graham 73
Steiner, George 2–3, 7
Sudnow, David 34
Superman, the 102, 110

Tanner, Kathryn 196
Taylor, Charles 151
theology 25, 32–3, 74, 99, 102, 106, 109–11, 136–9, 141, 144, 146–7, 178, 187–90, 194–5
Black theology 147–8
time 33, 81
Torah 59, 60n12
Tracy, David 139
transcendence 45–6, 49–51, 107, 128, 152
kinds of 44
Transcendent, the 57, 67
translation
  forms of 2–4
  marks of 4–17
  as epistemic act 4–6
  incommensurability of 7–11
  as 'other' 12–17
  historicity of 18
  'sentence' in 3–5
translator 11
  modes of 12–14
Trinity, the 28, 50, 57, 69, 118, 132, 152, 162, 177, 180–6
truth 19, 41–2, 47, 51–2, 55, 68, 87–9, 91–2, 95, 105, 109
  in religion 39, 47, 51, 55, 57–60, 64–5, 67, 69, 79, 88–9, 91, 115, 200–1

universals 8
university, the 91, 94n7, 199–200

Valparaiso Project 195–8, 200
Vedas 10–11
violence 58, 64, 125–7
vulnerability (as a Christian virtue) 145–6, 150

war (*see also* violence) 120–8, 130–4
just war 120–7, 133–5

Ward, Keith 168, 182, 189
Webber, Andrew Lloyd 29
Webster, Alison 149
Weil, Simone 128
Westcott, B. F. 136
'windows' towards reality 41–7

wisdom 189, 192, 194, 196n5, 202
Wittgenstein, Ludwig 42, 201–2
women (in theology) 148–9
worship (*see also* music) 25–7, 29